MW00933580

In Pursuit of Polymaths: Understanding Renaissance Persons of the 21st Century

by Angela J. Cotellessa

B.A. in Communication and Psychology, May 2003, University of Southern California
M.A. in Communication Management, May 2006, University of Southern California

A Dissertation submitted to

The Faculty of
The Graduate School of Education and Human Development
of The George Washington University
in partial fulfillment of the requirements
for the degree of Doctor of Education

May 20, 2018

Dissertation directed by

Michael J. Marquardt
Professor of Human and Organizational Learning and International Affairs

The Graduate School of Education and Human Development of The George Washington University certifies that Angela Cotellessa has passed the Final Examination for the degree of Doctor of Education as of February 27, 2018. This is the final and approved form of the dissertation.

In Pursuit of Polymaths: Understanding Renaissance Persons in the 21st Century

Angela Cotellessa

Dissertation Research Committee

Michael J. Marquardt, Professor of Human and Organizational Learning and International Affairs, Dissertation Director

Tracy T. Arwari, Adjunct Professor of Research Methods, Committee Member

Ron Sheffield, Adjunct Professor of Leadership and American Studies at Christopher Newport University, Committee Member

Dedication

To all those people who are striving to become their best, truest, fullest selves, to those who pursue the broadness and diversity of their humanity, to the aspiring polymaths of the world: I deeply respect and support your paths. This work is dedicated to you, the brave and curious explorers of life. My hope is that the pages you read here help you on your journey towards the expression of your most authentic, expansive self.

> Do I contradict myself?
> Very well then I contradict myself;
> (I am large, I contain multitudes.)
>
> -Walt Whitman

Acknowledgments

I have many people to thank who have supported my journey to becoming Dr. Cotellessa.

First, this dissertation would not be complete without acknowledging the role that my grandparents, George and Georgia Meyers, played in it. They always made me believe in my own capacity to achieve any goal I set for myself and provided endless support in immeasurable ways throughout the entire course of my life to help me realize myriad dreams. Without their positive, sustained influence, I am not sure I would ever have attempted to even obtain a doctoral degree; and so, much of the credit for this dissertation belongs to them, my primary role models in life and my beloved heroes. Mamaw and Frampa, you are both legends to me and I will be forever grateful for having you as my grandparents.

To my Lily Georgia: I feel as if I should share this with you, an honorary member of HOL/ELP Cohort 27, and my dissertation co-author in spirit. I became pregnant with you while I was a doctoral student, cared for you through my coursework and through comprehensive exams, and navigated my dissertation journey with you by my side. However, no accomplishment I could ever achieve in my education, career, or elsewhere will ever compare to the pride I take in being your mama. I love you deeply, unconditionally, and forever.

To my husband, Joe Cotellessa: part of why I was initially drawn to you as a person is because I believe you are a polymath. Whether it is quoting Shakespeare, enjoying classical music or reggae, expressing yourself through your photography, building an IT network, leveraging your Eagle Scout capabilities by always being prepared for a disaster, driving a snow plow, or training a dog, you are a Renaissance man at heart. Your ability to teach yourself, learning and doing anything you set your mind to, is inspiring to watch. Also, our wedding vows said, among other things, "I promise to be supportive to help you achieve your goals and dreams," and I thank you for supporting this big dream to earn my doctorate. (But don't worry, I will not expect you to call me Dr. Cotellessa.)

To my kind mother-in-law Sue, wonderful brother Paul, and dear friends, Mineko, Peg, Claire, Len, Jessica, Krista, Tiffany, Sara, Steve: your unending support and friendship over the years has enabled me to counterbalance the stressors of a doctoral program with camaraderie, connection, and a sense of encouragement. You are all my pillars. Whether a blood relative or not, whether you live near or far, I consider you all my family forever. I also want to thank, specifically, my cohort mates, Lynn and Michael, for being such wonderful classmates. And I also thank my boss, Dr. Wells, for her support of pursuing my doctorate.

To my dissertation chair, Dr. Marquardt: thank you for believing in my topic and in me. Your expert guidance along the way made my work immeasurably better. Plus, you have been a pleasure to work with, and I have learned so much from you working on this dissertation and beyond. I respect you tremendously both as an intellectual and as a very good human being.

To my committee members, Dr. Arwari and Dr. Sheffield: thank you for your expert refinements and support throughout this process. It has been a true pleasure to work with each of you.

I also thank all the polymaths—though their identities must remain anonymous—who allowed me to interview them as part of this research. Each and every interview was truly a privilege to be a part of as a researcher. I honor each of your polymath journeys.

Abstract

In Pursuit of Polymaths: Understanding Renaissance Persons of the 21st Century

This phenomenological study focused on the lived experiences of modern day polymaths. The constructs of openness to experience, identity, self-directed learning, polymathy or multi-disciplinarily, and intrapersonal functional diversity were used to frame the research. The primary theoretical lenses of this study are based on Identity Theory and Social Identity Theory. The inquiry focused on accomplished polymaths with careers spanning both the arts and sciences. The participants' narratives provided insights regarding how they became polymaths and what their experiences as polymaths have been like.

The population for this phenomenological study was found using snowball sampling (also called chain or network sampling). Interviews with thirteen participants were conducted using a modified version of Seidman's (2013) method, focusing on (1) life history, (2) details of the experience of being a polymath, and (3) meaning making of being a polymath. Through applying Moustakas' (1994) phenomenological data analysis methods, a total of twelve themes emerged. In addition to the twelve themes, textural and structural descriptions were presented that helped to elucidate the essence of polymathic experiences.

Seven conclusions were drawn from this research: (1) to be a polymath, one must accept not fitting in the typical box and perhaps even embodying apparent contradictions; polymathy is being intrapersonally diverse, (2) polymaths are exposed broadly, think creatively and strategically, and juggle their many interests and obligations through effective time management, (3) being a polymath can make life richer, but it can also be quite difficult, (4) polymaths are excellent at being creative and solving problems creatively, (5) polymathy develops due to a combination of nature and nurture, and polymathy is maintained in adulthood by a willingness to continue to work to improve oneself through self-directed learning, (6) polymath identity is discovered from not fitting in; polymath identity can be difficult to fully own and to explain to others, (7) family and financial resources impact the emergence of polymathy. A number of recommendations for theory, practice, and research are provided as well.

Table of Contents

List of Figures

List of Tables

Chapter 1: Introduction

Overview of Chapter

Since the Renaissance began in the 14th century, we have been fascinated by the great people who could excel in both the arts and sciences: famous examples of such polymaths include Michelangelo (painter, sculptor, architect, poet, engineer, scientist), Thomas Jefferson (politician, scholar, lawyer, philosopher, naturalist, astronomer, archaeologist, horticulturist, linguist, and inventor) and Albert Einstein (physicist and violinist). Over the centuries, there have always been individuals who were different, unique, able to live almost paradoxically yet comfortably in two different worlds at the same time. These are people who have dramatically changed the world in which they lived because of their unique abilities and impactful contributions.

How did polymaths like these come to be this way? The biographies of Michelangelo, Jefferson and Einstein indicate that they were self-directed learners. Are current day polymaths self-directed learners as well? What other characteristics do they possess? Perhaps not all polymaths reach the level of achievement or acclaim like Michelangelo, Jefferson, or Einstein did—but what can we learn from modern day polymaths who may also have the potential to positively change the world?

Polymaths may be known by other descriptors: Renaissance men (and women), polyhistors, people high in openness to experience, individuals with high intrapersonal diversity, intellectuals with diverse domains of knowledge, multi-disciplinary scholars, multi-potentialites, being a generalist rather than a specialist, "jacks of all trades," orthogonal thinkers, protean men/women, *Homo Universalis* (universal person), people with multi-creative potential, or being an integrative thinker. All of these terms or phrases describe, at least to some degree, someone who has a wide breadth of knowledge and/or skills but who also has deep expertise in a number of disparate areas, who is open to broad experiences, can be a divergent thinker, and can solve problems in creative ways as a result; these types of people (albeit ones who are very strong examples of this way of being) are the focus of this dissertation.

In past centuries, it was very common for people to have a wide range of expertise across different fields, but the Scientific Revolution made it much harder for someone to maintain mastery over different areas (Arbesman, 2013). "Scientific knowledge exploded in size, mainly due to the application of the scientific method to our surroundings…we made sense of our world by dividing information into manageable portions and distinct areas of proficiency" (Arbesman, 2013, p. 2). The downside of people specializing is that knowledge became more fragmented. "We chose to know more and more about less and less. We may have expanded what we as a society know—but it was at the price of no single individual being able to truly know it all" (Arbesman, 2013, p. 2).

Unfortunately, in modern day, there are few incentives for people to try to become to become polymaths; we live in a society and time where the major paradigm is that of specialization (Shavinina, 2013). In fact, specialization is seen as a requirement for adult success (Shavinina, 2013) and the more deeply one specializes, the more money they are likely to earn (Wiens, 2012). Although there is an important role for specialists in our society, there are limitations to what they can do; further, the problem with deep specialization is that those specialists may get entrenched in their own, limited points of view which negative impacts creativity and innovation (Wiens, 2012).

Aldous Huxley said in a 1959 lecture entitled "Integrated Education," that "A man of letters, can I think, perform a valuable function in the world at present by bringing together a great many subjects, by showing the relationships between them. It's a question of building bridges." He said that taking a very narrow specialized approach to knowledge and life is a sort of "celibacy of the intellect" which can be quite problematic by creating a partial, fragmented view of the world. The tunnel vision of a monomath, as opposed to a polymath, does not adequately solve the problems of our complex time.

Further, polymaths who can bring together disparate ideas and create new insights are valuable because an organization that is able to create knowledge—especially on an ongoing basis—has a unique capability to support continuous organizational improvement (Tsoukas and Mylonopoulos, 2004). Indeed, knowledge creation is valuable to organizations and helps them obtain and sustain a competitive edge (Boisot, 1998; Bryant, 2005; Grant, 1997; Spender, 1996; Tsoukas and Mylonopoulos, 2004). In fact, Spender (1996) has argued that the two primary goals any organization has are the generation and application of knowledge. Knowledge creation is critical in organizations to be able to compete in the marketplace and evolve and adapt over time (Brockman and Morgan, 2003; Smith et al., 2005; Swan et al., 2002, Vissers and Dankbaar, 2002; Zollo and Winter, 2002). How does an organization go about creating new insights and innovations? Polymathic individuals who can support knowledge creation by harnessing information from disparate fields and bringing them together are in a unique position to develop new innovations and insights and add great value to the organizations for which they work—assuming organizations know how to harness, or at least allow, a polymath to add value in this way.

Statement of the Problem

We do not know much about modern day polymaths. But we do know that they can contribute greatly to society, and so the development and support of those with polymathic potential should be encouraged. Currently, however, polymaths—though valuable for organizations and society more largely—are not adequately understood and therefore their skills are not fully leveraged. Further, we do not know how current polymaths came to be that way. What helped them become polymaths? What impediments were in their way to becoming a polymath that they had to overcome? How could organizations more fully utilize their talents? How can they be supported to make the greatest contributions in our world?

These questions are relevant because problems facing humanity in the modern era are frequently very complex and often involve multiple dimensions, not all of which can be solved within a single discipline or narrow, limited silo (Terjesen and Politis, 2015). Examples include global health challenges, international development needs, difficulties with the economy, environmental crises, etc., which cannot be solved by any single organization, government, person, or field of study (Young & Marzano, 2010). As a result, humanity must pursue bold ideas and innovative tactics to solve major, unanswered societal problems (Colquitt and George, 2011) which "requires multi-disciplinary lenses, multiple theoretical perspectives, and novel methodologies and data sources" (Terjesen and Politis, 2015, p. 156). Indeed, "the world's problems require a multi-disciplinary skillset—that is, the combination and involvement of several academic disciplines or professional specializations to a topic or problem" (Terjesen & Politis, 2015, p. 151). This is where polymaths can add unique value.

Despite the need for this way of thinking, few incentives exist for individuals to become multi-disciplinary experts (Terjeson and Politis, 2015). In other words, there is a need for these types of people to help solve serious global problems, but no real societal support for them to become this way. Posited differently, the problem is, we (as society) need more polymaths, but do not know how to do this; for people who have polymathic potential, we do not understand how to foster their full development. That is why it is so important to better understand their experience, so we can understand what would be needed to support the development of more polymaths in the future. This study aims to add value particularly in this way.

In the modern workscape, "we desperately need people with the ability to see big picture solutions. That's where being a polymath has certain advantages" (Wiens, 2012). But the dominant ideology says that the way to expertise is in exclusivity and that it is better to limit skillsets, so we have deep expertise in one area with more focus in that one field rather than having intellectual dexterity (Terjesen and Politis, 2015), interdisciplinary approaches become less valued (Arbesman, 2013). Further, there is a general belief in society that "skills and knowledge do not transfer across domains" (Shavinina, 2013, p. 62), which further encourages this kind of narrow specialization.

What is worth considering beyond the fact that we live in a society where specialization is typically rewarded, is how this is juxtaposed with the larger context in which we currently live: in the information age—in an economy based on information computerization—where so much information is readily available. Indeed, the proliferation of technology that humanity has seen in the late 20th century to current day, and the rise of digital culture more generally, has been a significant force that impacts the potential for polymathic thinking. Because information is more accessible to the masses (because of modern technologies), strategic thinking across domains that uniquely integrates and synthesizes information becomes more possible. In other words, even though we live in a time that rewards specialists, we also live in a unique time when modern technologies make it easier for people forge connections among ideas from disparate disciplines.

Specialist approaches come at the cost of fostering multi-faceted thinking, experiences, and expertise and undervalues the genius of generalists. Innovative connections that are made possible through cross-fertilization of ideas becomes much more difficult if experts remain in single silos. On the other hand, polymaths are "equally likely to contribute to both the arts and the sciences and either consciously or unconsciously forge links between the two" (Sriraman, 2009, p. 75).

Specialist careers may limit experiencing the fullness of life. On the micro level of analysis, for people who lack intrapersonal diversity, they may experience their narrow careers as cages of specialization. John Dewey (1916) in Democracy and Education talked about the diversity of individual talent "and for the need of free development of individuality in all its variety" (p. 106). If society continues developing and supporting specialists—if individuals become little cogs in big wheels—are they losing something essential? What happens to their ability to experience their full humanity and achieve fulfillment in life?

Further, there are big pay-offs for multidisciplinary solutions to problems. Scholar Roger Smith (2014) who himself holds a Ph.D. in computer sciences as well as a Doctorate in business administration said it well:

> But in a world where most single-discipline problems have been solved, the big pay-offs are in solutions to multi-disciplinary problems that call for individuals and teams who can integrate the skills and perspectives of many fields. Real value comes from people who can build within themselves the skills and capabilities to approach these new problems. What's needed today are modern Leonardos, individuals who can extend themselves beyond their formal training and integrate skills to match the diversity of the difficult problems to be solved.

Both approaches have value, but there is imbalance. Generalists and specialists think differently and approach problems in different ways; both have value. The social fabric requires both. However, in our society, in this age, the generalist is undervalued while the specialist is rewarded—and this scale has gotten quite unbalanced. Intellectual and experiential diversity is undervalued in the current era and this is a problem.

Gap in the literature. Another problem besides society's support of specialists rather than generalists is that there is very limited literature on what leads someone to become a polymath. There is literature describing some individual polymaths—one at a time—although there is a dearth of literature studying numerous polymaths together to find common themes among them; in this way, there is a gap in the literature. Of the literature that does exist, it looks mostly at polymaths from centuries past; there is scant literature aimed at understanding polymaths that exist in modern times.

No centralized body for polymaths. Further, there is currently no reputable, centralized body that certifies who is a polymath and who is not; right now, designation as a polymath is pretty much based on self-reported identity or through scholars identifying others as being polymaths. However, there do currently exist some organizations that promote polymathic ideals. For example, there is a scholarly journal out of MIT Press called *Leonardo*, which is a peer-reviewed, academic journal focused on forging connections between science and technology to the arts and music. At the University of Southern California, there is an Academy for Polymathic Studies that encourages students there to understand relatedness between disciplines, and students are taught how to think instead of what to think. Since 1981, another organization called Renaissance Weekend has held non-partisan retreats intended to build bridges among innovative leaders from diverse fields. The University of California Santa Cruz Institute of the Arts and Sciences supports collaboration across disciplines through interdisciplinary residencies. Although these examples of organizations that promote polymathic ideals do exist, they do so in relative isolation from one another. And there is currently no centralized body (like Mensa, the high IQ society) to certify who qualifies as a polymath; thus, this is an area for future development.

Purpose of the Study

The primary purpose of this phenomenological study was to help fill in the literature gap by better understanding how polymaths in the 21st century got to be adept in multiple, disparate areas—what motivated or led them to do so—and more generally what their experiences are of being this way. In a world that typically rewards specialists much more than generalists (Terjesen and Politis, 2015), this researcher wanted to understand what leads someone to take the generalist path and what they experience from doing so—whether good or bad, enriching or difficult. Of particular interest, this researcher also aimed to understand how their varied skillsets impacts their ability to solve real-world problems creatively (or not) as well as how their identity emerged in relation to and how it has been impacted by their polymathy.

This study explores the shared experiences—common themes—among a variety of different polymaths. To gain a better understanding of these individuals, their experiences, and in general, the phenomenon of polymaths, the constructs of openness to experience, polymathy or multi-disciplinarity, and intrapersonal functional diversity are used. Although participants in this study do not necessarily know each other, it was assumed that they will have some shared experiences among them which will help us to understand the experience of polymaths in the 21st century.

Research Questions

Subsequently, the primary research questions guiding this dissertation research are as follows:

- RQ1: What is the lived experience of polymaths?
  - Sub-question: What is it like being a polymath? How does it feel?
  - Sub-question: How does polymathy impact creativity and creative problem solving?
- RQ2: How did polymaths come to be that way?
  - Sub-question: How did polymaths discover their identity?
  - Sub-question: What in a polymath's environment impacted them becoming a polymath?

Statement of Potential Significance

According to Root-Bernstein (2009), the study of polymathy only began in the 19th century by J.H. van't Hoff, who later won the first ever awarded Nobel prize for Chemistry. Van't Hoff had a hypothesis that "the greatest scientists, unlike their less able colleagues, displayed their imaginative ability outside of science as well as within it" (Root-Bernstein, 2009, p. 685). So, this is an area worth understanding—there is value in understanding it—because polymathic thinking can improve innovation and advances in myriad fields (which will be discussed more later in this dissertation).

This research offers contributions to knowledge for both scholars and practitioners alike. For instance, this research adds a new perspective to a somewhat limited body of knowledge on the subject and takes a new perspective in doing so. There is ample literature exploring the individual experiences of one polymath at a time, but almost no literature that aims to find common themes among different polymaths. Of the literature that does exist, much of it looks at Renaissance men from history; very little looks at Renaissance persons living in the 21st century. Regarding polymaths who do exist in current day, there is scant scholarly literature exploring how and why they got to be that way and what their experiences are as a result. In fact, "very few (if any) attempts have been made to isolate the qualitative aspects of thinking that adequately describe" the term polymath (Sriraman, 2009, p. 75). This research contributes to the literature by helping to fill in these gaps.

This study also adds a new perspective to the literature on diversity. Understanding individual, intrapersonal diversity or polymathy is important so that discussions about diversity do not exist only at the meso and macro levels, but also the micro level of analysis—for more complete and thorough understanding of diversity and its impact at all levels. In fact, Harrison & Klein (2007) have said that most research on diversity is flawed because it defines diversity too simply. In the absence of a full understanding of intrapersonal diversity, we take the risk of not valuing and not developing something that could potentially have a very powerful, positive impact on individuals and organizations. Indeed, diversity as at the "forefront as an important management and research concern" (Roberson, 2013, p. 3) so it is worth having a full, robust understanding of it—including diversity that can exist within individuals themselves.

This research is also significant for practice. Further understanding of this phenomenon may help to create clearer pathways designed to nurture future polymaths. This study provides information to help guide their way as well as for academic advisors, career counselors, Human Resources professionals, etc. who may be advising or working with existing or aspiring polymaths. Indeed, having more polymaths in the world would be beneficial for us all; it would create better intellectual resources for humanity to solve the complex problems we now face, globally, as well as the problems that will inevitably arise in the future, so it is important to understand how to foster their fruition and development. These types of people can bring unique perspectives to solve problems in creative ways. Understanding how people got to be polymaths and what their experiences are is valuable in the event that individuals, organizations, or governments may want to support the development of polymaths more in the future to combat and solve problems we face as individuals, in organizations, governments, and more generally, as a species.

This research also has implications for how to recruit, retain, and motivate polymaths in the workplace. Organizations may attract very talented people who are polymaths, but those polymaths may become bored or feel underutilized in the organization; this may lead to poor retention of polymaths. It is important to help understand what keeps a polymath fully engaged in the workplace so that their gifts can be fully leveraged. This research helps answer the question, what can organizations do to support and encourage polymaths?

For individual practitioners who want to experience the benefits of being a polymath, this study helps uncover what makes someone become a polymath in the 21st century—the thinking and paths they took to get there—and what the benefits and drawbacks of it are, which may help inform their professional development and career path. For individuals who choose this path, there is evidence to show that it may increase the richness of their contributions to their practice, for example, by shaping their ability to creatively solve problems better than individuals who have had a narrower focus over the course of their careers (Bunderson and Sutcliffe, 2002).

In addition to providing information, this study may also provide inspiration for aspiring polymaths. Indeed, a final benefit of this research will be to uncover more about these exemplars of greatness and perhaps inspire others to pursue similar breadth and depth of learning and experiences and to embrace lifelong learning.

Conceptual Framework

The below conceptual framework attempts to depict the estimated relationship between a polymath's identity, experience, and learning. The framework suggests that one's identity influences what experiences one has, which in turn impacts what one will learn (i.e., through self-directed learning). The cycle repeats itself, and what one learns will in turn affect one's identity, which impacts future experiences, which impacts learning further. In other words, the newly formed identity will be influenced by what is then selected to learn, and the pattern continues indefinitely. Of course, this relationship between identity, experience, and learning will influence the choices a polymath makes in their self-directed learning; so self-directed learning is a significant factor in this framework.

Figure 1-1: Theoretical Framework

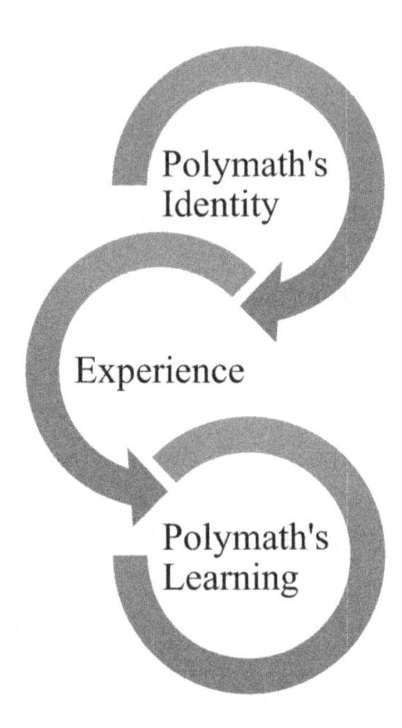

Brockett (1983) defined self-directed learning as "a disposition to engage in learning activities where the individual takes personal responsibility for developing and carrying out learning endeavors autonomously without being prompted or guided by other people" (p. 16). Self-directed learning can be further described as a process that the learner him- or herself controls; indeed, the learner takes responsibility for his or her own learning (Guglielmino, 2008). Since learning is fundamentally an individual behavior, self-directed learning could be considered the most valid form of learning, since it is most tailored to individual needs, from the individual's own perspective. Self-directed learning is especially relevant when studying polymaths since there is no organization, person, or societal values influencing the person to necessarily become polymathic; this is a choice they make on their own. What they learn impacts how they think of themselves—their identity.

Erikson (1950) believed that identity is not formed once, but rather is developed over time. Symbolic interactionists like Mead (1934) and Cooley (1902) believed that the self is a product of social interaction because people understand who they are in relation to their interactions with other people. Further, since people interact and are part of various different groups, they may have many distinct selves based on the different groups to which they belong and whose opinions matter to them (Hogg, Terry, & White, 1995). So, an individual's identity is not just one thing, but a composite of various identities merged together, impacted by both internal and external forces, all of which may shift over time. Ibarra (2005) has also written about how as what one does professionally changes, identity co-evolves along the way. This is very much in line with the idea of being a polymath with multiple areas of expertise, developed over time.

Summary of Methodology

Since this researcher aimed to uncover the lived and shared experiences of polymaths, this study was most suited to a qualitative approach, specifically using the phenomenology methodology. Creswell (2007) explained that phenomenology is used to describe the collective understanding of multiple people with regard to their lived experience of a phenomenon (i.e., the phenomenon of being a polymath). Further, Moustakas (1994) said that phenomenology is a tool to provide deep understanding and to create new knowledge. Indeed, phenomenologists try to understand lived experience—that is their main goal (Van Manen, 2014). Someone reading a phenomenological study should come away with the feeling, "I understand better what it is like for someone to experience that" (Creswell, 2013, p. 62).

However, using the phenomenological approach adds something more beyond just describing phenomenon; it allows for the researcher—the primary instrument of the study—to interpret the findings and make sense out of the phenomenon (Creswell, 2007). That said, the researcher—as the primary instrument of the study—should aim to be as objective as possible and let the data speak for itself to the greatest extent possible. There are several ways of doing this. One process is called *epoche*, which means that the researcher refrains from personal judgment (Moustakas, 1994). Any prejudices or assumptions the researcher has should be *bracketed* which involves temporarily setting aside those viewpoints (Merriam & Tisdell, 2016). However, "the extent to which any person can bracket his or her biases and assumptions is open to debate" (Merriam & Tisdell, 2016, p. 27). For this reason, this researcher provides a subjectivity statement in Chapter 3 of this text which will expose this researcher's involvement and interpretations in the research.

Beyond epoche and bracketing, other strategies used in phenomenological research include *phenomenological reduction*, which aims to isolate the phenomenon under study to comprehend it at its core essence (Merriam & Tisdell, 2016). *Imaginative variation* is another tool towards objectivity; this involves trying to view the data from different perspectives, looking at it from all angles (Merriam & Tisdell, 2016).

Population. In terms of the population to study, this research is not pertinent only to a specific industry or type of career since polymaths exist in various domains by definition. Accordingly, I used specific criteria for what makes a Renaissance man and sought out individuals meeting those qualifications for further study; this is known as two-tier sampling (Merriam & Tisdell, 2016). Due to the nature of polymaths—that they are somewhat unique in modern society—this research involves a *unique sample* since polymaths have "unique, atypical, perhaps rare attributes" (Merriam & Tisdell, 2016, p. 97). In order to obtain appropriate subjects, I also used what is known as snowball, chain, or network sampling; this is a strategy that involves finding a few key interviewees and asking them to refer me to other participants – like themselves – whom I could also interview (Merriam & Tisdell, 2016).

Naturally, some people may be polymathic to a lesser degree while others are true exemplars of polymathic living. Because this study aims to understand the experience of true polymaths, only those individuals who are the greatest examples of polymathy were be studied. The below image aims to depict this goal; it shows that there may be a larger population of people who exhibit some polymathic traits; however, for the purposes of this study, the smaller, truer core will be studied. People who are distinguished in at least one field (arts or sciences) but who also have skills in the other area are the target audience for this study. Participants may have started out as a single-disciplinary expert but over time grown their skills in multiple areas; it is not a requirement that they became distinguished in both areas at the same time.

Figure 1-2: Target Population

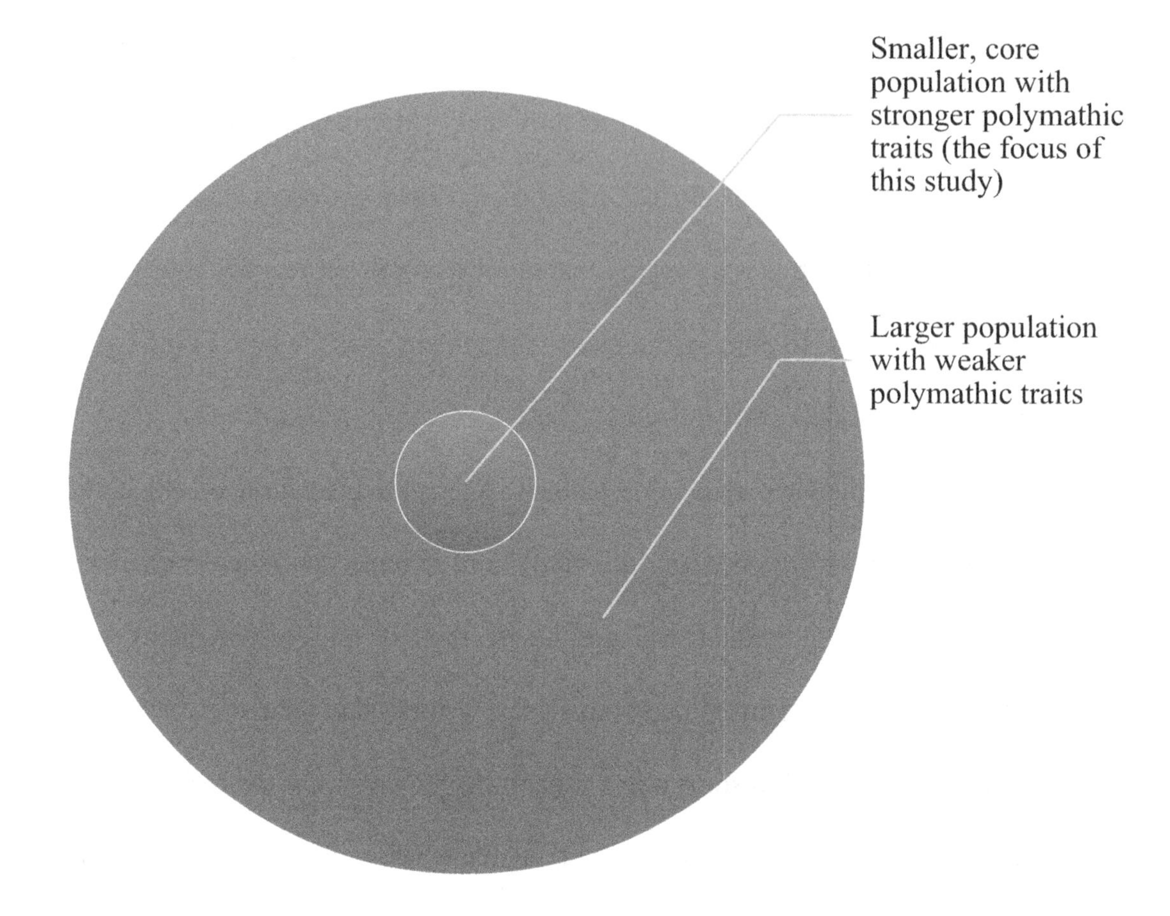

For this study, this researcher interviewed a diverse group of individuals from different ethnic backgrounds, ages, and socioeconomic statuses. Approximately half of participants were male and half were female. A total of 13 polymaths were interviewed, when saturation occurred. Saturation occurs in research when the researcher begins hearing the same responses and no new insights are being provided (Creswell, 2007).

Data Collection and Analysis. A total of 13 individual polymaths, roughly half male and half female, using pre-established selection criteria, were interviewed using an interview protocol prepared, tested, and approved ahead of time. Interviews were audio recorded and later transcribed. Interviews were conducted in person, over telephone, or through video conferencing software (such as Skype and FaceTime). To find themes among the different interviews, this researcher coded the data to find trends in the data, which are summarized in Chapter 4.

Limitations

There are a number of limitations with any study. Below are some limitations specific to this study, given its use of phenomenology:

- Researcher as key instrument: all qualitative research is interpretative in nature; the researcher is involved with participants directly, which introduces a variety of strategic, ethical, and personal issues regarding the process (Locke, Spirduso, & Silverman, 2013). Accordingly, researcher-induced bias is a risk in phenomenological research, which is why researchers should "explicitly identify reflexively their biases, values, and personal background, such as gender, history, culture, and socioeconomic status that shape their interpretations formed during a study" (Creswell, 2014, p. 187).
- Generalizability: phenomenology as a research methodology has some limitations. For instance, findings from qualitative research such as phenomenology may be internally generalizable, but findings are not generalizable from the sample studied to the larger population. However, "generalization in a statistical sense is not a goal of qualitative research" (Merriam & Tisdell, 2016, p. 96).
- Summaries of experiences: The nature of this research required interview participants to be introspective and retrospective regarding their experiences of

being Renaissance persons. Information is provided indirectly and is filtered by the interviewees (Creswell, 2014). Further, people may selectively recall information and the very presence of the researcher may bias their responses (Creswell, 2014). In addition, different people may have varying capabilities to be articulate and perceptive (Creswell, 2014). These are some additional limitations of this research.

- Sample: This phenomenological study involved interviewing people who have native English fluency; this means, essentially, that they may not have spoken English as their first language, but they are able to communicate just as well as someone whose first language was, in fact, English. People whose first (and potentially only) language is English are also eligible to participate, of course. Because this researcher speaks English fluently and does not speak any other language fluently, and also because there are downsides to conducting an interview in another language and then having to translate it (which can lead to information being lost or changed in translation), this research will not be conducted using other languages besides English. That is a limitation of this particular study since only participants who speak English fluently may participate.

Delimitations

The delimitations of this research include that only polymaths are being studied (and, for example, not outsiders who may have observations based off of experience or interactions with polymaths). The number of polymaths studied (13) is another delimitation. And the specific polymaths chosen – the diversity of their backgrounds and the specific experiences they as individuals have had – is another delimitation. The way interviews were conducted – using the English language, as well as the various formats (in-person, via telephone, or video conferencing) are additional delimitations that this researcher chose to utilize in this dissertation research study.

Definition of Key Terms

Below are several different key concepts discussed throughout this dissertation; descriptions of each are provided here (in alphabetical order) for reference, though they are covered in more detail later in the dissertation:

- **Creativity/creative problem solving:** Creative problem solving involves coming up with approaches and solutions that are new to the solver or even new in the context of history (Boden, 2004). For a solution to be considered creative, it must be useful, correct, and valuable (Amabile, 1983).
- **Identity Theory:** Identity theory aims to explain individuals' role-related behaviors and takes into consideration how society impacts the individual (Hogg, Terry, & White, 1995). The focus is on the personal, micro level of analysis, but it takes into consideration societal influences on the individual.
- **Intrapersonal Diversity:** The current scholarly literature on intrapersonal diversity focuses on functional intrapersonal diversity, which has to do with someone's professional experience—specifically, how much they are either a narrow specialist with limited experience in a range of functions versus a broad generalist whose prior work experience spans a number of

functional areas (Bunderson and Sutcliffe, 2002). In other words, someone who is functionally intrapersonally diverse has a wide "breadth of functional experiences" (Bunderson and Sutcliffe, 2002, p. 875) and considers how diverse the "functional areas within which they have spent the greater part of their careers" is (Bunderson and Sutcliffe, 2002, p. 878). "This approach to conceptualizing functional diversity rests on the assumption that each member brings a specific functional perspective to a team, a perspective gained through experience that is typically weighted toward a particular function" (Bunderson and Sutcliffe, 2002, p. 878). While interpersonal diversity "captures the differences in experience sets across" people, intrapersonal diversity is a "measure that captures difference within" one person (Huckman and Staats, 2011, p. 311). It has to do with the "extent to which members' prior experiences are individually heterogeneous or homogeneous" (Chiocchio, Kelloway, and Hobbs, 2015, p. 333) and therefore is a very similar construct to being a Renaissance man.

- **Multi-disciplinarity:** Multi-disciplinarity "involves simultaneous application of the thinking of several sciences and disciplines, and also involves the study and research of a domain of reality being achieved from several angles, descended from the multiplied thinking of several sciences or types of education simultaneously" and is a form of "intertwining disciplines" (Gheorge, Dinu, & Laurentiu, 2014, p. 713). Used interchangeably in this dissertation with polymathy.

- Multi-disciplinarity is different from *cross*-disciplinarity, which involves a sort of cross-fertilization among disciplines, where "aspects of one discipline are explained in terms of one or more other disciplines" (Baveye, Palfreyman, & Otten, 1997, p. 3).
- Multi-disciplinarity is different from *inter*-disciplinarity, which "involves phenomena, concepts and general laws that are common to several disciplines, investigated with common methods and models, it analyses, highlights, in a varied context, multifaceted issues and diverse opportunities for knowledge of reality but also for educational purpose" (Gheorge, Dinu, & Laurentiu, 2014, p. 712).
- Multi-disciplinarity is different from *trans*-disciplinarity, a relatively new idea, which "corresponds to projects that involve academics from different unrelated disciplines as well as non-academic participants, belonging to various categories of stakeholders, to jointly create new knowledge and theory as they try to address a common question" (Baveye, Palfreyman, & Otten, 1997, p. 4).

- **Openness to Experience:** Openness to experience is part of the "Big 5" personality traits described by McCrae and Costa (1987). Besides openness to experience, the other four traits of the "Big 5" include extraversion, agreeableness, conscientiousness, and neuroticism (McCrae & Costa, 1987). Openness to experience is the "disposition to be imaginative, nonconforming, and unconventional" (Judge, Bono, Ilies, and Berhard, 2002, p. 765). It includes exploring multiple options, challenging assumptions, seeking different perspectives, combining different viewpoints, and actively evaluating different options (Shalley and Perry Smith, 2008). People high in the openness to experience personality trait are often more flexible and able to understand various perspectives more readily (Zhao and Seibert, 2006), and those people tend "to be imaginative, intellectually curious, and open to trying new things" (Burke and Witt, 2002, p. 712). A number of different studies over a period of many years link openness to experience with creativity at the individual level of analysis (McCrae, 1987; Feist, 1998; George & Zhou, 2001; McCrae & Costa, 1997).

- **Renaissance man/woman/person:** Used interchangeably with polymath; see definition of polymath.
- **Polymath(s) or polymathy:** The word polymathḗs, equivalent to polymaths in English, first appeared in English around the year 1615, with poly meaning "many" and mathḗs deriving from the word manthánein which means to learn; so a polymath is someone with many learnings (Dictionary.com). The term 'polymath' has been in use since at least the Renaissance and refers to very learned scholars who were distinguished not only by their unique genius in particular fields of interest, but also by their noteworthy ability to traverse different fields of specialization and to sometimes see their interconnections (MacLachlan, 2009). A similar

notion, multi-disciplinarity, draws upon knowledge from different disciplines (Choi and Pak, 2006). Polymaths who pursue different areas of knowledge tend to understand things more broadly, developing an appreciation for a variety of different fields, and also are able to enjoy the experiences afforded to them across those various fields (Lang, 2014). In this dissertation, I will use the terms polymathy and multi-disciplinarity interchangeably. Polyhistor is also a synonym Polyhistor for polymath. A working definition that I will use—in my own words—is someone who has great knowledge, skill, or command of two disparate areas (i.e., in the arts and sciences).

- **Self-directed Learning:** Given that the topic of this dissertation is about polymaths—people with varied learnings across different domains—the definition of self-directed learning that fits best is Brockett's (1983), which defines self-directed learning as "a disposition to engage in learning activities where the individual takes personal responsibility for developing and carrying out learning endeavors autonomously without being prompted or guided by other people" (p. 16).
- **Social Identity Theory:** While Identity Theory is more focused on the role of the individual, in Social Identity Theory, the emphasis is on groups of people (Stets & Burke, 2000). According to Social Identity Theory, social identity is "a person's knowledge that he or she belongs to a social category or group" (Stets & Burke, 2000, p. 225).

Chapter 2: Literature Review

Purpose

Overview of Chapter

Throughout this chapter, this author will first provide a brief synopsis of the methods of the literature review, and subsequently, the remainder—the bulk—of this chapter will be spent reviewing, describing, critiquing, and synthesizing the literature around the following constructs:

- Identity
    - Identity Theory
    - Social Identity Theory
- Learning
    - Self-directed learning
- Polymaths and Multi-disciplinarity
    - Openness to experience
    - Intrapersonal functional diversity
    - Creativity and creative problem solving

I end the chapter with a summary and inferences for forthcoming study.

Methods of the Literature Review

The literature review was conducted using the following search terms: intrapersonal and/or individual diversity, intrapersonal functional diversity, homogeneity and heterogeneity of experience, experiential learning, openness to experience, polymath, interdisciplinarity, Renaissance man. The bulk of the literature used was found around (1) openness to experience, (2) polymaths, (3) multi-disciplinarity, and (4) intrapersonal diversity. I used the following databases to explore these topics: ProQuest, J-STOR, PsychINFO, Academic Search Complete, and Articles Plus. Most of the cited literature in this chapter was published within the last 20 years. The oldest source cited is from 1902; the newest is from 2015—though the bulk of the literature cited herein is from the last 25 years. Selections of literature to use or not was based on its relevancy to the research topic.

Identity

When trying to understand polymaths, it is important first to understand identity since that is a phenomenon with which they will identify. According to one of the seminal scholars in this area, Erikson (1950) believed that identity is formed over time. In fact, he (1950), believed unlike the Freudian idea that personality is fixed in early childhood, that because people learn and grow, their identities regularly shift over the life span. In fact, he developed the "eight ages of man" model to reflect this belief. Erikson's (1950, 1963) eight stages are described in the table below:

Table 2-1: Description of Erikson's Developmental Stages

Name of the Stage	Description of the Stage
Stage 1: Trust versus mistrust	This stage occurs from birth to 1.5 years old, when an infant engages with the world orally. This stage is called "trust and mistrust" because this is when a baby learns to request attention, food, or help by crying and a caregiver will either meet the needs of the baby or not—therefore the baby develops trust or mistrust for the caregiver.
Stage 2: Autonomy versus shame and doubt	This stage occurs between the ages of 18 months and three years old and occurs as the child learns about physical and personal control. During this time, the child becomes less dependent upon others for their needs and survival and begins developing more control over their physical abilities such as walking and talking. Due to the increasing sense of self-control, independence and autonomy form and set the stage for the baby's confidence.

Stage 3: Initiative versus guilt	This stage occurs from age 3 to 6, when the child begins to exert control and power through their environment. Social expressions such as play allow the child to experiment with this sense of newfound power. Normal development in this stage leads the child to believe that they can influence peers and have confidence in themselves, functioning in the world. If the child does not develop normally in this stage, he or she develops feelings of guilt and shame.
Stage 4: Industry versus Inferiority	Stage four occurs from ages 6 to 12 when the child develops a sense of industry by creating things. It is during this stage that most children across the world begin going to school and children also learn about the fundamentals of technology (such as tools and weapons) and begin mimicking their use.
Stage 5: Identity versus role confusion	This stage occurs during adolescence when the person learns to explore different roles while still resolving issues from earlier childhood. At this time, the ego identity is formed and adolescents usually identify with a group or clans, whether by race, culture, or other types of appearance.
Stage 6: Intimacy versus isolation	This stage occurs during early adulthood when an individual starts to explore relationships with others more deeply through merging identity with others, intimacy, or other types of close relationships.
Stage 7: Generativity versus stagnation	This stage occurs between the ages of 35 to 60 when an adult begins sharing their knowledge with younger people. "Mature man needs to be needed "(p. 266) and so if that is not happening, the person may have a sense of stagnation.
Stage 8: Ego integrity versus despair	The last stage, which occurs in late adulthood, focuses on lifetime accomplishments as well as regrets and lost opportunities. During this time, an individual may either fear death because there is a sense of a life not fully lived, or there is a sense of acceptance for what was accomplished in the lifetime.

Aside from Erikson's model, there are two leading theoretical perspectives with regard to identity: Identity Theory, which is rooted in psychology, as well as Social Identity Theory, which comes from the field of sociology (Stets & Burke, 2000; Hogg, Terry, & White, 1995). There are similarities as well as differences between the two theories. For example, one primary similarity in both Identity Theory and Social Identity Theory, is that "the self is reflexive in that it can take itself as an object and can categorize, classify, or name itself in particular ways in relation to other social categories or classifications" (Stets & Burke, 2000, p. 224). In Social Identity Theory, this is called self-categorization while in Identity Theory, it is referred to as identification (Stets & Burke, 2000). Both refer to the same basic concept, however: that it is through self-categorization or identification that a human being forms his or her identity. In other words, we learn who we are (our self-concept) and about normative behavior acceptable in society in relation to others (Hogg, Terry, & White, 1995). "Both address the social nature of self as constituted by society, and eschew perspectives that treat self as independent of and prior to society" (Hogg, Terry, & White, 1995, p. 255). Below, more details are provided on each of these two leading theories.

Identity Theory

Identity theory aims to explain individuals' role-related behaviors and takes into consideration how society impacts the individual (Hogg, Terry, & White, 1995). The focus is on the personal, micro level of analysis, but it takes into consideration societal influences on the individual. It is closely tied with the symbolic interactionist view that Mead (1934) described, in which society affects social behavior because of society's influence on the self. Mead (1934) believed that others play a role in how we view ourselves. He considered the self as being composed of an I and me, which represent the subjective and objective components of identity. Whereas Mead viewed society as a "relatively undifferentiated, cooperative whole" (Stryker and Serpe, 1982, p. 206), Identity Theory posits that society is actually "complexly differentiated but nevertheless organized" (Stryker and Serpe, 1982, p. 206). Identity theorists call the multi-faceted components of the self as identities or role identities.

Symbolic interactionists like Mead (1934) and Cooley (1902) believed that the self is a product of social interaction because people understand who they are in relation to their interactions with other people. Further, since people interact and are part of various different groups, they may have many distinct selves based on the distinct groups to which they belong and whose opinions matter to them (Hogg, Terry, & White, 1995). So, an individual's identity is not just one thing, but a composite of various identities merged together, impacted by both internal and external forces, all of which may shift over time. These role identities provide meaning for the self, both because they refer to specific roles the person inhabits, but also because these roles allow them to distinguish from counterroles that they do not inhabit (Lindesmith and Strauss, 1956).

Social Identity Theory

In-Group and Out-Group. While Identity Theory is more focused on the role of the individual, in Social Identity Theory, the emphasis is on groups of people (Stets & Burke, 2000). According to Social Identity Theory, social identity is "a person's knowledge that he or she belongs to a social category or group" (Stets & Burke, 2000, p. 225). It is knowing what their in-group is, of which they are a part, and their out-group, of which they are not a part (Stets & Burke, 2000).

Self-Categorization and Social Comparison. There are two important sub-aspects of Social Identity Theory: (1) self-categorization and (2) social comparison (Hogg & Abrams, 1988). Self-categorization involves a person perceiving who they have similarities with while also accentuating perceived differences between the self and members of the out-group (Stets & Burke, 2000). Social comparison involves selectively applying this accentuation effect in order to enhance outcomes for the self; in particular, self-esteem would be enhanced, for example, by evaluating the in-group favorably and judging the out-group less favorably (Stets & Burke, 2000).

Whatever social categories an individual places themselves in exist in the structured society that we are all born into and are defined by their difference from other categories (Hogg and Abrams, 1988). Different groups have more or less power, prestige, status, etc. (Stets & Burke, 2000). Once a part of the society, individuals develop their identity or their sense of self, in large part, due to the social categories to which they belong (Stets & Burke, 2000). And because each person has a unique life experience, each person has a unique combination of social categories with which they identify (Stets & Burke, 2000).

Social Identity Theory is largely about how different groups relate and compare—in other words, how people see themselves as part of their in-group in contrast to the out-group (Stets & Burke, 2000). Further, people tend to evaluate the behaviors of their in-group almost entirely positively (Stets & Burke, 2000). One example of this consequence of this sort of behavior is ethnocentrism (Turner et al., 1987). People also tend to behave in concert with their in-group (Stets & Burke, 2000), so groupthink tends to be more likely when social identification is high (Turner, Pratkanis, Probasco, and Leve, 1992). Polymaths may be able to help combat groupthink because they are not viewing the issues from only a single disciplinary perspective.

Relevance. Since this dissertation research aims to understand the experience of a specific group of people—namely, polymaths—understanding thinking around identity serves as a basis for putting their experiences into context. The goal of this dissertation research is to understand their experiences—identifying as and living life as polymaths.

Identity Theory is more focused on the individual and how they are impacted by society, while Social Identity Theory is about identifying with a larger social category or group—and some polymaths may or may not identify with such a category or group. However, since some polymaths may think of themselves that way and perhaps even seek to identify and connect with other polymaths, although even the absence of an in-group for polymaths is still worthy of considering in the context of Identity Theory and Social Identity Theory.

How does a polymath recognize that he or she may be one, especially in a society where many people do not even know the word *polymath*? When a life-altering realization like this occurs for a polymath, that individual has to engage in *sensemaking* (Weick, 1995). Weick has suggested that the process of sensemaking is grounded in identity and is usually initiated from extreme experience (or realization); he also said that those people who seek to make sense of that situation (or realization) are often afraid to tell others out of fear of what others may think (i.e., they may not be believed). Further, polymaths who tout or promote their own intelligence, skills, and value may be seen as arrogant and could even be ostracized for doing so. So how is a polymath identity formed and shared?

In a world where we need more polymaths to engage in *sensegiving* (Weick, 1995) in order to solve the major problems of our time, a basic initial step is for those who are polymaths to first understand themselves as being a polymath and to acknowledge that they are in a unique position to add value to society. So, understanding issues around identity is crucial in trying to support the development and success of modern day polymaths.

Learning

Self-directed Learning

Self-directed learning is

> a self-initiated process of learning that stresses the ability of individuals to plan and manage their own learning, and attribute or characteristic of learning with personal autonomy as its hallmark, and a way of organizing instruction in formal settings that allows for greater learner control (Caffarella, 1993, p. p. 25).

Self-directed learning can be further described as a process that the learner him- or herself controls; the learner takes responsibility for his or her own learning (Guglielmino, 2008). This approach is a means by which we may "participate in our own self-formation" (Tennant, 2006, p. 53). This sort of self-direction in adult learning has also been referred to as self-planning, self-teaching, independent adult learning, and self-initiated (Owen, 2002). Mezirow said that "no concept is more central to what adult education is all about than self-directed learning" (1985). In fact, because learning is fundamentally an individual behavior, self-directed learning could be considered the most valid form of learning, as it is most tailored to individual needs, from the individual's own perspective.

Early Scholarly Research on Self-directed Learning. Early researchers Houle (1961) and Tough (1971) explained self-directed learning as something that occurs throughout the lifetime, even if informally. Houle's (1961) research focused on why adults who choose to engage in continuing education do so, as opposed to how they learned. He identified three kinds of adult learners: (1) goal-oriented, (2) learning-oriented, and (3) activity-oriented (as cited by McCreary, 1990).

Tough's (1971) research built upon Houle's. Tough (1971) looked at the self-planning learning projects of sixty-six adult learners. His research showed that learning that is widespread and systematic can occur, regardless of whether or not an instructor or traditional classroom is involved. Tough (1971) observed that "highly deliberate efforts to learn take place all around you" (p. 3).

Malcolm Knowles is another scholar who contributed to early scholarly discourse on self-directed learning around the same time as Houle and Tough. Knowles' (1975) research defined self-directed learning as

> A process in which individuals take the initiative, with or without the help from others, in diagnosing their learning needs, formulating goals, identifying human and material resources, choosing and implementing appropriate learning strategies and evaluating learning outcomes (p. 18).

Knowles' contributions to the literature on self-directed learning focused mostly on explaining what it is and how to implement it through using learning contracts. Knowles also said that self-directed learning is part of the natural process of human psychological development, involves individuals who take initiative in learning instead of simply waiting to be taught, and is an essential component in maturing. All three of these early, pioneering scholars' work tended to describe what self-directed learning is and expose how widespread it is among adult learners. It also outlined, to some extent, the process that adults go through to self-direct their own learning so that it could be applied by others.

Guglielmino's (1977) research on self-directed learners looked at the characteristics that people have who are ready to be self-directed learners. She posited that this type of learning consists of a complex interplay of attitudes, values, and abilities that impact whether or not an individual is capable of self-directed learning (as cited by

Merriam, Caffarella, & Baumgartner, 2007). Guglielmino (1977) said that self-direction in learning occurs in a wide variety of different situations, whether in a teacher-directed classroom or independent, self-planned learning.

Early approaches: Self-directed learning as a linear process. Early scholars like Knowles (1975) and Tough (1971) described self-directed learning as something very linear. It involved steps in the learning process including planning, initiative, diagnosis of learning needs, creating learning goals, identifying resources, selecting learning strategies, and then evaluating outcomes. Later scholars viewed self-directed learning as something more complex than this sort of linear process (and will be explained further, below).

Contemporary research on self-directed learning. A number of various researchers from more recent times have added to the scholarly discussion around self-directed learning. Each scholar tends to have their own definition of self-directed learning. For instance, Caffarella (1993) posited that self-directed learning could either be a self-initiated process of planning and managing one's own learning, but it could also be an attributed or characteristic someone has, or also a way of organizing instruction in formal settings to allow for others to control their own learning.

As another example, Candy (1991) considered self-directed learning not only a process but a goal and involves the interaction between a learner and his/her environment; because of the context, a person could be successfully self-directed sometimes and not at other times, depending on the situation. Candy's (1991) definition of self-directed learning is the "individual, non-institutional pursuit of learning opportunities in the 'natural setting'" (p. 23). Candy said that

> The relationship between self-directed learning and life-long education is a reciprocal one. On the one hand, self-directed learning is one of the most common ways in which adults pursue learning throughout their life span, as well as being a way in which people supplement learning received in formal settings. On the other hand, lifelong learning takes, as one of its principle aims, equipping people with skills and competencies required to continue their own self-education beyond the end of formal schooling. In this sense, self-directed learning is viewed simultaneously as a means and an end of lifelong education (p. 15).

Merriam and Caffarella (1999) categorized self-directed learning as having three basic goals, which could exist independently or in tandem: (1) enhancing the ability of adults to be self-directed in their learning, (2) promoting transformational learning, and (3) fostering freedom of choice and social action. As for this third point, it may seem unclear at first how self-directed learning relates to freedom and social action. However, "people whose lives are affected by a decision must be a part of the process of arriving at that decision" (Naisbitt, 1984). Candy (1991) believes that in a participatory democracy, there should also be participatory learning methods whereby learners are involved in all aspects of their own education, from assessing their own needs, designing their learning, and evaluating the learning outcomes. John Dewey (1916) would probably agree, as would Freire (1968). "Learning should empower a student to become a free, mature, and authentic self" (Savin-Baden and Major, 2004, p. 14).

Varying definitions. As discussed above, there are a variety of definitions regarding what self-directed learning is exactly—though the idea of individual learning is prevalent among all of them. Because of these varying definitions, it is clear that self-directed learning may be understood, explained, researched, studied, and summarized in various different ways; it is a multi-faceted concept.

Given that the topic of this dissertation is about polymaths—people with varied learnings across different domains—the definition of self-directed learning that fits best is Brockett's (1983), which defines self-directed learning as "a disposition to engage in learning activities where the individual takes personal responsibility for developing and carrying out learning endeavors autonomously without being prompted or guided by other people" (p. 16). Because polymaths are unlikely to be told by another person which disparate areas to become adept and perhaps even expert in, this definition—which stresses the independent, self-initiated nature of their learning—is most appropriate when studying polymaths.

Self-directed learning as an interactive process. In contrast to early scholars who viewed self-directed learning as a straight-forward, linear process, later researchers viewed it as being more interactive, i.e., because self-directed learning may not even be well planned, and the environment, opportunities, or characteristics of the learner all interact together and impact one's self-directed learning (Merriam, Caffarella, & Baumgartner, 2007). Further, although many adults are motivated to learn in order to get a job promotion, enter a new professional field, make more money, or gain more prestige (Rogers, 1989), Rossing and Long (1981) said that adult learners might also seek out learning opportunities not just to solve problems, but for the simple satisfaction and joy that can come from learning—whether what was learned is practical or not. But what is clear is that learning, even if it is self-directed, rarely occurs "in splendid isolation from the world in which the learning lives…it is intimately related to that world and affected by it" (Jarvis, 1987, p. 11).

Spear and Mocker (1984) created a model for self-directed learning as an interactive process and takes into consideration the interplay of opportunities people have in their environment, their existing knowledge, and also pure chance. Together, these factors shape one's learning experience. This model emphasizes that one's life circumstances heavily influence one's learning.

Garrison (1997) created an interactive model for the self-directed learning process and is multi-dimensional in that it takes into consideration the social aspects of learning, motivation to learn, and behaviors one uses to implement one's own learning. Garrison's model posits that self-directed learning is both a personal attribute and also a learning process.

Another way to understand the self-directed learning process is through an instructional lens. According to Grow's (1991) model, the goal is to help instructors guide learners with different levels of self-direction to be self-directed in their own learning. Grow (1991) describes four types of learners: learners in stage 1, who are low in self-direction. Stage 2 learners, who have moderate self-direction and are interested in learning. Stage 3 learners are involved learners ready and able to explore a topic with an effective guide. Stage 4 learners are very self-directed and able to plan, execute, and evaluate their own learning projects whether or not they have the help of an expert. Grow (1991) believes an instructor can have a role in all of these stages. Therefore, according to this model, self-directed learning could be placed upon a continuum which ranges from teacher-directed learning (or other-oriented learning) to self-directed learning at the other end of the spectrum.

Self-directed learning correlates. According to Lounsbury et al. (2009), those who have high levels of self-directed learning will tend to also have high levels of intuitiveness, openness, conscientiousness, career decidedness, emotional stability, optimism, work drive, extraversion, self-actualization, a realistic view, an investigative and artistic nature, life and college satisfaction, and will tend to use multiple different types of reasoning. There is also data to support a link between self-directed learning and success in academic settings (Bad-El-Fattah, 2010; Cherng-Jyh & Simon, 2009; Bhat et al., 2007; Schmidt et al., 2009; Smith & Morrison, 2006). Self-directed learning also allows for a large degree of personalization and diversity since students can design their own learning (Smith & Morrison, 2006).

Self-directed learning and self-actualization. Maslow (1970) believed that the primary purpose of learning is to work towards self-actualization. Maslow (1954) defined self-actualization as the desire to "become more and more of what one is, to become everything that one is capable of becoming" (p. 92). Similarly, Rogers (1983) correlated learning with self-improvement, saying that significant learning will creative positive growth and development in people. Both Maslow and Rogers supported learners to be active participants in their own development so they could work towards self-actualization, which represents the pinnacle of human achievement.

Summary and critique of the literature on self-directed learning. In sum, a variety of different researchers over the past six decades have attempted to describe self-directed learning, whether as a simple, linear, step-by-step process or a more complex interactive one. What is common among all of them is that in self-directed learning, the individual learner is at the forefront of their own learning as opposed to the onus being mostly on a teacher, tutor, mentor, or peers; the individual is more personally responsible for his or her own development. It is a complex and multi-faceted concept that emphasizes human capacity, the ability to change one's own behavior, and self-evaluation as opposed to these facets coming from external sources (Danis, 1992). This author did not find any articles regarding the self-directed learning of polymaths, however—hopefully this dissertation will help fill that gap by adding to the discourse around self-directed learning with particular focus on polymaths.

Polymaths and Multi-disciplinarity

Description

The word polymathḗs, equivalent to polymaths in English, first appeared around the year 1615 in Greece, with poly meaning "many" and mathḗs deriving from the word mantháneín which means to learn. So a polymath is someone with many learnings (Dictionary.com). A similar notion, multi-disciplinarity, occurs when one draws upon knowledge from different disciplines (Choi and Pak, 2006). Polymaths who pursue different areas of knowledge tend to understand things more broadly, developing an appreciation for a variety of different fields, and also are able to enjoy the experiences afforded to them across those various fields (Lang, 2014). In this dissertation, I will use the terms polymathy and multi-disciplinarity interchangeably.

Nature versus nurture. For many decades, there has been a debate in the literature regarding whether *nature* or *nurture* impacts personhood more (Ornstein, 1993). There is some evidence to indicate that polymaths become that way due, in part, to their environment. For instance, a number of studies have shown that there is little correlation between creativity and being innately gifted or talented; instead, the studies indicate that creative people are more broadly trained, have more avocational interests, and show increased abilities in those interests than the average individual does (Root-Bernstein, 2015). In STEM (sciences, technology, engineering, and mathematics) fields, the avocational interests of the most successful professionals are highly linked with skills in the fine arts such as painting or music, or literary accomplishments, or skills in trades such as woodworking, metalworking, electronics, or mechanics (Root-Bernstein, 2015). Given it seems possible that polymathy may be fostered in individuals—rather than simply being an inborn trait—it is worth understanding the phenomenon even more, since there can be great benefits to polymathic thinking and skills.

Comparisons in Time. In centuries past, it was very common for people to have deep expertise across a breadth of different fields (Ross, 2011). The openness to try everything, "to think, write, and discourse publicly about a wide variety of topics from poetics to politics, mathematics to medicine, was more common among intellectuals of the Romantic period than it is today" (Ross, 2011, p. 401). In that time period, polymaths were almost entirely self-taught lifelong scholars; they were intellectually curious about disparate ideas and liberal—rather than narrow—in the scope of their intellectual pursuits (Ross, 2011).

Polymathic attitudes were common among intellectuals in the Romantic Period as Romantics "took pleasure in wide-ranging, learned discourse and what they called 'improvement'" (Ross, 2011, p. 412). It was very common at that time for various cultural societies, colleges, public lectures, social clubs, and periodicals to provide opportunities for cross-fertilization of discourses which "encouraged polymathic and educational endeavors of various sorts, and prepared a space in the culture for new attitudes" and ideas and ways of thinking to emerge (Ross, 2011, p. 413).

In contrast, our age is an age of specialists and specialization (Ross, 2011); there are a few explanations for this shift. In the Romantic Era, disciplinary specialization was not a necessity because the volume of knowledge that individuals might try to study or obtain was manageable (Ross, 2011). Secondly, the educational system of the period supported more interdisciplinarity more so than the system today (Ross, 2011). The system in the Romantic Era focused on training resourceful students with mental discipline as well as intellectual confidence whose knowledge was expected to widen over their lifetime; mental versatility was the goal (Ross, 2011). There was a growing interest in self-improvement and usefulness at that time as well as a belief that the world—in all its variety—is man's to study and master (Ross, 2011). A third reason for this shift to specialization is because Romantic polymathy generated so much new knowledge very rapidly that disciplinarity and professional specialization became necessary (Ross, 2011). It was during the Victorian period that the era of specialization—which we still have today—began to emerge and the emphasis on wide, general knowledge began to wane (Ross, 2011).

During the Industrial Revolution – the age of Ford's assembly line circa 1913—the concept of division of labor became even more widespread and has evolved over time from being applied to physical labor to also intellectual labor—even labor done virtually (O'Neill and McGinley, 2014). Although efficient and economical, did this move to specialization come at a cost?

Although overall there has been a trend towards specialization in the modern era, not all organizations support this view. For instance, Jonathan Rosenberg, former Senior Vice President of Products at Google, said in an interview with Harvard Business Review's IdeaCast that at Google, they focus on hiring people dedicated to continuous learning as opposed to specialists "And the main reason is that when you're in a dynamic industry where the conditions are changing so fast, then things like experience and the way you've done a role before isn't nearly as important as your ability to think. So generalists, not specialists, is a mantra that we have internally that we try to stick pretty closely to. Specialists tend to bring an inherent bias to a problem, and they often feel threatened by new solutions."

Single-Disciplinary Versus Multi-Disciplinary Scholarship. Although the complexities of the modern era demand a more integrative and multi-disciplinary approach to solve them, individual scholars in the academic world are rewarded for focusing on one area very deeply, within a single discipline, and are discouraged from developing wide expertise in various different fields (Leahey, 2007). "The university institution is largely monolithic and path-dependent, perpetuating discipline-based scholarship and sometimes creating new niches that are even more specialized. Such hyper-specialization expands exponentially, often without an integrative moment" (Terjesen and Politis, 2015, p. 151). An example of this trend in academia is in the tenure and promotion process which rewards deep specialization (Terjesen and Politis, 2015). Most academic journals also lack multi-disciplinarity, and if they do, it tends to be in fields that are different but closely related, like accounting and finance (Terjesen and Politis, 2015). As a general rule—whether inside academia or not—disciplinary specialization is common in our time (Ross, 2011). It is somewhat counterintuitive that this would be the case given the myriad examples throughout history of polymaths' extraordinary contributions to the world.

Examples of Polymaths

Some examples of very famous individuals with wide intellectual interests or talents whose multi-disciplinarity led to paradigm-shifting innovations include Leonardo da, Erasmus, Benjamin Franklin, Galileo Galelei, and Francis Bacon (Terjesen and Politis, 2015). There are countless examples of societal contributions from polymaths both in centuries past as well as in modern day (Terjesen and Politis, 2015). In the next few paragraphs, I will provide a bit more detail of some noteworthy polymaths.

Of course, a dissertation on polymaths would not be complete without acknowledging Leonardo da Vinci. Leonardo da Vinci is one of the most prolific polymaths in recorded human history (Smith, 2014). He was a renowned painter, sculptor, musician, mathematician, engineer, architect, inventor, anatomist, geologist, cartographer, botanist, and author (Smith, 2014). "He was able to jump between all of these fields to make valuable contributions when they were still young sciences…he bridged the gap from one profession to another when it suited his curiosity and his insights." (Smith, 2014, p. 58-59). Concepts found in da Vinci's writings from 1425-1519 later influenced other great thinkers such as Copernicus, Galileo, Isaac Newton, and Charles Darwin (Smith, 2014).

A lesser known, but still impressive, polymath from a different century than da Vinci is Thomas Young (Robinson, 2005). He lived from 1773 – 1829, and in 1931 Einstein even paid tribute to Young in a brief foreword to Newton's *Opticks*. In 1973, the Science Museum in London said that "Young probably had a wider range of creative learning than any other Englishman in history. He made discoveries in nearly every field he studied" (Robinson, 2015, p. 291). Young made pioneering contributions to the study of light, ophthalmology, Egyptology, while also being a distinguished physician, an expert author on myriad subjects, a scholar of ancient Greece, and a linguist (Robinson, 2015). There were some downsides to his polymathy, however: "Young was restlessly curious. He generally moved on long before he had fully explored his intuitions and discoveries. As a result, his reputation suffered, which he well knew" (Robinson, 2005, p. 291).

Another example, but from contemporary times, is Michael Polanyi (1891 – 1976), a British-Hungarian researcher whose skillsets spanned fields including science, philosophy, history, politics, art, economics, literature, ethics, values, and religion (Terjesen and Politis, 2015). He said that much of the reason he was a polymath was because of his upbringing—he spoke English, French, German, and Hungarian languages as a child, studied many different subjects, and sought to "develop a diverse epistemology that supports multiple ways of knowing rather than a specific single method" (Terjesen and Politis, 2015, p 154).

As another example of a contemporary polymath, Vernon Smith, who withstood incredible institutional pressures in economics to keep confined to the discipline's boundaries ended up applying his engineering expertise to develop the groundbreaking field of experimental economics (Nobel, 2002). As a result, he received the Nobel Prize in Economics. When asked about this, he said he was inspired by an Enlightenment economist from Scotland, Adam Smith, who was a multi-disciplinary adventurer and Friedrich Hayek's belief that an economist who is only an economist cannot be a very good one (Smith, 2008).

Complex Problems are Multi-disciplinary

Although the dominant paradigm we currently experience in the 21st century is focused on singular discipline-based scholarship, the problems of the world require more multi-disciplinary approaches to solve them (Terjesen and Politis, 2015). Some examples of problems that will need multi-disciplinary solutions include addressing "sustainable development challenges such as climate change, widespread poverty, and gender inequality…cancer, terrorism, unemployment, AIDS, cybersecurity, and sustainable energy" (Terjesen and Politis, 2015, p. 152-153).

In fact, a dominant paradigm growing in more modern times revolves around Complexity Theory; in fact, Complexity Theory is touted as a leading scientific trend (Manson, 2001). Complexity Theory is an interdisciplinary theory related to Systems Theory. One of the things this paradigm says is that in a very complex system, solutions emerge (they cannot be predicted). The whole is greater than just the sum of its parts (Manson, 2001). Complexity Theory would advocate that problems are very complex—likely multi-disciplinary—and need knowledge from many different parts of the system in order to be solved (Manson, 2001).

Benefits of Multi-disciplinarity

Multi-disciplinarity provides benefits to society as well as individuals (Terjesen and Politis, 2015). For example, generalists are better at forecasting what will happen in the future (Tetlock and Gardner, 2015). And Root-Bernstein (2008) found that Nobel Prize laureates demonstrated creativity in several domains of work more so than those less eminent peers who tended to be more specialized. Similar to openness to experience, multi-disciplinarity is associated with a number of similar benefits, described below further.

Individuals can also experience professional and personal benefits from being polymathic. For example, researchers who are too specialized are less likely to get promoted (Leahey et al., 2010), whereas those who work in various disciplines tend to receive more citations (Leahey, 2007). Polymaths are more likely to be creative given their ability to draw analogies from disparate bodies of knowledge. People who have broad, varied experiences and exposure are able to ignite cognitive processes that increase creativity (Ward, 1995). Creativity scholars refer to polymaths as being highly creative people (Root-Bernstein, et al., 2008, Kaufman, et al., 2010) who are able to experience a broad array of disparate and unrelated—even paradoxical—activities. These people are open to novel experiences whether professionally or through hobbies (Csikszentmihalyi, 1996).

Multi-disciplinarity also gives way for new linkages and creativity to emerge; indeed, knowledge in one discipline can often inspire or be applied to other disciplines (Terjesen and Politis, 2015). Scholars such as Karl Weick, James March, and Jeffrey Pfeffer have made significant contributions in fields of education as well as management; the consistent them among them is that they are committed to understanding the myriad aspects of real-world problems regardless of disciplinary boundaries (Terjesen and Politis, 2015). In 1966, Cranefield examined 12 scientists who had helped to found the field of biophysics in the mid-1800's; Cranefield (1966) found that there is a positive association between the number of avocations that a scientist had and the number of significant discoveries they made. A later study done on 20th century scientists found that the most successful scientists, including 4 different Nobel laureates, tended to be engaged in the fine arts or an avocation around crafts when compared to their less successful counterparts (Root-Bernstein, Bernstein, & Garnier, 1995). Clearly, there can be great benefits from polymathic thinking and approaches, as these examples highlight.

On Curiosity

Polymaths are driven by curiosity; curiosity defines what it is polymaths do. In fact, in more recent times, the idea of "CQ," has emerged which stands for curiosity quotient, similar to IQ (intelligence quotient) (White, 2009). People who have high CQs are very inquisitive and open to new experiences (White, 2009). They like novelty, are good at generating original ideas, and tend to dislike conformity (Chamorro-Premuzic, 2014). These types of people are more likely to have high levels of knowledge acquisition over their lifetimes and that level of expertise means they may interpret complex situations into familiar ones. So, individuals with high CQs are often very adept at producing simple solutions to complex problems (Chamorro-Premuzic, 2014). In fact, there is a general consensus that creativity requires multiple resources within one person—the kind of "multiple resources" that a polymath would have (Amabile, 1996).

Curiosity can help individuals succeed. For instance, curiosity is associated with higher academic performance (Von Stumm, Hell, and Chamorro-Premuzic, 2011). People who are highly curious engage in deep learning and may be intrinsically motivated (have an internal locus of control) to study subjects beyond what is even required—beyond simple compliance; this intrinsic motivation may come from the values they hold, their upbringing, culture, etc. Many highly curious people become entrepreneurs; entrepreneurial people tend to be more curious, as well, and that is part of why they avoid traditional employment—because it is too boring for their hungry minds (Chamorro-Premuzic, 2014).

Regarding Self-Actualization

A number of different authors have equated openness and polymathic behaviors with the concept of self-actualization. For example, Abraham Maslow (1970), who is well-known for his theory regarding man's hierarchy of needs, believed that once the basic needs of a person are met (food, shelter, warmth, security, belonging, etc.), then and only then could a person can achieve self-actualization. His exact definition of self-actualization is "the full use and exploitation of [one's] talents, capacities, potentialities, etc." (Maslow, 1970, p. 150). This definition sounds very similar to polymathy. Maslow said that to be self-actualized is to be a "mature, fully-human" person. In fact, Maslow himself uses the phrase "open to experience" to describe those who self-actualize.

Though made popular by Maslow, a number of other authors have written about self-actualization. The term self-actualization was actually first introduced by Kurt Goldstein in 1939. To him, self-actualization was expressing one's creativity and pursuing knowledge while also positively transforming society. He said it is the only real motive people have: "The tendency to actualize itself as fully as possible is the basic drive…the drive of self-actualization" (Goldstein, 1939, p 350). Another author, Ernest Schachtel, (1959) also says that openness is tantamount to self-actualization. And Erich Fromm (1955) said in his book, The Sane Society, that "the whole life of the individual is nothing but the process of giving birth to himself." Arguably, this "giving birth" process could take place through exposure and finding one's authentic self through trial and error. And Kolb (2015) has argued that experience and exposure plays a central role in learning; polymaths are lifelong learners who get exposure across various domains. Indeed, this type of learning allows people to construct knowledge and meaning rooted in real-life experience (Yardley, Teunissen, and Dornan, 2012). Vygotsky's (1978) Zone of Proximal Development could also be used as a way to understand reaching one's fullest potential (self-actualizing).

The Downside of Multi-disciplinarity

Despite the benefits, there are drawbacks to being a multi-disciplinary expert. Obviously, one drawback is the amount of time and resources it takes to become expert in multiple fields (Terjesen and Politis, 2015). Different fields may also be associated with different value sets. For instance, the soft (social) sciences tend to be more open to qualitative research whereas the hard (natural) sciences prefer quantitative approaches (Albert et al., 2008); this contradiction of values could be difficult for some. Similarly, relative to single discipline scholars, multi-disciplinary experts tend to publish less and be less visible (Leahey, 2007). As a result, multi-disciplinary scholars may have a harder time gaining legitimacy (Terjesen and Politis, 2015).

Another downside is the difficulty involved in learning vast amounts of disparate information (Jones, 2009). "If knowledge accumulates as technology advances, then successive generations of innovators may face an increasing educational burden. Innovators can compensate through lengthening educational phases and narrowing expertise, but these responses come at the cost of reducing individual innovative capacities, with implications for the organization of innovative activity—a greater reliance on teamwork—and negative implications for growth" (Jones, 2009, p. 283). Jones (2009) suggests that the very nature of innovation itself is changing, with innovation becoming harder due to the vast amount of information that people must learn—which he says will also impact long-term economic growth.

Polymaths may be viewed negatively as well, given the society we live in tends to value single-discipline expertise (Terjesen and Politis, 2015). In fact, when a person, for instance, "seeks to operate outside a discipline's boundaries by contributing in two or more, others may perceive that as a violation of institutional norms, and may advocate for some sort of retribution or punishment" (Terjesen and Politis, 2015, p. 154) and they may even be marginalized and have resources diminished. So, in some ways, polymathy "may be a vice as much as a virtue in this age of specialization" (Robinson, 2006, p. 409).

Another downside of polymathic endeavors is that multi-disciplinary people may be so interested in many different topics that this can be distracting (Richardson, 2005). For instance, da Vinci did not always deliver on time and sometimes abandoned his projects completely; he started many projects that he never finished (Richardson, 2005). Aside from the unfortunate reality of unfinished work, this also led da Vinci to have some soured relations (Richardson, 2005).

Paths to Polymathy

For individuals who want to become more polymathic, there are a number of ideas for how to go about doing so—a craft to become a polymath. For instance, "At an individual level, an essential first step" to becoming a polymath is "learning how to learn" (Terjesen and Politis, 2015, p. 154). Another approach is to expose oneself to workgroups of people who have differing expertise and backgrounds so as to increase exposure to a broader set of perspectives (Taylor and Greve, 2006). One polymath, Laszlo Polgar, read biographies of 400 great intellectuals from different disciplines in order to help inspire his own polymathy. His multi-disciplinary education is in line with what Bloom (1985) claimed, which is that experts are made, not born, so it is entirely possible to develop one's expertise in one or several different disciplines. Terjesen and Politis (2015) have suggested developing deep expertise in one area first before trying to become expert in multiple arenas at the same time; in other words, a diverse skill set can be developed over time.

Leonardo Da Vinci was the quintessential Renaissance man and one of history's great luminaries—still revered even 500 years after his time. He was prodigious in an array of different fields including architecture, engineering, anatomy, and physical sciences, said that to develop a complete mind, one should "Study the science of art. Study the art of science. Develop your senses—especially learn how to see. Realize that everything connects to everything else."

Summary and Critique of the Literature in Multi-disciplinarity and Polymaths.

Taken as a whole, the literature on polymaths and multi-disciplinarity points to the fact that these types of individuals are particularly well suited to solve complex problems like those that exist in the twenty-first century. Perhaps one weakness of the literature is a limited number of experiments to test the belief that polymaths add value. Most of the articles in this particular literature stream provide anecdotal evidence for the values – and drawbacks—of polymathy and multi-disciplinarity. There is also a dearth of literature trying to understand the lived experiences of modern day polymaths.

Openness to Experience

Emergence of Openness to Experience in the Literature. The openness to experience literature first appeared in the late 1980's—or at least that is when it first appeared with that moniker. At that time, McCrae (1987) conducted a study, finding that openness to experience is positively related to divergent thinking and creativity. Two years later, Martindale (1989) published an article—perhaps responding to McCrae—by saying that he believed openness to experience and creativity are essentially the same thing. McCrae published another article in 1994, probably responding to Martindale's critique in part, which said that openness to experience is essentially a personality disposition that can lead to creativity, but that it is different from creativity itself. More recent and advanced scholarly work has been done beyond this initial debate, which will be described in further detail below.

Description. Openness to experience is part of the "Big 5" personality traits originally described by McCrae and Costa (1987). It is the "disposition to be imaginative, nonconforming, and unconventional" (Judge, Bono, Ilies, and Berhard, 2002, p. 765). It includes exploring multiple options, challenging assumptions, seeking different perspectives, combining different viewpoints, and actively evaluating different options (Shalley and Perry Smith, 2008). People high in the openness to experience personality trait are often more flexible and able to understand various perspectives more readily (Zhao and Seibert, 2006), and those people tend "to be imaginative, intellectually curious, and open to trying new things" (Burke and Witt, 2002, p. 712). A number of different studies over a period of many years link openness to experience with creativity at the individual level of analysis (McCrae, 1987; Feist, 1998; George & Zhou, 2001; McCrae & Costa, 1997).

Given this description, it is easy to understand why understanding openness to experience pertains to the study of polymathic approaches—indeed, they are very similar constructs. Openness to experience is a precursor to polymathic exposure; in order to have broad, varied learning experiences, it is of course necessary to be somewhat open to having them to begin with.

Openness to Experience Linked with Creativity at the Individual Level. Since that initial debate in the literature regarding what openness to experience essentially is, a number of studies have been conducted which all point to the relationship between openness to experience with creativity and innovation. For example, Shane (1995) said that openness to experience leads to more innovation (initiating new strategies) and that being open helps implement those new strategies as well. Olakitan (2011) also found empirical evidence showing a positive relationship between openness to experience and innovative behavior. Sung and Choi (2009) found similar data: "Consistent with previous studies…openness to experience exhibited a significant positive effect on creative performance…our finding offers additional empirical evidence that openness to experience enables people to move away from traditional beliefs and conventions and engage in novel and unique ways of thinking" (p. 952).

Several other studies connected openness to experience with improved thinking ability. For instance, Wolfradt and Pretz (2001) found a positive correlation between openness to experience and creative thinking. McElroy and Dowd (2007) said that individuals high in openness to experience will be more likely to pay attention to multiple influences when making decisions. And Mieg, Bedenk, Braun, and Neyer (2012) conducted a study looking at independent inventors in Germany and found that they show higher levels of openness to experience compared to non-inventors—showing that openness to experience is linked with an ability to think in inventive and original ways.

A few longitudinal studies have been conducted on openness to experience as well showing benefits over the long term. For instance, Helson et al. (1995) did a study over time and found that levels of openness, originality, and unconventionality in people at age 21 predicted their levels of creative potential at age 27 as well as their occupational creativity at age 52. Similarly, a longitudinal study of male graduate students by Feist and Barron (2003) found that levels of originality at age 27 predicted later lifetime awards (tallied when they were 72 years old). Together, these studies point to the possibility that openness to experience can lead to a lifetime of benefits, rather than perhaps just a few instances of usefulness on occasion in specific instances—making understanding the phenomenon even more significant.

Openness to Experience in Individuals Improves Their Team's Performance. In addition to finding a link between openness to experience and creativity at the individual level, there is evidence that polymathic individuals help their teams to perform better. For example, a study by Schilpzand, Herold, and Shalley (2011) found evidence for how individuals high in openness to experience can impact creativity for the teams on which they work as well. "This study examined the relationship of team members' openness to experience and team creativity. Results from a study with 31 graduate student teams suggest that openness to experience is significantly related to team creativity" (p. 55).

A number of additional studies have shown how openness to experience leads to better overall performance. For instance, McCrae and Costa (1997) showed that individuals who are open to experiences are better at absorbing information and combining unrelated information into new, useful insights. Another study by Bing and

Lounsbury (2000) showed that people high in openness are better at performing in unfamiliar environments.

Alternatively, one study found evidence for what can occur when individuals are low in openness to experience—and how that negatively impacts performance: "Individuals who were low in openness (i.e., close minded, myopic, non-creative, narrowly focused) and highly extraverted were rated by supervisors as manifesting the lowest levels of performance" (Burke and Witt, 2002, p. 718). The authors (Burke and Witt, 2002) go on to provide further nuance on the phenomenon: "Among introverted workers, openness was essentially unrelated to performance. Furthermore, individuals who were low in openness and low on emotional stability were rated by supervisors as manifesting lower levels of performance (than those high on emotional stability)" (p. 718). They (Burke and Witt, 2002) also found that "workers low in both openness and emotional stability were rated as the weakest performers" (p. 718). These authors also add nuance to the study of openness to experience by considering the interplay of introversion versus extroversion and emotional stability as well.

Openness to Experience Linked with Other Valuable Skills. A couple of studies describe openness to experience as a skill itself, but also point out that it is one which enables other useful skills to emerge, such as leadership. Kickul and Newman (2000) said that those high in openness to experience are more likely to emerge as leaders in a group since they are most likely to initiate new ideas, ask more questions, and share their opinions more freely. Oakes, Ferris, Martocchio, Buckley, and Broach (2001) said that openness to experience is an important quality for gaining skills (skill acquisition). Given these findings, openness to experience can be used not only in predicting performance in specific instances but also in predicting potential career progress over the longer term.

Openness to Experience Studied More Recently with Mediating Variables. More recent empirical work on openness to experience has gotten more nuanced and sophisticated. For instance, Ivcevic and Brackett (2015) found a mediating variable between openness to experience and creativity—that is, emotion regulation. "Emotion regulation ability appears to help individuals with high openness to transform their preference for new ideas and intellectual or artistic interests into creative behavior by enabling them to manage and influence emotions experienced in the course of the creative process…the present study showed that the relationship between emotion regulation ability and creativity is mediated by passion for one's interests and persistence in the face of obstacles" (p.484). This has implications for organizations or individuals who want to support the development of polymaths: part of empowering polymaths may not just be to encourage their openness, their exploration, and their creativity—it also may mean helping them from an emotional perspective to work through any emotional challenges or issues they may face in their journey as a polymath.

Another interesting study by Wenfu, et al. (2014) showed that those high in openness to experience have brains that show up differently on scans. "Creative individuals had higher gray matter volume in the right posterior middle temporal gyrus (pMTG), which might be related to semantic processing during novelty seeking. More importantly, although basic personality factors such as openness to experience, extroversion, conscientiousness and agreeableness all contributed to trait creativity, only openness to experience mediated the association between the right pMTG and volume and trait creativity. Taken together, our results suggest that the basic personality trait of openness to experience might play an important role in shaping an individual's trait creativity" (p. 191).

These two studies point to the idea that openness to experience does not exist in a bubble on its own. Openness to experience exists within complex individuals who are themselves systems—with various personality traits, emotions, and complex brains. It begs the question as well: did the openness to experience impact emotions and emotion regulation – or vice versa? Did higher gray matter volume in the posterior middle temporal gyrus lead to more openness, or did more openness to experience impact the brain? The literature does not specify the causal directionality in this regard and therefore is one critique of the literature.

The Down Side of Openness to Experience. Although openness to experience, on the whole, seems to be a positive trait for individuals to have – both for their own benefit and the organizations for which they work, there are some down sides. As one example, it can lead to career problems if those people high in openness to experience are not in suitable positions to match their personalities. For example, De Jong, et al., (2001) found that individuals high in openness to experiences tend to be dissatisfied in jobs low in skill variety; they become dissatisfied and frustrated if jobs are mechanical or unchallenging. This study is significant for practice; it may have implications for career counselors, staffing professionals, hiring managers, etc.

Summary and Critique of the Openness to Experience Literature. Taken together, this literature tells us that openness to experience and creativity are very clearly and positively related, whether at the individual or team level. This literature does not explain much in the way of why or how this is the case exactly; further, deeper explanation is needed in explaining why openness to experience and creative problem solving are so strongly and consistently correlated. The most recent research (around 2015) has taken this sort of approach; it starts pointing more to mediating variables or factors such as emotion and brain structure and how that impacts or interplays with openness to experience and creativity although it does not specify the direction of causality. So, some limited research has been done to show why openness to experience and creativity are so consistently linked—but further work needs to be completed to better understand the phenomenon in this regard.

Intrapersonal Functional Diversity

Description. The currently scholarly literature on intrapersonal diversity focuses on functional intrapersonal diversity, which has to do with someone's professional experience—specifically, how much they are either a narrow specialist with limited experience in a small range of functions versus a broad generalist whose prior work experience spans a number of functional areas (Bunderson and Sutcliffe, 2002). In other words, someone who is functionally intrapersonally diverse has a wide "breadth of functional experiences" (Bunderson and Sutcliffe, 2002, p. 875) and considers how diverse the "functional areas within which they have spent the greater part of their careers" is (Bunderson and Sutcliffe, 2002, p. 878). "This approach to conceptualizing functional diversity rests on the assumption that each member brings a specific functional perspective to a team, a perspective gained through experience that is typically weighted toward a particular function" (Bunderson and Sutcliffe, 2002, p. 878). While interpersonal diversity "captures the differences in experience sets across" people, intrapersonal diversity is a "measure that captures difference within" one person (Huckman and Staats, 2011, p. 311). It has to do with the "extent to which members' prior experiences are individually heterogeneous or homogeneous" (Chiocchio, Kelloway, and Hobbs, 2015, p. 333) and therefore is a very similar construct to polymathy.

Intrapersonally Diverse Individuals Think More Strategically. A body of literature has looked specifically at how intrapersonal functional diversity impacts a singular individual's ability to think in more strategic and useful ways. Burke and Steensma (1998) theorized that intrapersonal functional diversity leads people to think more broadly and therefore be less susceptible to bias in their decision making. Ten years later, Shibayama (2008) found that people with higher experiential diversity (or domain-relevant scientific knowledge and technical skills) in research groups helped foster both radical and incremental innovation.

Indeed, intrapersonal expertise diversity enhances how people learn and then innovate. Researchers who are more cognitively diverse are more likely to radically innovate when they have had broader expertise (Shibayama, 2008). Findings indicate that technological innovation can be facilitated through fostering one's own diversity. Similarly, Angriawan and Adebe (2001) found a positive relationship between the length of industry tenure of CEOs, their intrapersonal functional diversity, and the extent to which they scan the environment—which has positive implications for strategic decision making. Also, Hitt and Tyler (1991) found that executives who have broad functional backgrounds are better at evaluating options and making strategic decisions when compared to their counterparts who have narrower functional backgrounds. Lastly, Yap,

Chai, and Lemaire (2005) stated that intrapersonal functional diversity can foster innovation. What these studies tell us is that individual thinking tends to improve when people have more functional intrapersonal diversity.

Intrapersonally Diverse Individuals Perform Better. Beyond improved thinking ability, individual performance also appears to improve with increased intrapersonal functional diversity. For instance, Rulke (1996) found that MBA students perform better when they are part of a group of functional generalists rather than functional specialists. And people who have broad experience in a variety of functional domains also earn higher salaries and get promoted more than those who do not (Campion, Cheraskin, and Stevens, 1994).

Intrapersonally Diverse Individuals Make Their Teams Better. Now that I have addressed studies looking at single individuals, I will review a variety of articles looking at diverse teams and how being diverse impacts the team. For example, Bantel and Jackson's (1989) study found that functionally diverse teams tend to be more innovative. They also said that heterogeneity of functional (work) experiences and education level were the strongest predictors of innovation on teams. These researchers also concluded that functionally diverse teams are better at collaboratively developing clear plans and strategies. So, at the group level, teams whose members have more functional diversity are able to think more innovatively and collaboratively (similar to individuals who are diverse being more innovative). This is in line with Levi (2001) who said that functionally diverse teams have less groupthink.

There are also a couple of studies that address how individuals who are diverse impact the teams they are on—specifically in the team's ability to think better, as a whole. For example, Cannella, Park, and Lee (2008) said that "Intrapersonal functional diversity enhances information sharing on top management teams, improves 'sense making,' and leads to better integration of available information. Within-member breadth of experience directly increases group-level information sharing, which leads to enhance decision making" (p. 769-770). They also say that the effects of intrapersonal diversity become more positive as environmental uncertainty grows.

Similarly, Park, Lim, and Birnbaum-More (2009) found further evidence that individuals who are intrapersonally diverse can be of great value to the teams on which they work. Teams consisting of "multi-knowledge" individuals (when a person understands multiple functional areas) are more likely to understand the skills, strengths, and capabilities of other team members. Because of this, individual team members share information more easily with one another, thus producing better information sharing among team members, as well as more shared understanding on the team. Their research confirmed that the more multi-knowledge individuals on a cross-functional team, the more innovative the team is—essentially due to more information sharing.

Huckman and Staats (2011) tried to describe why these findings are true. They hypothesized that a team's level of intrapersonal diversity positively affects team's performance, particularly when the situation demands that the group change. Their rationale: "With more diverse individual experiences, team members might map current problems to past experiences more accurately or use different cognitive representations more effectively to define and solve problems in new ways" (p. 2). Huckman and Staats (2011) posit that, "when cognitive problem-solving demands are high, diverse experience may improve performance by enabling access to a wider base of knowledge and improved information processing" (p. 324).

Day and Dragoni (2015) said that increased intrapersonal diversity better creates leadership capacity; teams who have intrapersonally diverse leaders may fare better than teams who have leaders with less intrapersonal diversity—regardless of how easy or difficult those experiences are, or whether they are work or non-work experiences—both can enhance leadership capacity. Bunderson and Sutcliffe's (2002) findings suggest that intrapersonal functional diversity "has significant and positive implications for team processes and performance" and therefore "organizations can benefit considerably by seeking and developing management teams composed of individuals who are functionally broad and not just narrowly specialized in a single functional area" (p. 890). They also say that intrapersonal diversity is most powerful for project team performance in volatile and uncertain environments, more so than stable ones (Bunderson and Sutcliffe, 2002).

The Downside of Diversity. Although most studies pointed to the value of intrapersonal functional diversity on a team, one study did say that functional diversity across a team can create an environment in which more conflict might occur (Knight, et al., 1999). People who have developed a niche (in other words, those who lack intrapersonal diversity) may have less competition in the workplace; in other words, by picking a career specialization early in one's career and staying with it, individuals can develop a competitive edge for themselves, given we live in an age of specialization. So, people who are generalists may not have that sort of advantage in the workplace. Some may also perceive having a résumé with a wide variety of positions to be unfocused or undedicated. These critiques are worth noting; but on the whole, the literature focuses more on individuals with intrapersonally diversity being an asset, and less of an obstacle or difficulty to avoid.

On Developing Intrapersonal Diversity. There are two main ways that one can develop intrapersonal diversity. The first way is through unplanned exposure or incidental learning. Incidental learning is unplanned, unintentional learning (Cahoon, 1995). In other words, by simply living life, individuals are bound to be exposed to a variety of different types of thinking, behaviors, people, places, experiences, roles, jobs, etc. The learning that takes place as a result can happen through observation, socializing with other people, or solving problems (Cahoon, 1995).

In contrast, another way that intrapersonal diversity can be developed is through purposeful design. Individuals can decide to expose themselves on purpose to enhance their experiences and capacities. This can be considered a life-design process (Setlhare-Meltor & Wood, 2015). Whether or not someone becomes more intrapersonally diverse can be either by chance or by design; choice and effort can lead to increased intrapersonal diversity as well as all of the benefits it brings.

Given that people are "constantly in the process of change and development" (Ornstein, 1993, p. 8), it is worth considering, then, how those individuals can proactively, consciously choose what they are exposed to which may cause them to change and develop further; in other words, people can choose to design who they become, on purpose. "Life experiences have a profound effect on the cultivation of the self," and it is therefore worth considering "how can one guide one's life to enhance one's development" (Ornstein, 1993, p. 9) and how we can "remake ourselves through conscious choice, even in adulthood" (Ornstein, 1993, p. 12).

Summary and Critique of the Literature on Intrapersonal Diversity. On the whole, the literature on intrapersonal diversity links it strongly with the ability to creatively solve problems. The literature focuses on functional intrapersonal diversity which has to do with the extent to which someone is a generalist or a specialist in their career, but it does not consider other types of diversity that might exist within a single individual but outside the confines of one's job requirements; this is a major gap in the literature and an area for future study.

Creativity & Creative Problem Solving

Creativity is important to consider when studying polymaths because it relates to the ability to do divergent thinking (Gibson, Folley, and Park, 2009). The type of creativity that is made possible through polymathic approaches is valuable; creativity is indeed important, especially in the face of complex problems. Creative problem solving involves coming up with approaches and solutions that are new to the solver or even new in the context of history (Boden, 2004). For a solution to be considered creative, it must be useful, correct, and valuable (Amabile, 1983). "The Big Five trait of openness to experience has been theoretically and empirically defined as a general disposition for creativity" (Ivcevic and Mayer, 2006, p. 68). Creativity is related to change and leadership: "imagining change requires creative thought and leading change requires creative behavior" (Harding, 2010, p. 52).

At the individual level, creativity is now considered a core competency (Shalley, Zhou, and Oldham, 2004). In fact, in recent years, efforts have been underway to understand how to develop capabilities to be innovative so that such educational interventions can be implemented for gifted children so that they will grow into adult innovators (Shavinina, 2013). Other scholars such as Beghetto and Kaufman (2009), however, believe that "all students have multi-creative potential" to contribute across unrelated domains, if only teachers could help them realize their potential (p.39). Root-Bernstein (2015) argues that "the knowledge and skills required to be creative are, in short, learnable" (p. 203).

Nevertheless, creativity is one of the most important factors affecting individual performance in various domains of work (Sung and Choi, 2009). In fact, "considerable evidence demonstrates that creativity promotes individual task performance" (Sung and Choi, 2009, p. 941), which in turn impacts organizational innovation and effectiveness (Amabile, 1996; Scott and Bruce, 1994).

In addition to being valuable at the individual level, creativity is critical at the organizational level, as well. Creatively solving problems is necessary for an organization to be effective (Oldham, 2002) and creativity is increasingly seen as a factor for economic growth for firms (McWilliam, 2008). Creativity helps teams solve problems by allowing for divergent perspectives (Barczak, Lassk, and Mulki, 2010). Creativity also allows for society to evolve and advance because "being creative is most fundamentally about advancing change in or about something" (Harding, 2010, p. 51). When studying polymaths, it is tantamount in some ways to studying creativity since part of what defines polymathy is the ability to learn across various domains of one's own choosing.

Summary and Inferences for Forthcoming Study

In this chapter, I have summarized, critiqued, and synthesized the literature from the following streams of scholarly study:

- Identity
    - Identity Theory
    - Social Identity Theory
- Learning
    - Self-directed learning
- Polymaths and Multi-disciplinarity
    - Openness to experience
    - Intrapersonal functional diversity
    - Creativity and creative problem solving

I have provided evidence for the value of these approaches, covered some nuances of each topic as it pertains to my research topic and questions, and also addressed the "downsides" of each of these constructs.

The overall strengths of this body of research, as a whole, is that it is mostly in agreement—indicating that it can be accepted as evidence, on the whole. There is no major debate in the literature on these topics; there seems to be consensus for the most part (aside from some lack of consensus on one specific definition of what self-directed learning is).

The major downfalls are that (1) the literature claims that there is a relationship between these creativity and openness to experience, intrapersonal functional diversity, and multi-disciplinarity, but does not do a very thorough job about explaining why this is the case exactly (the direction of causation, etc.). There are some correlations found in the scholarly literature, but the direction of causation is not well understood (i.e., levels of openness to experience and brain structure). Another weakness of the literature is that intrapersonal diversity is described but only focuses on professional, functional intrapersonal diversity and neglects to address other parts of what make up individual diversity outside of the career. In order to get a sense of that further, one has to look to other literature streams such as that of polymaths and multi-disciplinarity—it is not covered under the construct of intrapersonal diversity. The literature on polymaths exists, though it focuses on individual polymaths (mostly men) instead of finding themes among various different polymaths. There also is a dearth of literature aimed at understanding how modern-day polymaths got to be that way in a workscape that does not necessarily reward that kind of approach to career and, more generally, to life. The literature on openness to experience is the largest body of work among the various related but slightly different concepts reviewed herein; the openness to experience literature is quite vast and well-studied.

The literature reviewed in this chapter underscores the fact that people are multi-dimensional, and any study of human beings needs to be integrative, taking into consideration all parts of personhood. Indeed, within each human individual, there may be multiple selves. An individual who has an inquiring spirit with broad expertise in disparate domains in the modern era are a type of rogue adventurer because we live in a day and age that does not necessarily develop, support, or reward this type of exploration. Polymaths have unique, bricolage combinations of knowledge—a sort of intellectual bi- and tri-lingualism, and a clear commitment to lifelong learning.

Instead of knowledge being sequestered by specialists, generalist learners like polymaths create connections and seek synthesis among disparate streams of knowledge and among varied experiences and in doing so they create innovations which advance the larger society forward in significant and historic ways. "By building bridges today between disciplines, the greatest benefactors are the potential innovators of tomorrow" (Sriraman, 2009, p. 85). Given the importance of creativity, creative problem solving, and innovation in order to solve the world's difficult problems of today as well as those that will arise in the future, it is important to study this unique group of people who have skills that put them in a unique position to help solve such problems. Think of the impact a polymath like Da Vinci had on our world. What would our world look like if there were thousands of Da Vincis?

Chapter 3: Methods

Overview of Chapter

The purpose of this phenomenological study is to develop a deep understanding of the experience of polymaths in the 21st century: what dispositions or traits, values, experiences, relationships, or ways of thinking led them to pursue polymathy, and what they experience as a result of their polymathy. Given that we live in a society and time where specialists are typically valued more so than generalists (Terjesen and Politis, 2015), the high-level objective of this study was to uncover why some individuals choose this alternative path to their careers and lives and to understand what their experiences are as a result. The constructs of identity, openness to experience, polymathy or multi-disciplinarity, and intrapersonal diversity will be used to frame this study.

This chapter is organized into the following sections:

- Overview of Methodology
    - Qualitative Orientation
    - Phenomenological Inquiry
    - Researcher as Primary Instrument
    - Theoretical Perspective
    - Research Questions
    - Research Design
    - Population and Data Collection
    - Verification Procedures
    - Data Analysis & Interpretation
- Human Participants and Ethics Precautions

Overview of Methodology

Qualitative Orientation

Because the purpose of this study aimed to uncover "the meaning of a phenomenon for the participants involved," this research was most suited to a qualitative approach (Merriam, 2009, p. 5). Qualitative research is most appropriate in cases when "a problem or issue needs to be explored" (Creswell, 2013, p. 47). This study, aimed at understanding the experiences of polymaths, is not suited to a quantitative approach; "quantitative measures and the statistical analyses simply do not fit the problem" (Creswell, 2013, p. 48).

Phenomenological Inquiry

The type of qualitative method selected for this study is phenomenology. The purpose of phenomenology, at a high level, is to capture the essence of a lived experience by studying a number of different individuals who have that experience in common (Creswell, 2007). (The purpose of this specific study was to understand the experience of polymaths.) Moustakas (1994) said that phenomenology is a tool to provide deep understanding and to create new knowledge. Indeed, phenomenologists try to understand lived experience—that is their main goal (Van Manen, 2014). Someone reading a phenomenological study should come away with the feeling, "I understand better what it is like for someone to experience that" (Creswell, 2013, p. 62).

Phenomenologists use language (through interviews as the primary method) to understand their subject: researchers using the phenomenological methodology ask questions and interviewees provide responses using language (Seidman, 2013). In fact, "the aim of phenomenology is to transform lived experience into a textual expression of its essence" (Van Manen, 1990, p. 36). Therefore, phenomenological researchers understand participants' lived experiences through the use of language and through meaning-making (Seidman, 2013). Interestingly, Schutz (1967) has argued that an experience itself does not have meaning; it is through "acts of attention" and "intentional gaze," through reflecting upon one's experiences that meaning is actually made (p. 71 – 72). Reflection through the use of language is therefore a critical component of the meaning-making process to deeply understand experiences.

However, phenomenology is more of an art than it is an exact science. Phenomenological researchers must "resist the urge to follow a recipe and instead, embrace the open searching, tinkering, and reshaping that this important work requires" (Vagle, 2014, p. 10). Phenomenology is concerned with experiences at their core essence based on the internal experiences of participants; however, there is "no denial of the world of nature, the so-called real world" (Moustakas, 1994, p. 46). Objectivity, facts, and realism presumably have been the pillars of the natural or hard sciences, "yet ultimately the natural sciences operate from ideal principles in that they presuppose that objects that exist in time and space are real, that they actually exist, yet there is no evidence that objects are real, apart from our subjective experience of them" (Moustakas, 1994, p. 46). Nevertheless, phenomenology looks at the intersection of individual experiences but also considers the real world's social structures in which those individual experiences exist.

This study used transcendental phenomenology in particular, based off of Husserl's approach (1965). Transcendental phenomenology "emphasizes subjectivity and discovery of the essences of experience and provides a systematic and disciplined methodology for derivation of knowledge (Moustakas, 1994, p. 45). It is called "transcendental" "because it adheres to what can be discovered through reflection on subjective acts and their objective correlates" (Moustakas, 1994, p. 45). In other words, transcendental phenomenology looks at how objects are constituted in pure or transcendental consciousness.

Researcher as Primary Instrument

Using the phenomenological approach allows for the researcher—the primary instrument of the study—to interpret the findings and make sense out of the phenomenon (Creswell, 2007). That said, the researcher—as the primary instrument of the study—should aim to be as objective as possible and let the data speak for itself to the greatest extent possible. There are several ways of doing this. One process is called *epoche*, which means that the researcher refrains from personal judgment (Moustakas, 1994). Any prejudices or assumptions the researcher has should be *bracketed* which involves temporarily setting aside those viewpoints (Merriam & Tisdell, 2016). However, "the extent to which any person can bracket his or her biases and assumptions is open to debate" (Merriam & Tisdell, 2016, p. 27). For this reason, this researcher provides a subjectivity statement later in Chapter 3 of this text, which exposes this researcher's involvement and interpretations in the research.

Beyond epoche and bracketing, other strategies used in phenomenological research include *phenomenological reduction*, which aims to isolate the phenomenon under study to comprehend it at its core essence (Merriam & Tisdell, 2016). *Imaginative variation* is another tool towards objectivity; this involves trying to view the data from different perspectives, looking at it from all angles (Merriam & Tisdell, 2016). These strategies will also be used in this research.

Theoretical Perspective

Given that this researcher was the primary instrument in this study, it is worth exposing this researcher's theoretical perspective and worldview. Specifically, this researcher has a subjective epistemology, which posits that the world does not have only one reality or truth; this researcher believes instead that reality is in the eye of the beholder—that it is internally constructed and therefore completely subjective. In other words, different people having the same experience would interpret it differently. There is no single "true" experience of polymathy.

Accordingly, this researcher has an interpretivist theoretical perspective, which seeks "culturally derived and historically situated interpretations of the social life world" (Crotty, 1998, p. 67). Interpretive research acknowledges that reality is only understood through social constructions like language, consciousness, shared meanings, and instruments (Myers, 2008). "People create and associate their own subjective and intersubjective meanings as they interact with the world around them" (Orlikowski and Baroudi, 1991, p. 5). In other words, though it was this researcher's intention to uncover the real, lived experiences of polymaths, it is understood that those experiences may not represent "the truth" for all polymaths since each polymath perceives the world from his or her own unique, subjective perspective.

Research Questions

The primary research questions guiding this research is as follows:

- RQ1: What is the lived experience of polymaths?

- RQ2: How did polymaths come to be that way?

Research Design

The purpose of this study was to understand the experience of polymaths. Accordingly, this study explored the shared phenomenon (polymathy) among different participants using purposeful sampling. Purposeful sampling involves the researcher setting boundaries on the study regarding who is studied and when they are studied—which is done in a purposeful and intentional way (Maxwell, 2005; Miles & Huberman, 1994).

Population and Data Collection

This researcher interviewed a total of 13 polymaths. This research used a purposeful, snowball sampling strategy, interviewing participants who met the criteria outlined below:

Tier I: Necessary Qualifications to Participate in the Study

The below five criteria are standards that every single interviewee in this study was required to meet in order to participate:

- All participants must identify as a polymath (or whatever term they feel comfortable with); they must be able to acknowledge that they have polymathic skills and abilities in both the arts and the sciences and be able to provide evidence of this. Evidence includes being able to articulate supporting data to validate their claims.
    - For the purposes of this research, a polymath is someone with varied interests and skill sets across disparate areas. Study participants must be able to articulate why they identify in this way and provide evidence to

support this claim. For instance, a qualified polymath for this research would have significant experience and/or skills in both the social sciences as well as the hard sciences (more than simply dabbling in them). If one is as a job (i.e., in the social sciences) and the other area is pursued as a hobby (i.e., the traditional sciences), that is acceptable; the idea is that the person is comfortable in both worlds as well as successful in both.

  - A potential difficulty of finding participants to participate in this study included that they may never have heard the word polymath, and may not consciously think of themselves that way, even if they realize that they have a very broad and diverse skill set; their identity as a polymath may not be fully formed and labeled as such. As a result of being asked to participate in this study, it may put people in a position to consider if they are, in fact, a polymath and there may be implications (albeit positive ones) for how they view themselves. Because of this factor, this researcher at times had to convince people that they qualified for participation in the study based on their skills and experience.

- Participants must have had at least two unrelated, disparate career paths in both the arts and sciences over their lifetime and provide evidence of this (i.e., not a narrow career focus with a high degree of specialization).
- Participants must consider themselves more of a generalist rather than a specialist, professionally (over the course of their career) and have evidence for this.

- Participants must be at least 30 years old and no older than 64; they must be active in their careers (i.e., not retired). The reason for these upper and lower bounds is because someone must be old enough to have had achievements in his or her career the arts and sciences, and a person in their teens or twenties may not have had enough time to fully develop in this way. People older than 64 are typically retired or nearing retirement, and since this study aims to understand polymaths who are in the prime of their polymathic experiences, individuals 65 years old or older were not invited to participate. These ages also coincide with Erikson's (1950) stages of development since, according to Erikson, adulthood begins at 20 and ends around age 64 when people transition into "maturity." Although adulthood begins around 20, however, 20 years olds have not had enough time to develop into true polymaths, thus the age minimum for study participants is 30.
- Participants must have native English fluency.

Tier II: Desirable Qualifications to Participate in the Study

The below additional criteria were the preferable standards for participation in the study, but were not strict requirements for participation:

- Participants may have had disparate hobbies over the course of their life, interested in many subjects (and not just superficially) and have evidence of this.
- Participants, as students, may have been very interested, curious, or adept in more than one field of study (particularly if those areas of study are very different by nature).

- Participants may identify as independent, self-directed learners/thinkers who like to continue learning and growing across various domains of knowledge and articulate why they identify this way (provide evidence).

An effort was made to have maximum variety in terms of participant demographics. This researcher recorded demographic information for each interviewee, including education level, age, race, and sex. Participants were solicited through a combination of e-mail and telephone requests and were pre-screened to ensure they meet the selection criteria outlined above. See "Appendix A: Solicitation to participate in the study" for what participants were e-mailed to request an interview with them.

Interviews. Data was collected using interviews as the primary method. In terms of interview platforms used, seven interviews were conducted using Skype (video conferencing). One interview was conducted using Facetime (video conferencing). Four interviews were conducted over the telephone. One was conducted in person. Most interviews were approximately 90 minutes in length.

In terms of interview modalities, the original intent was to do interviews via video conferencing or in person, and only use the telephone as a last resort. Four of the 13 interviews ended up needing to be conducted over the telephone, however. For instance, for a couple of the interviews, we tried to connect using Skype and had bad connections—I was unable to hear some of what was being said. In those instances, I made a judgment call that it was better to have a clear connection over a telephone line, so I could clearly understand what was being said, as opposed to trying to force the interview to happen using Skype. I did not want to lose the opportunity to collect data by forbidding use of the telephone for the interview. In another case, the interview was conducted while someone was at their work office, and so they only had access to the telephone. I had to work around the limitations that participants had with regard to technology. Of course, video interviews provided another level of information to me, as I was able to read their body language, see facial expressions, etc. and this information was completely missing from the interviews that were conducted over the telephone.

All interviews were audio recorded and later transcribed by a third party transcription company, and then reviewed by this researcher for accuracy. All participants received an email with the transcription document attached and were provided the opportunity to review it to edit (add, delete, or correct) the document (member-checking). However, only one participant out of thirteen actually reviewed the transcript and provided some feedback to refine it.

Hand-written notes were kept during and shortly after each interview on any noteworthy observations and important comments as part of a post-interview reflection journal. Those notes were later reviewed and considered as part of the findings in this dissertation, though the bulk of what was analyzed here is the exact quotes from the participants themselves.

At the beginning of each interview, this researcher referred to the prepared interview protocol that includes an opening script, which explained the purpose of the study and asked them if they had any questions. The script also included a request to record the interview for later transcription. The interviewer assured the participants that their identity will be kept confidential. That interview protocol is included in this document in Appendix B. Interviews were semi-structured based off of the interview protocol as a guideline for the conversation. Beyond recording the interviews, this research also took notes of pertinent observations regarding body language, tone of voice, or other relevant feedback as part of data collection techniques. A post-interview reflection journal (Maxwell, 2005) was created so this researcher may capture additional thoughts and observations and subjective reactions following each interview to enrich the analysis. Once interviews were transcribed and coded, original audio recordings were destroyed to further safeguard the participants' confidentiality.

Verification Procedures

As mentioned before, the primary purpose of this phenomenological study was to understand the experience of modern day polymaths. As such, a number of different trustworthiness techniques were used in this study: (1) a subjectivity statement (provided in the next section), (2) peer reviews, and (3) member checking. In order to promote reliability, field notes were kept (Creswell, 2007). Post-interview reflection journals or field journals allow for the researcher to engage in sensemaking with regard to their subjective experience before, during, and after each interview (Maxwell, 2005).

Subjectivity Statement. Although epoche may never fully be attained, researchers should still attempt to bracket any known biases (Moustakas, 1994). Accordingly, it is worth noting that this author has a deep admiration for polymaths and is in fact an aspiring polymath herself. This is based on experiencing the benefits that broad experiences have brought to my life in terms of adding richness, understanding, and knowledge. This researcher believes that polymathy is a powerful and valuable way of being in the world, whether for professional purposes or for personal growth and fulfillment. In the past, when I have met polymaths, I have usually very drawn to them.

In other words, by default, I have a positive orientation towards polymaths—this could be considered a bias. This is important to understand in the context of this qualitative study.

Data Analysis and Interpretation

A total of 13 polymaths were interviewed one time each, approximately 90 minutes in length per interview. The interviews were semi-structured, following a pre-developed interview protocol but some probing questions were added in the interviews as appropriate. Confidentiality was and will continue to be maintained for all participants, and interviewees all read and signed a consent form (see Appendix C: Research consent form) before interviews began.

Many steps were taken to ensure the data was properly analyzed and interpreted. Three pilot interviews were held in April 2017 to test, validate, and refine the interview protocol. This step also helped this researcher gain familiarity and comfort with the protocol in a test environment to ensure that actual interviews for the research would come across as smoothly as possible. This experience also allowed the researcher to practice adding probing questions to further gather relevant data, although the primary intent was to ask subjects the same questions, as outlined in the interview protocol, to keep the interviews fairly consistent in the approach taken.

Further, this researcher was the primary instrument in this phenomenological study and it is nearly impossible to avoid all bias completely. However, I made every attempt to remain neutral and open in gathering data and in analyzing findings. I did this by stating in the opening script that there are no right or wrong answers and that it is my desire for interviewees to feel comfortable in being completely honest. I also asked open-ended questions (rather than leading questions), used my body language and tone of voice to help participants feel comfortable, and spoke the minimum amount of possible so that the focus be on what the interviewees think. I asked questions regarding the positive sides of polymathy as well as the negative aspects of it in an attempt to understand the full experience of polymaths, rather than eliciting a one-sided version of the experience.

Member checking is another tool that was used. Once interviews were transcribed, those transcripts were sent to each pertinent interviewee to validate what was heard. This step helped to ensure that the raw data was accurately captured to the greatest extent possible. This step also provided an opportunity for interviewees to correct, delete, or add information as appropriate.

Once interview transcripts went through the member checking process, relevant data was pulled out of each transcript and was put into a codebook. The codebook included a table with the following four columns: (1) major theme, (2) participant pseudonym, (3) direct quote as it relates to the major theme, and (4) analysis and synthesis across interviews. Organizing the salient points out of the transcriptions in this way helped elucidate findings by clustering themes which were used to develop textural descriptions of their experiences (Moustakas, 1994). It is from those textural descriptions that structural descriptions emerged so that the essences of the polymathy phenomenon could be understood (Moustakas, 1994). "Texture and structure are in continual relationship. In the process of explicating intentional experience one moves from that which is experienced and described in concrete and full terms, the 'what' of the experience, 'towards its reflexive reference in the how of the experience' (Moustakas, 1994, p. 79).

Additionally, two peer researchers, both holding doctoral degrees, who were not engaged in the study also served to validate the data analysis process by reviewing data and the process and comparing them with the researcher's conception of dominant themes emerging from those transcripts; a third party objectively verifying the themes will helped ensure findings were accurately understood. That said, these peer researchers did not do their own independent review and analysis of the entire data set.

A post-interview reflection journal/field notes were kept to enhance the data and analysis as appropriate. For example, the respondent's body language, tone of voice, or other relevant feedback was noted as well as the researcher's subjective observations on how the interview went, overall. Though subjective in nature, these field notes helped add perspective and richness to the data analysis process.

Moustakas (1994) describes phenomenology as a research approach that captures the essence of a group of people's common experiences (the phenomenon under study—in this case, polymathy), synthesizes those different people's various experiences into a description that summarizes their collective experiences. For the purposes of this research project, the Moustakas (1994) approach was adhered to; his sequential approach is itemized in the below table:

Table 3-1: Moustakas (1994) Sequential Process for Phenomenological Research Analysis

Step 1	Describe the researcher's experience with the phenomena under study (subjectivity statement)
Step 2	Create a list of significant or noteworthy statements from the transcribed interviews
Step 3	Cluster those significant or noteworthy statements into meaning units or themes together
Step 4	Write textural descriptions of each cluster based off of and using the quotations

Step 5	Develop a structural description of how each of those experiences happened
Step 6	Prepare a synthesized description of each theme, combining the textural and structural descriptions in order to understand the essence of the experience

Transcendental phenomenology, as described by Moustakas (1994), should include bracketing. In bracketing, the researcher sets aside their pre-conceived notions about what they anticipate finding in the research or other forms of personal bias. However, Van Manen (1990) has argued that bracketing is not really possible in an interpretive study. This is why a subjectivity statement has been provided, exposing this researcher's relationship to the topic under study. After all, the primary intent of phenomenology is to describe experiences—the main goal of phenomenology does not lie in the explanations or analysis (though still part of the process). Description of experiences should retain, as much as possible, the "original texture of things, their phenomenal qualities and material properties. Descriptions keep a phenomenon alive, illuminate its prescience, accentuate its underlying meanings, enable the phenomenon to linger, retain its spirit, as near to its actual nature as possible" (Moustakas, 1994, p. 58 – 59).

Human Participants and Ethics Precautions

There are a number of precautionary measures that were taken to ensure the study is ethical. First, this researcher took Collaborative IRB Training Initiative (CITI) CITI Human Subjects Training. Then, this study was reviewed by George Washington University's Internal Review Board (IRB) to ensure the research is ethical and that it would not do any harm to human subjects involved in the research; research was only conducted once the project received formal approval from IRB. Additionally, participation in the study was completely voluntary and participants could end their involvement at any time if needed, though nobody did this. Their identities have been kept confidential by using a pseudonym for each participant; only this researcher knows who participated in the study, and which pseudonym is used for each individual. The table containing this data was kept on a password-protected computer that only this researcher knows how to unlock. In order for participants to know that this was done, a final copy of this dissertation will be provided to each participant. Each time someone was interviewed as part of this study, this researcher fully explained to each person the intent of the study verbally so there is complete transparency. Each interviewee was also provided with a written description of the intent of the study (see Appendix B: Research Consent Form) and was asked to read and sign a it (and a copy was provided to them as well to keep). Signed forms are being kept by this researcher but participants also have digital copies as well. The form includes contact information for George Washington University's IRB in the event the participant has any concerns. Techniques of member checking as well as peer reviews of data interpretations also support ethical research and were applied in this project.

Chapter 4: Results and Analysis

Overview of Chapter

This chapter describes the findings that emerged from phenomenological analysis of the audio recordings and subsequent written transcripts from interviews with thirteen polymaths. Interviews were conducted over a period of two months, followed by a period of four weeks of intensive data reduction, analysis, and synthesis. Chapter 4 also provides an overview of how the research was conducted. This chapter also presents demographic and biographical data for all the participants to provide a deeper context of the findings.

This chapter consists of two sections which, together, present the findings of the study. Section one presents the findings using coding and thematic analysis of the data, while section two employs Moustakas's (1994) phenomenological method using individual meaning horizons, invariant meaning horizons and themes, as well as individual textural and structural descriptions of polymath experiences. The chapter ends with a textural-structural-synthesis, or essence, of polymath experiences.

Section One: Coding and Thematic Analysis

Review of Analysis Method

The two primary questions guiding this research are: (1) What is the lived experience of polymaths? (2) How did polymaths come to be that way? The sub-questions nested under those two primary questions included: (1) What is it like being a polymath? How does it feel? (2) How does polymathy impact creativity and creative problem solving? (3) How did polymaths discover their identity? (4) What in a polymath's environment impacted them becoming a polymath? This chapter provides answers to these questions based on the experience of modern-day polymaths.

The study involved a sample of thirteen participants who were found through snowball sampling. The first interviewee was found through a podcast she hosts—that is how I learned of her. Based on knowledge she shared in the podcast, I realized she is a polymath. I asked her for an interview and she said yes. Later, she asked a number of people she felt were qualified for the study if they would also let me interview them, and I was able to interview several people as a result; that was the first "snowball" that occurred. Later, another, separate snowball occurred; a colleague knew some people he felt would qualify, sent an email to them about my study, and I got several of those individuals to let me interview them; that was a second "snowball." Some other participants I found on my own based on information I discovered on the internet; I reached out to them and asked for an interview, and many of those people allowed me to interview them.

Participants were screened for qualification for participation via a combination of email exchanges and telephone conversations. A total of seven possible participants who were willing to participate were turned away because they did not meet the qualifications for participation.

The interviews were conducted using an adjusted version of Seidman's (2013) approach; each polymath was interviewed a single time (not three times), but the interview was broken down in three main sections based on Seidman's methods: (1) life history, (2) details of the experience of being a polymath, and (3) meaning making of being a polymath.

Profile of the Participants

Thirteen accomplished polymaths agreed to participate in this study. Each met the requirements for participation as described in Chapter 3. Within these restrictions for participation, however, there was a rich variety of ages, professional backgrounds and interests among the participants. Not surprisingly, no two interviewees had identical career paths or polymathic capabilities—each person was unique in their own ways, including having unique combinations of skills, interests, ways of expressing their thoughts, etc.. Below are specific demographics of the interviewees:

- **Gender:** Of the 13 polymaths interviewed, 7 were female and 6 were male.
- **Locations:** Ten interviewees were born and raised in the United States of America. Two were born in other countries (Russia and England) but living in the USA at the time of the interview. One was born, raised, and living in a foreign country (Germany) at the time of the interview. Of the participants currently residing in the USA, three were living at the time of the interview in southern California, two were living in New York state, one was living in Georgia, one resides in Texas, one in Maryland, one in Illinois, one in West Virginia, one in Pennsylvania, and one in Rhode Island.
- **Age:** The age range of participants was from 30 to 56 years old—a total span of 26 years. The average age across all participants was 39 years old. Table 4-1 below outlines the specific ages and genders of all the interviewees:

Table 4-1: Ages and Genders of Participants

Pseudonym	Age	Gender
Felicity	30	F
Svetlana	31	F
Trinity	32	F
Wendy	33	F
Levi	35	M
Sebastian	35	M
Sarah	37	F
Hunter	38	M
Caroline	41	F
Dianna	42	F
Karl	47	M
Henry	55	M
Kevin	56	M

- **Levels of expertise:** The goal of this study is to understand the experience of true polymaths—individuals who are the greatest examples of polymathy this researcher could find to interview. Many of the polymaths interviewed as part of this research are indeed extremely accomplished, some even with somewhat public personas. Many have won distinguished awards in their fields. Several are successful published authors – whether writing books for public consumption or writing articles for both scholarly journals and non-scholarly text for magazines or websites. One polymath interviewed as part of this research is a former White House staffer (political appointee). Several interviewees are podcast hosts. At least one has been a guest on a popular television show. Several participants have done TED talks. Their identities must remain anonymous for purposes of this research, of course—but indeed, they are all impressive people in their own ways. The below chart gives a brief synopsis of their major STEM achievements as well as their achievements in the arts by person.

Table 4-2: STEM and Arts Achievements of Each Participant

Pseudonym	STEM Achievements	Arts Achievements
Felicity	• Ph.D. in Neuroscience from a top-tier university • Science Communicator for a large and well-known company • Founded a neuroscience education and outreach website	• Accomplished (and exhibited) photographer. • Hobbies have included ballet and piano
Svetlana	• Works as a Producer for a scientific federal government agency in the virtual reality field • Skilled in coding, designing websites, and producing videos	• Bachelor of Fine Arts degree in Film, Video, and New Media • Prior professional musician with two albums (and radio-play) • Classically trained pianist and self-taught guitarist • Hobbies include reading, writing songs, drawing, painting
Trinity	• Master's degree in Business • Works as a Financial Analyst	• Bachelor of Arts degree in Technical Theater • Worked in theater as a lighting designer and set designer • Artwork has been on display in a gallery • Hobbies include painting, crocheting, running, herbology, wildcraft medicine, Native American ceremony, and welding/blacksmithing
Wendy	• Bachelor's degree in Math, Master's degree in Business from an Ivy League University • Executive at a technology company	• Podcast host, writer, entrepreneur, board member of several foundations/councils • Accomplished professional singer and pianist

		• Hobbies include triathlons & marathons, traveling, politics
Levi	• Bachelor's degree in Physics • Ph.D. in Physics • Physics researcher • Physics professor	• Professional magician (deception artist) • Theater/magic professor • Podcast host • Hobbies include carpentry, cooking, sports, video games, bartending, reading, refereeing for women's roller derby, trivia
Sebastian	• Technologist • Founder of a conference revolving around technology issues as they relate to choreography	• Master's degree in Choreography • Accomplished and lauded choreographer • Professor of choreography at an Ivy League university • Speaker/lecturer, including doing a TED Talk • Show producer • Previously in a band • Previous puppeteer • Hobbies: Reading and following politics
Sarah	• Master's degree in Business • Master's degree in Architectural Acoustics (a type of engineering) • Former CEO and co-founder an organization that puts together events exploring the intersection of arts, technology, and entrepreneurship. • App developer	• Bachelor's degree in Music from Ivy League university • Master's degree in Vocal Performance • Former professional opera singer • Hobbies have included music directing, various sports (field hockey, tennis), and acting
Hunter	• Bachelor's degree in Physics • Master's degree in Electrical Engineering • Previous nano-technology engineer/scientists. Holds numerous patents related to nanotechnology. Published author of 15+ different articles in scholarly journals related to nano-technology.	• Bachelor's degree in Music • Professional musician at prestigious opera house • Adjunct professor of Music • Hobbies include home improvement, exploring the outdoors, and writing

Caroline	• PhD in Pure Mathematics from a very prestigious university • Theoretical mathematician. • Math professor.	• Published author of several popular books • Columnist for a famous newspaper • Entrepreneur who founded a non-profit organization revolving around music • Classically trained and accomplished pianist • Speaker (including doing a TED Talk and appearing on television) • Hobbies include baking and flamenco dancing
Dianna	• Digital strategist • Speaker at conferences particularly around the topics of technology and digital strategy	• Master's degree in Instructional Design • Has worked at the White House, for the Oscars, the Super Bowl around experience design • Speaker (including doing several TED Talks) • Hobbies have included traveling, pets, soccer, and toastmasters
Karl	• Creative coder, computer programmer, website developer, graphic designer • Co-founder of an organization related to sharing technology and knowledge	• Previously worked in marketing • Artist in Residence for a well-known company • Hobbies include photography, flea markets, old bookstores, thrift stores, jigsaw puzzles, collecting and labeling things, old electronics
Henry	• Executive dealing in the area of fisheries and conservation issues	• Bachelor's degree in Russian Studies • Previously a professional musician • Hobbies include dog agility training, hunting, guns, auto slalom racing, cycling, travel, reading, brewing beer, photography, the mathematics of art,

		accomplished visual artist, sculptor, trumpet player
Kevin	• Bachelor degree in geology • Master's degree in geology • Geologist, environmental consulting	• Former professional chef • Received Project Manager of the Year Award at his agency • Hobbies include photography, rock climbing, cave diving, woodworking/cabinetry, stained glass art, motorcycles, and collecting antiques

The below table summarizes by interviewee and by theme, which types quotes from specific participants were used in finding the themes. Boxes in gray note that the quotes were used from that person in the analysis. Boxes in white indicate that the person may not have talked about the subject at all, or might have only briefly touched upon the idea—inasmuch as what was said was not usable herein.

Table 4-3: Themes by Participant

Theme	**Felicity**	**Svetlana**	**Trinity**	**Wendy**	**Levi**	**Sebastian**	**Sarah**	**Hunter**	**Caroline**	**Dianna**	**Karl**	**Henry**	**Kevin**
Polymath Definitions	■	■	■	■	■	■	■	■	■			■	
Identity	■	■	■	■	■	■	■	■	■		■	■	■
Others' Opinions & Social Considerations	■	■	■	■	■	■	■	■	■	■	■	■	■
Career	■	■	■	■	■	■	■	■	■	■	■	■	■
Finances			■	■	■	■	■		■		■		■

Family													
Voracious Learning													
Confidence & The Imposter Syndrome													
Creativity													
Happiness													
Time Management													
Nature vs. Nurture & Level of Effort													

As the above chart shows, five of the themes were discussed by every single participant. Those five themes related to other people's opinions & social considerations of polymathy, career implications of polymathy, impact of family on polymathy, being a voracious learner, and the nature versus nurture and level of effort it takes to be successful as a polymath. The other themes were not addressed by every single participant but were discussed by enough participants that I still considered those themes significant and worthy of inclusion in this study. If I would have only focused on the five themes that every single participant discussed, and left out the other seven themes, a lot of rich, valuable information would have been omitted herein. So, all twelve themes were included, though the above chart makes it clear the number of participants who discussed each theme or not.

Theory (Etic) and Inductive (Emic) Codes for Bridging Constructs and Data

Creswell (2007) defined Emic codes as a set of rules that incorporates the views of participants. Alternatively, Etic codes are those that are taken from theory and included by the researcher. Etic codes in this study include the constructs of openness to experience, identity, self-directed learning, polymathy or multi-disciplinarily, and intrapersonal functional diversity. The primary theoretical lens of this study is based on Identity Theory, based on the work of Erikson (1950). Erikson believed that identity is not fixed—that it changes throughout a person's life. Social Identity Theory (a subset of Identity Theory) was also used as a theoretical basis for this study. The study leveraged the unique capabilities of the qualitative methodology, namely phenomenology, to understand the lived experiences of current-day polymaths.

Findings

Chapter 4 findings are presented from both macro and micro perspectives, including attribute, descriptive, in vivo, and thematic coding. Raw data—in the form of direct quotes from participants—is presented to illuminate the emergent themes. I employed Moustakas' (1994) method of analysis to analyze the phenomenological data. First, I pulled out all statements from the transcripts relevant to the participant's experience. In this process called horizontalization, each comment held equal value. Second, I gathered all non-repetitive, non-overlapping statements. It is these statements that are the invariant horizons of the experience. Third, I grouped invariant horizons into themes. Fourth, I used invariant horizons and themes to build an individual textural description of each participant's experiences, including word-for-word verbatim quotes. Fifth, I built individual structural descriptions of several participants' experiences based on the individual textural descriptions. Sixth, I built a textural-structural description of the essences of several sample participant's experience, to include the invariant constituents and themes. Lastly, I used individual textural-structural descriptions to create a composite description of the essences of lived experiences for all participants as a whole. This description was the heart of the lived experiences found in the polymaths who participated in this study.

Descriptive Coding

According to Saldana (2009), descriptive coding is meant to "summarize in a word or short phrase the basic topic of passage of qualitative data" (p. 70). This is done through coding in order to understand the essence of experience. Analysis of the data included coding it into major and minor themes using a codebook structure in order to discover the research findings. The codebook included columns for the direct quote, name of the interviewee, general theme the quote fit into, and a space for this researcher's thoughts on analysis and synthesis across quotes within that theme. When printed, the codebook findings from all the interviews took up 117 pages; there was a significant amount of thick, rich data to be analyzed. Individual codebook entries ranged in length from a short phrase to an entire paragraph of verbiage. Microsoft Excel was use for this purpose, which allowed for the data to be sorted by either theme or by interviewee or both. It also allowed for specific words to be searched and found in the database. The first attempt at categorizing the data resulted in 60 constituent categories, which were then refined down to 12 themes, based on similarity. The below illustration aims to depict how the original 60 constituent categories were narrowed down into 12 different themes:

Figure 4-1: Synthesizing 60 Initial Categories to 12 Themes

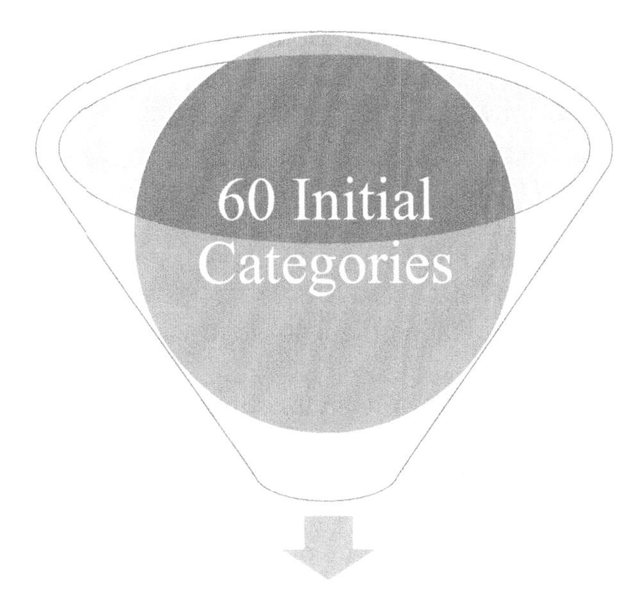

The 12 themes found from the 13 interviews are as follows:

1. Theme One: Polymaths Define Themselves as Experts Across Disparate Disciplines
2. Theme Two: Polymath Identity Emerges from Not Fitting in A Box
3. Theme Three: Being Polymathic Impacts One's Social Experiences
4. Theme Four: Polymaths Have Difficult Career Choices
5. Theme Five: Financial Resources Can Both Hinder and Promote Polymathy
6. Theme Six: Polymaths are Shaped by Their Families
7. Theme Seven: Polymaths Are Voracious Learners
8. Theme Eight: Polymaths are Quite Confident but May Also Experience "Imposter Syndrome"
9. Theme Nine: Polymaths Self-Identify as Highly Creative
10. Theme Ten: Polymaths Cannot Be Happy as Narrow Specialists

11. Theme Eleven: Effective Polymaths are Effective Time Managers
12. Theme Twelve: Polymathy is Due to Both Nature and Nurture but Polymathic Excellence Requires a Level of Effort and Attention

Each of these themes will be described in more detail below.

Theme One: Polymaths Define Themselves as Experts Across Disparate Disciplines

One of the first questions that participants were asked in the interviews was how they would define what a polymath is. Given their unique experience living in the world as polymaths, their answers showcased a few emergent themes, including that being a polymath is being more than a dabbler—it involves more than simply being interested in various things, but actually following through on interests and developing expertise and excellence at them. Along these lines, Wendy's definition of polymathy is:

> You have developed a level of expertise in multiple fields and have continued to pursue it in some degree of excellence....I think there's a difference between people who are going to work in different industries and kind of cobble together a multi-disciplinary zig zag path and polymaths...I would say polymaths would be specifically people who have built very discrete skill sets in multiple fields at a very high level and continue to pursue them...separate from people who have been able to build a career across different industries.

There was a consensus among interviewees that to be considered a polymath, there needs to be some level of expertise and accomplishment the person has had; dabbling or trying something a few times does not mean someone is a polymath.

Other definitions of polymathy included that polymathy involves having a unique career across disparate domains. According to Levi, a polymath is "Somebody who has a multitude of skills in various fields, which to the average onlooker, if you will, appear to be completely disparate fields." Having skills in disparate areas could create unique synergies, as Trinity pointed out: "I define a polymath as someone who has passions that they pursue in two completely different areas and that informs them in both so that it's actually synergistic, better at each because of the other."

Sometimes a polymath may combine their interests into a unique job. Sarah said, "The thing about the polymath thing is, I don't know how it is for other people, but for me it's really about combining interests." Similarly, Trinity said that being a polymath means "you're able to make connections across modalities and across subjects."

Another common theme among the definitions of polymathy include being someone who is not easily defined by any single field. The idea of "not fitting in a box" came up numerous times throughout the interviews. Felicity said, "I guess the way I would categorize who I am is somebody that doesn't fall into one of those buckets of being a particular person with a particular career picked out. So, I think it's somebody that excels in many different areas that normally we would categorize in different subjects." In sum, polymaths define polymathy as having a combination of expertise across disparate, perhaps even unexpected, domains.

Theme Two: Polymath Identity Emerges from Not Fitting in a Box

In every single interview, the subject of identity came up as a major topic of discussion, whether it was identity that the participant felt connected to, not connected to, or simply being aware of what others may think of their identity. This was expected, and why Identity Theory and Social Identity Theory were used a theoretical basis for this research. There was a range, of course, regarding how strongly interviewees identified as a polymath (using that word, anyway). In fact, several attendees had never even heard the word polymath before. All participants, however, did identify with traits/behaviors of being polymathic; some felt more comfortable referring to him/herself as a "Renaissance man," or "multi-interested" or "being polymathic" (rather than being "a polymath"). The below graphic attempts to depict the spectrum of how weakly or strongly someone identifies with being a polymath; interviewees for this dissertation ranged from not identifying as a polymath at all (not using that word anyway), to completely identifying as a polymath.

Figure 4-2: Polymathic Identity Spectrum

No Identity as a Polymath **Complete Identity as a Polymath**

To show the wide range of how strongly or weakly someone identified with polymathy, consider these two examples. Trinity highly identified with the term polymath and said that she first realized this part of her identity around the age of 5 but developed a deeper understanding of it in her teens: "I think the first time I was cognizant of [my polymathy] was in kindergarten, which sounds kind of obnoxious but it's true. I actually attributed being polymathic to being a Gemini probably until I was in my late teens. I just thought it was because I was a Gemini, two people, I'm just smooshed…I am, you know, this fun-loving artist and also this hardcore logical science person…and that's how I kind of rationalized it to myself." On the other hand, Karl did not identify with the term polymath at all: "I would never call myself [a polymath]. That's kind of boasting or something. At least, I guess, it's something, an ideal to strive for, right? I don't know. I'm just multi-interested. I've never labeled myself."

Several interviewees said they do not feel like they "fit in a box," and so "labeling" themselves is not something they like to do. Felicity shared, "I've never been a fan of falling into a bucket, so for me to have to categorize myself it's a little odd."

Many polymaths interviewed for this research preferred to be without narrow labels. Caroline said that she considers polymathy normal and good, and that if anything, it is the narrow specialists—the monomaths—that should require qualification.

This precise phenomenon may be part of why polymathy is not discussed more in society—because the simple act of identifying as a polymath constitutes classifying someone who may prefer to not be put into a category—someone who is used, in fact, to defying categories. In other words, identification as a polymath is almost an oxymoron, since polymaths may have many identities, while the construct 'polymath' is a way of encompassing many possible identities under one umbrella label. Calling someone a polymath is, in a way, an attempt to put a multi-faceted, unique identity into a single word. This works for some polymaths and feels uncomfortable for others. Although polymathy essentially means having many types of knowledge and skills, it is still a *single* label, which is precisely something that may feel uncomfortable for some, though certainly not all, polymaths to adopt.

While identification as a polymath varied in degree from person to person, what was consistent for interviewees was a sense that they must be thoughtful about how they explain who they are, which could be quite difficult. For instance, Karl said "I struggled [with] what am I exactly? …It was always hard to explain people what I'm doing. That is kind of a constant in my life…Yeah, there was never, 'Yes, I am this.'" The idea of a "personal brand" came up as something that interviewees had to thoughtfully consider. Many participants said that it is frequently hard to fit in, but at the same time, sometimes they would want to "play up" their differentness to stand out, on purpose. In fact, it was this differentness that typically helped their identity to emerge. Caroline said she wished everyone was a polymath, and that she could be surrounded by others all the time who had polymathic capabilities; to her, her own differentness was at the same time an honor and a challenge, since it is mostly a singular journey at this point in her life.

Several polymaths said that they realized they were different—that he or she had a unique identity—in relation to their differentness from others. For example, Henry said he thought everyone was like that (polymathic), until he realized they were not; he thought polymathy was just normal. Participants shared various other stories, including of not being believable given disparate skill sets, not being as narrowly focused as others who were able to gain expertise and get joy out of the pursuit of single-disciplinary specializing, sticking with multiple interests more than counterparts did as they got older—many examples that showed that part of how polymath identity seems to arise is through social comparison. Some polymaths who were interviewed were bullied as children. A polymath's differentness could be both an advantage and a disadvantage, depending on the situation.

This observation regarding identity formation emerging through social comparison mostly fits in with Social Identity Theory, discussed in more detail in Chapter 2, but with a key difference. Briefly, Social Identity Theory says that social identity is "a person's knowledge that he or she belongs to a social category or group" (Stets & Burke, 2000, p. 225). Interestingly, the way that a person develops their identity as a polymath is through ***not*** fitting into a group. Further, there is no defined group of other polymaths with which the single polymath can associate with or co-created a sense of shared polymathic identity. Whereas Social Identity Theory says people find their identity by fitting into a group, polymaths may find their identity by not fitting very well into any single group. This is a significant finding of this research and may be useful as an addendum to add an additional layer of understanding to Social Identity Theory: that some develop a sense of identity from belonging to a social group, whereas others may form identity from precisely not fitting in any particular group very well.

As it relates, part of polymath identity formation may be due, in part, to experiencing a struggle to define oneself. Trinity shared, "'What are you going to be when you grow up?' I still don't know how to answer that question because I want to be everything and nothing." Others may view parts of the polymath identity as contradictory. Wendy said, "And so at an art school, I found this identity as a mathematician which became very clear to me, that yes I am both and, and those are not inconsistent." Svetlana said that she would have had an easier time with her own identity if polymaths were discussed more in society:

> I think that it's not really reflected in society enough. So I don't really have anything to compare it to. I think I do now in the world that I'm in and with the friends that I have. But that was always a struggle growing up too and even in school, in college. Being like 'What do I compare myself to?' Like 'Who is the person that I want to be like?' And I was asked that and I can't answer it, because there weren't a lot of people going out there and saying these things in a very direct way that I was able to latch on to. Because the kind of lectures and things that we were going to, again, they were mutually exclusive. It was either like going to a lecture at the Field Museum about a science research project. Or going to a lecture at my university about this person that's been creating art for the past 25 years. But there was no one that was talking about both of those things in a way that made it work…No one really held my hand through those thoughts and I was really young so I wasn't able to truly process. But I do feel like just hearing those words from someone is impactful at an early age. And I make it a point to speak to a lot of elementary schools especially about what I do because their reaction, in fact last year I did it in this class about an hour north of LA. They wrote me handwritten, like 100 letters for being at their career day and they were saying thank you, which is the cutest thing in the world and one of my prized possessions. But a lot of the content of their letters were like, 'Hey, [Svetlana], thank you for speaking to us. Now we know that we can be an artist and work in science.' And they kept up. That was a point that they understood and were repeating back to me and I just felt that that was something that made me very

> happy....even just the idea of telling kids that you can be a combination of ridiculous things that no one tells you are possible. You could be a rock guitar playing doctor. That's okay, you can be both of those things. And in fact, that it's all over the place. One of the original members of Queen, the guitarist, works for NASA actually. Brian May. And it's incredible. And I'm like, 'Why doesn't he do more lectures?' Because that combination is super insightful. He's a rocket scientist and he used to be in Queen. It's like, I find that fascinating."

What became clear is that identity formation for many polymaths is a process of self-realization that may be easy for some polymaths, but very difficult for others—especially when the larger discourse around career implies that specialization is the route to professional success, and the idea of polymathy is almost never discussed in society in general, but especially amongst youth, as a potential option worth striving for.

It appears, then, that polymath identity arises out of (1) noticing oneself being different from non-polymaths, or noticing one does not fit well into any single group, and (2) going the polymath journey mostly alone, not only because there is no defined group of polymaths with which to join, but also because each polymath is so unique; it would be nearly impossible to find a group of similarly constituted polymaths. Some polymaths have do not have a descriptor, title, or more generally, language, to describe the phenomenon that they were actually living; not all polymaths are fully comfortable and conscious of their polymath identity.

This can make finding a sense of place and a group identity very difficult. Sebastian said, "I guess one of the emotional realities of not fitting in anywhere is that it's really exhausting to create your own sense of place. ...Again, I say that with a great deal of consciousness insomuch as my sense of place as a straight white dude is, like, everywhere." Even if there was a group of polymaths, each of them would likely be singularly unique—so while they would have a shared identity as polymaths, they would also have unique sub-identities regarding what made each of them a polymath. As a result, polymathy appears to be a fairly lonely journey, a singular exploration, that only people willing to exercise some level of bravery and muster up confidence in themselves seem to be able to navigate.

For all the polymaths interviewed as part of this research, there was no choice to become and stay a polymath, though. It was simply that the other route, monomathy, was not palatable, not even an option really, not something they would have wanted to ever pursue. To someone with polymathic tendencies, the idea of focusing in a single area feels like an impossibility—simply not an option—too uncomfortable.

A polymath needs a variety of experiences to be happy, and if they cut out part of who they are, it feels like something is missing. Sarah said,

> I totally feel like I would be missing a big chunk of myself. Even now, I'm not singing much right now and I really feel like kind of discombobulated and out of sorts and I think it's got to be related to that in a way because there's this thing that I've identified or rather has been a big part of my identity for so long, and then not to do it for a couple years is like ... At first you don't realize it, the effect that it's having, and then after a while you're like, oh, yeah, this thing that I used to be really good at that people thought of me when they thought of this thing or when people thought of me, they thought of this thing, if you're not doing it anymore, it's kind of stops being part of your identity and then it feels like you're missing something.

Wendy said that she thinks people who are naturally polymathic who try to force narrow specialization on themselves may face unfortunate repercussions later on in life: "I think there are a lot of people going through mid-life crises because they cut off parts of themselves very early in school or in their career and you know I think that kind of dissatisfaction with life and career that a lot of people have in their thirties and forties…when they say is this all there's going to be? I think a lot of that is a symptom of forcing yourself into a narrow identity early instead of embracing all of the things that you might have been or still could be."

Along the lines of not necessarily making a choice to become a polymath, but in a way, not having any other option, several participants credited their polymathy, to some extent, to random encounters—chance meetings where opportunities presented themselves, and the polymath chose to pursue them, thus broadening their base of experiences, knowledge, and skills. Of course, accepting these opportunities involves a relatively high level of openness to experience. Levi said he became a polymath by

> Accident, pure accident…. all of these things that I've gotten into randomly...And all these little things that I've done…just luck, and just willing and wanting to take that chance when the opportunity presents itself…I think it's stupid luck in a lot of cases for me. I think that kind of makes ... Well, don't get me wrong. I mean, the very first thing that was instilled in me from an early age was, 'Learn. Go keep learning. Keep learning. Keep asking why.' I mean, my mom taught me how to read and write and speak, and my dad took over, taught me the science and the math, and then of course, he got me interested in baseball. But I was always taught about learning, and I'm happiest when I'm learning something. I've realized that about myself, so that's a big part of it, and I think that that's why I've accrued this bizarre skillset…And I guess that's in my own nature, but it was instilled. It was instilled, and the rest has just been the chance to learn X, Y, or Z. And of course, it's on me to take the advantage when it shows up, but everything I've done that's been strange has been just an unbelievable roll of the dice. You're in the right place. Here you go… I've been super lucky, which makes me boring in a lot of ways.

In some ways, some polymaths' identity was not something they thoughtfully created or even purposefully forged with forethought; it was dependent on meeting people who made introductions, opened doors, and planted seeds. But it also required an openness to pursue opportunities when they presented themselves. And so it appears that polymathy identity and the construct of openness to experience are, in fact, strongly linked.

This may also help explain why polymathy is not something with more discourse surrounding it—because no polymaths who were interviewed decided one day to become a polymath. It does not appear to be something they heard of and decided to aspire towards necessarily, though those type of people may certainly exist. One story line from the interviews is that polymathy happened over time, to some extent by chance, and whether individuals realized they had even become polymaths seemed almost beside the point. Others felt they were destined for polymathy. Regardless, the point was to explore, enjoy, and learn—and there was less focus on labeling their interests, skills, and various knowledge bases with a word such as being polymathic—especially when the emergence of their unique personhood was in the hands of chance encounters, at least for some of the polymaths interviewed.

Some polymaths talked about having completely disparate career paths that never crossed, while others were able to combine their various interests, to coalesce them into a unique professional role. This has implications for their identity formation, because not all polymaths are the same in this regard; some polymaths work in a field leveraging combinations of their interests blended together, and some polymaths have more siloed interests that do not interplay in concert necessarily—though they may possibly help inform one another in creative ways at times.

In sum, the bottom line regarding polymathy identity is that it develops through social comparison, by not truly fitting in with any other single group. This is a significant finding of this research and may add a more nuanced layer for consideration in Social Identity Theory. The other significant finding is that polymathy is not discussed much in society as an identity that one could adopt, and so the level of identification with this construct varies widely, with many accomplished polymaths not identifying strongly with the term, even if they can see that they fit descriptors of the word. Polymaths do not belong to any shared group to co-create a polymath identity together, which impacts individual experiences of polymathy.

Theme Three: Being Polymathic Impacts One's Social Experiences

A significant theme amongst all participants had to do with identity—from the perspective of what others think of them—their identity as perceived by others, socially. Being a polymath can make social interactions richer but also more challenging sometimes. This section will explain more about the impact of polymathy on one's social experiences.

One specific area of challenge polymaths face has to do with being thought of as ostentatious. Many polymaths were cognizant of the fact that if they share information with others about all their capabilities in various realms, that may be construed as bragging which could "put off" other people. Kevin shared that if he shared too much about his skills and capabilities, "It sounds like you're bragging." Kevin shared that he may downplay his capabilities at times in order to have a pleasant relationship with another person—without intimidation or coming across as bragging.

Svetlana described herself as being someone deeply interested in understanding other people but feeling like no one truly understands her. While on one hand, she wants to be deeply understood, this is juxtaposed with the sense that she must oftentimes censor what she tells people about herself so that the information is easily digestible for others. Svetlana said, "It can be a little bit lonely I guess because I don't always think people can understand where I'm coming from…just like on like a very human level, I think that the way that I like to connect with people is very complex and I want to know them so well." She was not alone in this sentiment.

In fact, most of the polymaths interviewed alluded to not really feeling understood—at least not fully. This is the polymath's dilemma: they rarely feel understood from the outside, though they would like to be. But at the same time, to attempt to be understood, they frequently must simplify the complexity of their identity. They censor themselves. Everyone to some degree may censor what they share about themselves, given the setting or the people involved. Of course, self-censorship is not unique to a polymath.

What may be unique to the polymath are the reasons behind why they must censor themselves. A polymath may censor him or herself to try to be understood more easily and/or to not threaten or "put off" other people who might otherwise be intimidated by the accomplishments and capacity of a polymath. An accomplished polymath may censor him or herself to avoid being considered a braggart. What is noteworthy is that people in general usually share more about themselves order to be understood; polymaths, to be understood, seem to share *less*, or perhaps must share different versions of stories about themselves to different people, depending on the context and the relationship.

This precise difference is an important finding of this research because it may explain why polymathy as a subject is not more frequently discussed in our society; polymaths who openly share their capabilities or who address their identity as a polymath, may not be well received by others or may not be well understood, and so the person withholds information about their polymathy—and thus, polymathy as an important topic of discourse remains largely in the shadows. If a polymath wishes to remain unfettered by difficult social interactions, sometimes it is easier not to share too much about who they are, at least not very thoroughly, especially with someone they are just meeting.

There are some additional aspects of being a polymath that others might perceive as negative, and which polymaths must navigate. For instance, polymaths may feel some pressure to stick to a single identity, which is not in their nature, and over time, they may change—dropping and adding identities, perhaps—and this can have ramifications on their social connections. Trinity said,

> Especially in an intense jag about one thing and switch to another, can be really disruptive for friendships and relationships, people that form a friendship thinking that you're one thing and aren't willing to see you as something else as you shift. I think more so in the art world…no in the science too like…there are people in the moment who are like 'Oh you're an artist,' get a bias and think you can't be really serious about math if you're also wasting your time doing art. The view that the other side is a waste of time...it's very easy to disappoint people who aren't polymathic who want you to spend 100% of your time on something and it's not in my nature.

There are other challenges a polymath must navigate, as well. For instance, several participants talked about concerns they have regarding others viewing them as flighty, not committed, or not focused, given their disparate skill sets, careers, and/or interests, and in some cases, relatively short job tenures. Wendy shared,

> From a personal branding point of view, there are I would say a fair number of people who might look at my career and call me flighty or a dabbler or someone who does a lot of things and sees that as not being committed or loyal to any one of them. Part of the struggle of the polymath is deciding what story you tell to whom… [And] the spotty kind of breadcrumbs of your story are not entirely in your control all the time. Or if you work very hard to tell that story, and I do…it can sometimes be perceived as being a self-promoter or like someone who is kind of working extra hard to talk about themselves all the time. So there's this balance between, 'I want to make sure you guys understand how these things fit

> together' or why I keep these different worlds in my life…but the second I make the effort to tell that story you see that as self-promotional. And if I don't take the effort to tell that story you see me as flighty. So, it can be hard, like how do you tell a story that says 'I am very committed to this world. I also am very committed to this world. And I've built a life and a discipline and a practice that allows me to have both of those facts be true.' [A polymath] has to be very thoughtful and strategic about how they tell that story about the different parts of their lives.

There was also an element of polymathy being viewed negatively by others, and polymaths having to explain their choices. Sarah said,

> I feel like I'm constantly having to defend what I want to do… Even though my family, and even to some extent, friends, you know, people that have chosen a path that's a little bit more traditional according to what society considers normal in terms of career…I think it's hard for them to understand sometimes the well-rounded polymathic choices. It's just hard. You have to craft a version of the story that can help them understand. Like I couldn't just say, 'I'm just interested in tons of things and I want to try everything.' I think if I said that, they'd be like, 'Well, you can't try everything in life.' Something like that which is kind of a downer. And my, I don't say this, but my actual response would be, 'Why the hell not?' You know, I've got one life to live. But most people don't do that. And don't value that in life. That's just not one of their goals. Because yeah, I kind of want to try everything.

Felicity shared similar challenges of telling the story of her polymathy to others: "The view that people have of you that you're not focused. That has not worked in my favor many times." Felicity went on to say that by not focusing only in her field that she believes others perceive her as less of an expert: "The expectation is if you consider yourself an expert in something, like I would consider myself an expert in neuroscience, I got a PhD, right? Yet if I talk about the extra-curriculars that I do, or my other interests, somehow my expertise withers." Polymaths may be viewed as not committed, flighty, or distracted by others who value narrow specialization. It can be challenging for a polymath to explain their identity to others who may have these sorts of negative views.

As a result of these types of challenges, for some polymaths particularly in the workscape, it has been easier to not share aspects of their personality and capabilities if it did not directly pertain to their work or did not align with the representation of themselves they wanted to express; in this way, they only present a portion of their true selves on the job. Levi said, "When I introduce myself to [people], and they're like, 'Well, what do you do?' And I go, 'I'm complicated,' is usually my answer. I know I have to guard [my polymathy], otherwise, I'm going to overwhelm people… There's definitely something to be said for, again, hiding yourself a little bit, making it easy for people to digest. People over there only need to know I'm a physicist. That's all they need to know…It makes it a little easier in some respects, but in most respects, they have no idea what else I'm capable of." When polymaths do venture into sharing more pieces of themselves, they reported that it should be done with careful consideration and in small doses.

While being different from the norm can certainly be a challenge for polymaths to navigate, at times, their differentness could also be an asset. Several interviewees talked about playing up their separateness at times, to market themselves, to stand out as unique in a group, or to get attention (if that is what they desired at the time). Wendy said, "I probably played up my opposition to the group more than I necessarily felt in the moment because that's what set me apart. And that's also what helped me develop my brand, so to speak. By choosing to stand out versus to try to blend in and find what I had in common I think that allowed me to develop very specific identities that set me apart and kind of embrace that differentness." Similarly, Sebastian said, "There have been numerous times in my career where I have understood the supply and demand of my then-field and understood that unless I represented myself and my expertise in a particular way, I was going to be a commodity. So, I would do ... let's call it research, positioning, whatever, to represent myself either against type or to a certain kind of type that I thought was more employable, more bankable, more prestigious…My career has been beautiful largely because I don't feel tied to any particular vision or version of myself."

A couple of interviewees even talked about it being fun to shock or surprise people with aspects of their personhood that would be unexpected by others. Levi said, "It's fun and it's kind of nice, because you feel like you're opening up and exposing your real self, because come on, science is only half of me. It's nice to be able to share your full self. But yeah, there's always the shock. That's kind of fun. But it's not what I'm looking for when I'm telling people. It's because I'm trying to share something with them, like a passion or an interest." In this way, sharing bits of their background and capabilities that people would not expect to be true was something that could be enjoyed; though it was also something they had to be careful to expose this only to people with whom they felt comfortable enough to do so. Svetlana, though, said that when others are surprised about her various skills that she feels defensive at their level of disbelief. So, the same behavior from others—namely, surprise at someone's polymathy—could be interpreted in different ways by different polymaths—positively by some, negatively by others.

As it relates, some polymaths gave the impression in interviews that they wish they did not have to be concerned with what other people think of them—especially if it was something negative the person thought of them. Several participants mentioned that they do not have to explain their choices to other people or at least should not have to worry about how others respond to their polymathy. That should not be their "problem." However, while they shared this value of honoring who they are without concern about what others think of them, the impression the polymaths left overall was still that to some extent, others' opinions do impact them to one degree or another, even if through a "halo effect" of being in their "atmosphere" as Dianna put it.

Of course, each interviewee had their own comfort levels with their polymath identities. Some people very strongly identified as a polymath while others' identity as a polymath were more tenuous. Some people realized their identity as a polymathic person at a very young age, while others were just recently realizing this part of their identity. A few interviewees did not identify with the word "polymath" whatsoever, though they did identify with the traits and behaviors of a polymath. Felicity said that several other people viewing her as a polymath and using that word was impacting her identity more and more over time, which was helping her to feel more comfortable with her identity as a polymath (and this was something she liked).

But just as identity as a polymath could be encouraged by others in this way, it could also be discouraged as well. For instance, Trinity gave an example of how her college major was impacted by the opinions of their academic advisors, in particular. In this case, the advisor suggested the Trinity study art as a single major, and not double major in engineering; she followed that advice. While a single person's opinion might help someone begin to own their polymath identity more, as mentioned in the previous paragraph, a single person's opinion could also sway someone in a direction so as to dissuade their polymathic pursuits as well. On the other hand, another participant, Wendy, had an academic advisor that prevented her from dropping her math major (which she wanted to do after receiving a grade of a B in a class.) What was clear amongst all the interviews, nevertheless, is that polymaths do not exist in the world in a bubble; they are impacted by others' opinions of them, whether an academic advisor or otherwise, and what others think that they should do, at least to some degree. Though their identity is something they own themselves, others do have an impact upon it.

In that vein, regarding social considerations of polymathy, a very dominant theme found in this research is that one of the great strengths that a polymath develops as a result of their polymathy is an ability to connect with many different types of people. The rationale participants gave for this was that essentially a polymath has a broad base of experience and knowledge, which makes it easier to find common ground with people, i.e. someone they are just meeting for the first time. Being a polymath may mean that friends or colleagues one has are more diverse in terms of interests and capabilities as well. Wendy summarized these sentiments:

> In any group of people, in any setting, I can find a thing to talk about. I can like find a way to connect with literally anyone… It certainly has made my friend group pretty awesome. I have an orthogonal network to the one that most people have… So, I think [my polymathy] kind of broadens just from like a social capital point of view, you know, who I can bring to a table, whether it's like connections or just like you're looking for an expert or a resource or a job offer or whatever it is, I can sort of bring in a different set of lenses. [I have] an incredible emotional intelligence that allowed me to read people and read groups and you know read a room and adapt because you know I sort of mentioned, you feel like you have multiple identities as a polymath – and you do.

Similarly, because a polymath can employ multiple ways of understanding the world, several polymaths (Trinity, Caroline) said that they can figure out how someone else thinks—even if they do not think the same way themselves—and this puts them in a good position to be able to interact effectively with that person. Trinity said, "Being able to learn people...I can learn a person and figure out how they think and why they think and be able to interact with them on a level where they're comfortable and I don't see that as being non-authentic, I just see that as using data to be able to have a better interaction. And so I think part of that exceling is because I can interact with people on the logical level if that's how they are and I can interact with people on a feeling or artsy level and it's authentic in both worlds."

This ability also adds a level of richness to the polymath's social life, because of the broad social milieu with which they can engage. Kevin said, "It makes for an interesting life. I am able to have a meaningful engagement with a pretty broad group of people that I guess most people don't have as many different subgroups to be part of…I think there are some intangible benefits that are associated with understanding something about whatever's going on in the world or amongst your friends and being able to participate with them. There's not a whole lot of things that I don't have some familiarity with and I like engaging with people so that's on a day to day basis, I guess that's probably the greatest benefit is I feel very comfortable engaging with folks wherever they are."

At the same time, the downside of their polymathy—regarding social settings—is it can be frustrating, at times, when interacting with others who have a more narrow, limited view of issues. Levi said, "Sometimes it's frustrating, because I see things in ways people don't, and to me, certain things are obvious, and I get frustrated when people don't see them." Hunter made a similar comment: "I find myself getting much more quickly frustrated in situations" with people who are "extremely, narrowly educated." He said, "There's the narrowness of experience, and then there's being narrow-minded. And they're not a perfect overlap, but there is some of that Venn Diagram there, and I think it's generally super unhelpful."

Another consideration is how polymaths fit in socially. While on one hand they can find common ground with anybody to connect on or talk about, they also feel like they do not fit in. This is a paradox of polymathy: they can connect socially with anybody, but never feel like they fit in completely in a social group. What's more, they do not necessarily find many other people who are like they are. Sadly, several participants (Trinity, Sebastian) talked about being teased of bullied as children—not fitting in with others, even from a young age. Trinity said that this sort of "bleak reality" pushed her even more into her mind as a child. Sebastian, who was also bullied as a child, was inspired to achieve excellence as a sort of "revenge" against those who had hurt him.

Most interviewees did say that they enjoy associating, whether professionally or personally, with other polymaths. Some of them seek out other polymaths, while others said they do not. Regardless, being able to spend time around other polymaths is something that helped some interviewees feel more comfortable—like they could be more of their real selves around others who have similar polymathic tendencies. Polymath to polymath social milieus were described, overall, as being deeper than relationships with non-polymaths. Being with other polymaths also provide an opportunity to learn from someone who might also be "fascinating" as well, given their unique experiences and perspectives. Caroline said, "Yes, I do [associate with other polymaths], because I like people who are interested in lots of things and who are interested enough to pursue them deeply." Similarly, Svetlana said, "Meeting people that are a very interesting combination and I'm immediately drawn to them."

Polymaths do also, of course, associate with non-polymaths. Relationships with non-polymaths often require some degree of self-censorship, though, which is a sort of burden that a polymath may have to navigate. On the other hand, some polymaths preferred to spend time with single-issue specialists because those are the people they said they could learn from the most. Karl said, "The polymath is sort of the parasite of the expert. I am drawn to people that are really, really good at one thing. ...I would much rather learn a lot about somebody who's at the top of their field than talk to somebody else who's dabbled in a lot of different stuff." It seems, naturally, there are both benefits and drawbacks for a polymath to engage with others who are also polymathic, versus people who are not.

Theme Four: Polymaths Have Difficult Career Choices

Career preparation starts in school, and several polymaths talked about the disconnect between educational values in their youth, and career expectations in adulthood. A few different interviewees mentioned how confusing it was to be raised as a child who was encouraged to explore and try different things—to explore broadly, to then get to a certain point in their schooling – or be out of school – and feel pressure to pick one career area and specialize.

Many polymaths had phases of pursuing STEM jobs and then later pursuing artistic opportunities, while others were able to creatively combine their interests. Being able to figure out how to integrate interests was something only some polymaths have been able to figure out how to successfully do, though. Sarah shared:

> It was from decently early on, it was just like, oh, yes, you're a Renaissance person. That's what we called it. And that was ... It wasn't like anybody tried to have me be any different. That seemed like that was a really great thing. Later on in life it was like, 'Oh, now you're supposed to focus.' And I was like, 'Wait, what? You raised me this whole time...' You know, like in fact, our school system in many ways in both secondary school and college, I think, trains people to be ... In a way to be polymathic during school, and then suddenly you're supposed to get one job that does one thing, like one very focused specific thing. And it's like, that's crazy. You didn't prepare me to do one thing. In order to get into college I had to have all these hobbies and stuff and now none of that's important anymore? And that was tough. It took me a couple of years to be like, 'Oh, wait no. I refuse. I shall not focus.' You know, I'm not going to do that. I'm going to do a bunch of different things and I'm going to figure out how to combine them if I need to... It wasn't just that I didn't like opera. It's a larger phenomenon with me. It wasn't that opera wasn't the thing and acoustics is the thing. It's that they're too focused.

Certainly, being a polymath with many interests and capabilities, it can be difficult to navigate a career where specialists are typically rewarded and perceived as more successful, more expert. Narrow specialists may be preferred to fill vacancies, for instance, which can make polymaths' careers more challenging, especially in landing desired jobs. Karl said his polymathy makes his career "harder, probably…I have to fight harder to get visibility in the first place and then credibility in the second place."

Once in a position, though, many polymaths felt that they offer tremendous benefits to their employers; some respondents viewed their polymathy as something that made their career better because they were interesting to companies and the respondents had more to offer to an employer—it made them marketable. For example, Henry said, "I think [my polymathy] has made it easier for me to have a rewarding career…In terms of performance on the job it has made it easier for me because I think that it has allowed me to function at a fairly high level in an organization. I have never had a job when I did not have access to the top person in an organization, and I think that part of that is because my characteristics as a polymath tend to get me thinking at that level, and to be able to make a contribution at that level." Similarly, Trinity shared "Job market wise it's a huge benefit because I offer to an employer much more than what's on my resume and the ability to form connections and pull things from different arenas, think critically. I really think that critical thinking goes hand in hand with being polymathic, making connections across different parts of the brain."

Despite the many benefits polymathy brings, it also brings a certain burden, particularly when it comes to making career decisions. Trinity shared,

> The idea of picking one career was just horrible, picking one major was horrible…It's made my professional life easier and richer but it has made my professional decision making more difficult. So, once I'm in the profession or job or whatever I'm doing it's definitely easier because I have more to draw on – more tools in your tool kit – and they're readily accessible. But to make decisions about career profession I think it's more difficult because there's more options.

It seemed that many polymaths chose one career for a period, and then gone onto a second career in another field—having seasons for certain types of work—whereas other polymaths tried to juggle a career with side-gigs, or they might have tried to merge their interests into a single job through an entrepreneurial venture of some sort.

Indeed, several participants found ways to integrate their interests in both the arts and sciences/STEM into a unique career path. Caroline shared, "Building my career, I had to think much harder about how to get a career that was going to be fulfilling for me. I think my greatest personal success, I still view it that my greatest personal success is in succeeding in doing that, and not just languishing in the standard career that I started with because it would have been easy to just go with that because there was a blueprint and because it was safe."

Being a polymath also made some people's professional lives harder, especially as they tried to tell the story of who they are, and to make it easily understandable to others. Sebastian described his career as "squirrely." For some, employers might find the narrative of the "buffet of their career," as Dianna put it, less appealing. For example, Sarah said she had applied to a senior-level job which she was quite qualified for, but was not selected for it because they only wanted to hire someone who had done that specific job – for a long time – already (instead of putting someone in the job who had a variety of different but relevant experiences as it pertained to the job at hand). It is true that a specialist, in comparison, may have more deep expertise than a polymath—though a polymath brings a wider perspective and a larger toolkit to solve problems in the workscape.

The "toolkit" idea was raised in several interviews. Which approach was valued by an employer—the deep expert or the broadly minded polymathic type person—mostly depended upon the organization. Some polymaths felt marketing themselves as a broad polymath made impressing an employer or possible employer harder, while others found it to be an asset in this regard.

Many of the interviewees talked about not fitting in a box, and often employers try to have employees do just that. Svetlana said, "Being placed into boxes at work, where it's like, well you're like this, you do this. So kind of struggling with that." Even once they are in jobs, employers may pressure polymaths to fit into a certain mold, to fit the requirements of a very specific job. This can certainly be very problematic for a polymath who enjoys variety if their job demands more narrow focus.

Many of the interviewees also said that their employers do not know how to leverage their different skill sets. Levi said that nobody even really knows what all his skill sets are (other than himself). "I don't think anybody knows what my full skillset is.

My skillset goes in so many different directions, I couldn't imagine having everything I can do be useful to a job, you know? I mean, leverage my full potential would mean somehow keeping me happy...I wish I knew how to take advantage of my own full potential. I'd probably have another job already if I could figure out how to make it all work together." Wendy said she became an entrepreneur in order to use more of her talents: [Being a polymath] "has made my professional life richer and more complicated…My employers distinctly have not known how to leverage my skillsets which is why I became an entrepreneur… I'm not willing to stay in a place that wants to put me in a box and only asks for that part of me. So I think there's a huge opportunity for organizations to rethink how they use talent."

While many polymaths felt underutilized on the job, one felt overtasked. Trinity reported feeling very used and over-tasked by her employer, especially because she is so capable of doing so many different things; but even though she can, that does not mean she should be expected to juggle many different roles. She said,

> I was told to be careful of working so high above my pay grade, but I couldn't help it…Forgive the crudeness but sometimes when you hire a polymath you're like a wet dream for the employer because they can do so much. Rather than having an employer that can leverage the skills, I'd rather seen an employer who can set boundaries for the polymath. The other side of the sword of unceasing curiosity is unceasing workload and/or constant tasking… I can do a lot. I can design your logo, fix the code in your software, I can talk that customer off a cliff and back into our arms and I can tell you how to save money while doing all those things but that doesn't mean I should be doing all those things.

As a result, part of her challenge at work is to set boundaries regarding what responsibilities she will take on or not. In sum, there was a range of polymaths being underutilized at work as well as being over-tasked in some cases; some of the polymaths interviewed, however, did have positive experiences at their current jobs and felt they were able to bring their talents to work quite nicely.

Suggestions for Employers: A couple participants gave suggestions for how employers could support polymaths more. One interesting suggestion that came up from several respondents was that job rotations to learn multiple skill sets is something that would appeal to them—and this is something that organizations might consider to attract and develop more polymaths. Job rotations would allow for the curiosity in polymaths to be satiated and for them to have a sense of continual learning and growth in their skill sets—something of value to a polymath or really anyone with a sense of curiosity or a growth mindset. Variety also appeals to Karl, who said, "That kind of idea that you would do the same stuff for the rest of your life is horrifying… the idea that you might have a job for life, or if you do this then you will continue doing this. That never worked for me… Give me freedom, give me interesting challenges."

Another idea, this one from Wendy, suggested was to have a polymath focus on their assigned job for 75% - 80% of the time, and then allow flexibility with the rest of the work hours for the polymath to initiate new projects and explore ways to add value. Caroline echoed this idea, saying that employers should "allow flexibility in the way that people develop their own roles in the system. I think that once you allow people some autonomy and flexibility, then they will play to their strengths. Because who doesn't want to play to their strengths?" This may be a way for companies to allow employees to use their strengths to the benefit of the organization, while still having the employee execute the core duties of their position.

Several polymaths talked about micromanaging being a management technique they would not respond well to. Dianna suggested that the best way for an employer to leverage a polymath's talents is to give them a goal to achieve and grant them autonomy to make it happen:

> The [employers] who understand that putting me on multiple projects and unleashing my creativity and giving me autonomy have seen fantastic results. The ones who look at somebody like me and are like, 'I don't even know what box to put you in,' and then they try to force me into a box, it's been miserable for everybody… The best way to set [me] up for success is to give [me] a goal and get out of [the] way. And that doesn't mean I'm going to not include people, or I'm not going to respond to feedback, but it's, don't micromanage. I think the biggest way to douse the fire of a polymath is to micromanage them. The way you succeed is you give them a goal, and you give them guardrails, and you check in on a regular basis, but you don't get in her way.

Svetlana also talked about how horrible it is to be micromanaged as a polymath. She said, "The one thing that drives me completely up the wall is when someone is trying to stand over me and micromanage my stuff. Because I think with anyone I think that leads to a lack of trust in the person that you're hiring. And I think that's okay to some extent, checking in and whatever. But I've definitely [had] experiences where it's like 'okay, you do not need to hold my hand through this'…I think it's more of like a sense of trust in the confines of a job."

Wendy, herself an entrepreneur, suggested that polymaths do well in certain types of environments and not others. She said,

> The places where I've seen polymaths successfully integrate multiple sides of them into actual companies or organizations are either places like Google X where it's kind of this creator's lab space where you get to come in and define what your pieces are and how you relate to all the other projects, and they're very kind of futuristic focused. Or in places like startups, particularly early stage startups where they really need people to wear multiple hats and they're open to you know…you show up and then you kind of write the job description based on what you're capable of doing and what you're interested in doing. I think

> polymaths best utilized in spaces that are undefined or less defined. It's probably disruptive in a world where they want you to perform the status quo. I think it's very hard to successfully integrate polymaths into defined jobs in defined functions and defined sort of business units or problems or whatever. I think academia works well I think labs work and I think the futuristic or startup world or whatever, works. Like innovation things. But if you just try to plop someone into a marketing job it's probably going to be disruptive to have a polymath say, 'But I also dance ballet can we find ways…' and you're like, 'Okay you can do that ballet on the side, but it's not really relevant here.'

Theme Four Summary: In retrospect, there were not many all-encompassing themes that applied to the majority of participants regarding how polymathy and career relate—it seemed each experience was its own unique narrative—except for four dominant themes, which did apply to all interviewees without exception:

1. First, the impact of polymathy on one's career trajectory is significant (whether positively or negatively)
2. Second, for polymaths, a narrow, focused, specialized career would not fit for them, though the idea of specialization is commonly the dominant message people hear about how to advance and succeed professionally. One respondent said that such a circumstance be "horrifying." Even having to focus on the same type of task all day is something polymaths may try to avoid, preferring instead, variety. So, whether on a daily basis, or a career-long basis, variety is important for all polymaths.
3. Third, organizations who want to leverage the full skill set of polymaths should give them freedom, flexibility, and leeway in their work to allow the polymath to add value using their strengths. One person called it "unleashing" their talent on the job. Micromanaging was mentioned several times as something that a

polymath would have trouble dealing with and which would severely stunt the ability of a polymath to make the greatest contribution possible.

4. Four, polymaths who could not find the right job working for someone else often ends up creating their own job as an entrepreneur. To avoid workplace difficulties, a number of polymaths interviewed as part of this research became entrepreneurs in order to be able to combine their skill sets in unique ways, with some degree of freedom and autonomy. Becoming an entrepreneur is fraught with risk and challenges to overcome, though; it is not necessarily an easy route either. Others were able to find employers who give them enough flexibility in their roles to be able to enjoy the job enough to stay for a while. In fact, some interviewees were in jobs they were not happy in, and shared that they were looking for alternate employment opportunities.

Theme Five: Financial Resources Can Both Hinder and Promote Polymathy

There are a number of different financial considerations – both positive and negative – as it relates to being a polymath. For example, financial, familial resources impacted the kind of education that participants were able to have—and this education impacted their polymathy early on in their lives. Trinity shared, "My parents made the conscious decision that was very painful for them to live as the poorest family in a wealthy neighborhood, so I could have the best schools."

In a way, polymathy can provide a means to advance up the socioeconomic ladder. Trinity shared further:

> I wanted out of blue collar world, I wanted out of the socioeconomic class my parents were in. I wanted out of a house that was rife with drug abuse. I wanted out of a house that was rife with domestic abuse. I wanted out of feeling less than everybody else. I wanted to feel like I fit in. I wanted to have things that were

> not knockoffs. I wanted to climb…I read Oliver Twist and Dickens and I saw myself in those characters and I was bound and determined to climb up out of it. I studied wealthy people, I would go the mall and people watch. That person has social status, how do they carry themselves? What are they wearing? It was scientific in the way I studied people because I wanted to fit in with a class of people…I went to a very wealthy college where I didn't fit in… It was never an option to me to not be able to climb socially. I feel like I haven't climbed to the point where I want to, no, I'm not there yet. But I have a map and I have a plan and I also…I know what's enough for me. And I'm not scared of being lower either…so I think that's freeing. Some people climb and climb and can't stop because it's never enough.

Trinity also shared that she used her various talents over the years to generate an income, so for her, polymathy was a way to obtain better financial standing. In fact, for some, their financial situation might have inspired them to pursue their polymathy to the fullest.

As it relates, some people credited their becoming polymathic to the fact that they did not have much money to pay other people to do or fix things, or provide services to them in general, so they had to figure it out on their own. Wendy shared, "Growing up without much money….it forces you to be scrappy and creative and get comfortable without much of a safety net. I think the forcing function of not having a ton of resources at each of these stages was a great blessing in disguise that forced me to say, 'What do you have?' And 'Where is your scrappiness, your creativeness, your network? Okay, get back in the game.' And build that resilience a lot faster." And then later in life, when resources were more plentiful, a continued benefit of polymathy is being able to save money due to being able to do more work themselves. Kevin said, "The stuff that I either make or repair, that allows us to save a bunch of money and maybe live better, which was my understanding originally of why you [became polymathic]."

Being a polymath means that there are more options, more ways, for someone to earn a living. Caroline shared, "There's no end to the ways in which I can be useful and appreciated and earn a living doing things that I love." Wendy said something similar to this but brought in the idea of having a safety net, financially, through her polymathy: "I feel like I have more optionality and more kind of irons in the fire to do that should a life change happen, or should an economy change happen. I feel like I have a safety net in my polymath skills that I maybe didn't have or don't have from like a financial or family perspective. And quite honestly that may have been what drove me to continue to develop multiple skill sets and multiple networks and multiple paths…I am never quite certain which came first, the chicken or the egg there."

Having limited funds, in a way, forced them to develop polymathic skills which continued to pay off over time (something that they value in themselves). On the other side, having financial resources allowed others to pursue their polymathic interests. Being polymathic with number of different sources of income and a "portfolio career" with "side hustles" also can create a sense of financial security, in having diversified skill sets and income streams. Wendy said, "I have like seven different sources of income. My financial planner loves me. But it's a meaningful amount. It's like 30% of my income comes from these so-called side-hustles, which is nice to have kind of a diversification of income streams, should anything happen."

Interestingly, Karl spoke about being sort of financially at the mercy of his interests at any given time, and that what money represents to him is freedom. "Obviously just as my interests change, also my finances change. That's the one thing I noticed, financial freedom is very important. The more financial freedom I have, the more creative I am and the more happy I am. Even though, money is never the main goal. I would never say, 'Oh, I have to take this job, because I can buy me a car.' It only buys me freedom to then say, 'Now I don't have to do this for ... I can do whatever I want for the next six months.' I buy me freedom, I don't buy me things."

Several participants talked about the negative financial aspects of being a polymath. Two participants, Sebastian and Dianna, talked about how privilege plays into the ability to become polymathic—that it takes a certain level of societal privilege to become educated, expert, accomplished, etc. Sebastian that it might in some ways being polymathic might disempower some people if what they want to do is focus narrowly, but they cannot afford to do so—in which case they are sort of forced into some sort of polymathic endeavors. (However, this researcher would add that doing small side jobs does not make one a polymath.)

On a related note, Sarah said that being a polymath has been very expensive, especially the multiple degrees she paid for pursuing her different interests. She, along with several other participants, mentioned that they are in debt. Indeed, most gave the impression that they were not particularly wealthy, despite the level of success they have had professionally. Levi said that he would be able to pursue his polymathic areas of interest (and expertise) more if he had more funds available to do so: "I mean, I guess maybe this is where money becomes a limiter, because, you know, could I go and do more magic? Yes. How would I do that? I would buy more books. I would go to more lectures. I would travel around the world to study with people I've met only briefly."

For interviewees such as Trinity and Sebastian who are parents, they feel some pressure to monetize their skills to gain resources for their household. Trinity shared, "I could recognize life is a balance and it's not all about money, it's really not. Now I have a kid it's a lot more about money." Similarly, Sebastian said that,

> I cannot stop consulting. I cannot stop writing or speaking, because our household will ... We just don't have the money for it. I just need to continue working. We're upwardly mobile and relatively comfortable. It's not like we are independently wealthy or have a terribly massive savings account. So, it just wasn't an option for me to stop with the polymathy. I couldn't stop. There's a kind of forever hustle that I've become increasingly comfortable with. Or maybe comfortable is not the right word. Accustomed to? Where I understand that if I were to stop the hustle, if I were to stop sort of sharking my way through my career, I think the polymathy would stop. I think that my ability to work in between fields is a function of kind of ... not desperation exactly, but it's a certain necessity, if self-driven or external.

As a father, Sebastian felt pressure to use all his various talents to make money for his family to the greatest extent possible, while also juggling the demands of parenthood.

In sum, finances are either something that can force, facilitate, or limit polymathic exploration—it just depends on the situation at hand. What is common amongst all the interviewees, though, is that money has a relationship with polymathy in one way or another; it is something that polymaths must consider along their life journeys. Money has a unique and complicated relationship with a polymath.

Theme Six: Polymaths Are Impacted by Their Families

Family was something that every single interviewee discussed as a factor impacting their polymathy in one way or another. For most, their family supported—or at least allowed—their polymathy and in many cases, was reported as the biggest reason for polymathic tendencies beginning to emerge in childhood. In some ways, it seemed the way that families encouraged polymathy the most in their kids was simply to have no expectations but support the child's free exploration of their various interests. (Please note: family is defined broadly here as parents, siblings, children, or significant others.)

It seems that the greatest support parents could offer a polymathic child is simply to let them explore their interests; being neutral to allow a child to pursue their interests seems the most common thread amongst interviews in terms of what allowed a child's polymathic tendencies to emerge. Hunter shared that being polymathic

> Probably requires having parents that are very open to a lot of different things you want to do. They never really pushed me specifically to do anything. And they also never discouraged me from specifically doing anything. It was just very much like, 'What are you interested in? Cool, we'll support that.' Which certainly made it a lot easier to go off and do a lot of different things. It's interesting now, being in the field I am, I am surrounded by a lot of colleagues who had parents that were like, 'You know, from the age of four, you're going to start playing the violin, and that's all you're going to do.' And that's a very different experience growing up as a kid, you know? I know it definitely sucks some of the joy out of it. It's a whole lot different when you get to feel a sense of agency and autonomy over what you're exploring.

Levi shared similar sentiments, sharing "I think a lot of it did have to do with my parents always taking care of me and giving me the chance to be whatever I wanted to be. They were pretty non-judgmental."

Many different polymaths had parents who would actively teach their kids about various subjects or get involved if the child showed interest in learning about something in particular. In this way, parents sometimes took an active role in helping explore the child's curiosity. In other cases, the parents simply allowed the child to explore independently. Both seemed valuable to respondents. Kevin said, "I go back probably to my dad who, if there's anything that I picked, he would be interested in it with me."

Of note is the fact that many participants mentioned that they had parents who were very different, for example, an engineer father and an artist mother (or another combination of parents with different skillsets). Caroline said that she feels she is a mix of her two parents who are very different from one another. As it relates, no interviewees said that they had parents who are very similar in terms of interests and capabilities.

In terms of family size, there was a mix of participants who were only children, as well as interviewees that came from a family with multiple children. For only children, it seemed that perhaps parents may have had more time to spend with that child alone, helping to teach and engage with them. For participants who grew up with siblings, in some cases it was a sibling (i.e., an older sister) who inspired the younger sibling to try to "keep up," which also encouraged the development of more skills and growth in the other child. Caroline said, "I think that having an older sister definitely helped me want to get better at things because I didn't want to lag behind her all the time." Svetlana mentioned that she had an older brother who really helped her a lot with math, which helped develop her skill sets. It seems whether it was parents or siblings, being able to learn from others in the family is an important aspect of what helped these polymaths as children be able to develop a strong base of information and an appreciation for learning, early on.

The families described throughout the thirteen individual interviews ranged from being full of other people with polymathic tendencies, to having no other polymaths in the family aside from the interviewee him or herself. It was more common, however, that the interviewee came from a family with others with polymathic tendencies—though the level of development of family members' polymathic skill sets varied. Sarah, who says she comes from a family with many polymaths, credits her mom for encouraging her polymathic traits early on in Sarah's life. She said,

> When I was a kid, my mom, we were talking about how I had all these interests and imagining what I would do when I grow up. And she was like, 'I used to play tennis, that was my main sport, and then I would sing a lot.' I sang in all the musicals in school and at church. And then I sang in the church choir. And I did solos almost every month at church in this big Presbyterian church that we belong to in Dallas. And so she was like, 'You could be a singing tennis player.' You know, which obviously is not a thing. But that's like, we were always talking about that. How to combine interests.

Worth noting is the fact that several different participants had childhoods that involved moving frequently; they all attributed that aspect of their childhood that spurred their polymathy more. Dianna said, "In third grade, though, we moved to Illinois from New Jersey, and my whole world was uprooted because my dad had to get transferred at his job...And we were there maybe six months, then we moved to upstate New York for a year, two different locations up there, so I had to learn how to be adapting to new friends, new situations, and that built in a resilience in me. ...I think the moving around in middle school fostered this resilience." Because moving frequently as a child required them to spend more time in alone-play and exploration, participants reported developing a sense of resilience, since each move required making new friends, which took time. Kevin said that moving around frequently made him more "independent."

Interestingly, family sometimes had a negative impact on polymathy. While family was frequently something that encouraged polymathy in interviewees as young adults, family sometimes also became a factor for suppression of polymathy later in adulthood as respondents tried to juggle the responsibilities of family life with the time demands of their polymathic interests. Several respondents mentioned having come from "dysfunctional" families. One respondent said that in her youth, her parents encouraged her polymathic pursuits, but as an adult, they were her biggest "roadblock," as they wanted her to pick one field and stick to it. Felicity said, "My parents are the biggest doubters of me. It's hard for them. ...They never encouraged my photography. But I don't know if they actively discouraged it. The great thing about my parents is that they always encourage education.....I would say they are my biggest roadblocks." In other words, exploration was fine as a youngster, but as an adult, it is time to focus in one area. Felicity went on to say, "They totally shaped who I am, and yet I as an adult need to be a very focused, career-oriented woman. ...What they think I should be doing with my time is different from what I know that I need to do with my time to fulfill both sides. They only want to hear about the job and the good girl stuff."

The impact of polymathy in a marriage and on parenthood can be quite a challenge to juggle. One interviewee discussed how his pursuing his polymathic interests was a strain on his marriage, since he would spend so much time on his individual interests, and not enough time with his wife. His resolution to this problem was to cut back on solitary pursuits and find more interests to pursue with his wife, together. He described his prior time-consuming exploration of his interests, alone, as "selfish" in the context of being married. Similarly, another interviewee discussed how being a father limits his ability to explore and exploit his polymathy to the fullest. Sebastian said,

> It's all the more complicated now that I'm a parent. I knew what success looked like ... I have known what success looks like in varying valances in my career over time. That ... and this is sort of trite and stereotypical, but it's true, your sense of self and your vision for yourself radically shift if and when you become a parent, even if you're a poor or an absent or a necessarily absent parent. The prioritization just shifts. ...I can't travel as much. I can't consult as much. I can't go to the work nearly as much. If I want to be the parent that I want to be, and potentially my children need me to be, I really need to say no a lot more. And as ... let's just call me a professional polymath, that's really fucking hard. We talked about other valances, but that difficulty ... My varying work brings in a lot of the money that pays a lot of our bills, so it is a financial and a psychic struggle to be the professional that I want to be while also being the parent that I want to be.

Taken together, it appears that being polymathic in the context of family life seemed a difficult to navigate, especially as an adult. It requires compromise. Interestingly, majority of interviewees did not have children. Only three of the thirteen interviewees shared that they were parents. Dianna shared, "Privilege; like the fact that I can jump from job to job because I don't have a spouse or a partner, you know, husband who needs me to have benefits, and I don't have kids that I have to do something for, I [don't] have to live in a certain area. There's a hefty amount of privilege involved in being able to bounce around as much as I do and try the things I'm trying." It may be the case that it is easier to become a polymath or maintain polymathy without children, though some polymaths do successfully juggle parenthood and their multi-faceted careers and interests.

As it relates, dating as a polymath—finding the right partner—seemed a challenge for several interviewees. This was not something that was asked about in the interview protocol, but several interviewees mentioned it on their own. Trinity said,

> It's hard to date…because normally you find someone who only fulfils one part of you or one aspect. It's hard….my experience has been it's hard…[My polymathy] definitely impacted who I chose to marry. I was explicit with my husband that I am a polymath because I wanted to marry someone who could handle me making sharp turns in my career and my life to follow passions that might seem disparate…someone who would not get easily shaken off, someone who was thrilled by it rather than terrified of it…

Finding a partner as a polymath seems difficult due, in part, to the fact that a polymath who has multiple unique aspects to his or her lifestyle and personality would require a partner who could understand and support that; finding such a person was not easy to do for the participants who talked about their love life. What's more, these interests and pursuits may change over time. Several respondents did mention finding partners successfully and maintaining long-term relationships with them, however. Based on what participants shared, it seems the key is finding a partner who is understanding and can be flexible as the polymath's identity (or multiple identities) evolves through the years.

Theme Seven: Polymaths are Voracious Learners

If there is a single essence of polymathy, it would be that they are very strong learners. But more than just being capable of learning, they have an apparent *appetite* for it. This section will review the role that formal education and self-directed learning played in the development of polymaths. This section also includes data regarding polymath curiosity and how reading plays into their hunger for learning. Lastly, this section addresses the desire polymaths have for change, newness, and variety.

Educational System: Many polymaths talked about how the education system impacted their polymathy. For example, a lot of interviewees said that there was a specific teacher or teachers who impacted their exploration of their interests, which helped them become polymathic. On the other hand, some said that they had experiences with teachers who discouraged their multiple interests and wanted them to focus more narrowly instead. Several participants attended boarding (high) schools, which they felt helped them become polymaths (for instance, having time in the evenings—while still in a school environment—to continue learning activities).

Because the school system, especially at the college level and up, requires a specific focus to earn a degree in a specialized field, one participant, Karl, opted not to go to college at all. Another participant, Hunter, decided to design his own sort of real-world Master's degree program similar to what he would have done if he was a part of a formal program (but without the expensive tuition). Sarah has three Master's degrees, evidence of her interest in various fields. Indeed, there was a broad range of experiences with the education system amongst the interviewees, but what was common among all of them is that their education, whether formal or self-taught, impacted their polymathy in one way or another. Trinity said, "The scholastic system is not set up to support being a polymath or at least it wasn't when I went through. It was focused on finding a track and focusing on it."

Several participants suggested some ways to improve the education al system, from a polymathic point of view. For example, one way to improve the educational system would be to make subjects that are taught more interdisciplinary instead of being discrete stand-alone topics; making more connections between what a student is being taught would be useful in terms of helping gain a deeper level of understanding and breaking down the siloes between subject areas. Two different participants talked about taking such a class, i.e. a physics class that requires building a musical instrument, or a class focused on interdisciplinary thought, and said how much they learned from and enjoyed those classes.

Sarah said she believes the school system already teaches polymathic principles, but that once formal schooling is finished, the "real world" expects more narrow specialization. She said,

> This comes back to my belief that we teach this ... Our school system is set up for polymathy in that we're literally taking like history class and English class and science class and whatever club. You're doing all these different things and then all of a sudden it's different when you get into the real world and people are like, 'Well, it's different when you get in the real world, and you're like, well, why? Why does school have to be so different from the real world? Why can't either school be modified to match the expectations of the real world or why can't we just operate in a way that's ... Why isn't it more acceptable to continue in the way that you did in school in terms of all your different interests and abilities?' It's just crazy to me.

Sarah notices a disconnect between the way youth are taught in school to learn about many different subjects, whereas in adulthood, this sort of approach is frowned upon.

Svetlana shared that she believes that the school system repressed her polymathic tendencies early on:

> I think [my polymathy] was being suppressed by the way that I was going through the educational system...I think it was because I was being asked to separate everything out. So, nothing connected with each other. So there was no logic between learning something in art and learning something in science...So I think that maybe at the end of high school is where I realized that I was good at both of these subjects but I kind of had to think about the rest of my education in a bit of a creative way to make it work in the way that I wanted it to work, instead of feeling crushed under the way that things should be and the mutual exclusivity of art versus science, which I don't really believe is a thing.

To Svetlana, learning about different subjects without any interweaving connections between them is problematic; she believes this is something that should change in the educational system—that there should be more interdisciplinary connections made for students.

Wendy shared her belief that the educational system could be used to identify more polymaths early on. She said, "I still stand by my assertion that I was probably born this way. But I do think that there are opportunities…through particularly I think education and how we approach teaching at least through K-12 that either would surface more polymaths or would at least teach this toolkit particularly around problem solving and discipline and self-actualization even to people who aren't necessarily polymaths themselves but could use the toolkit."

Most participants said that they did quite well in school, though a couple said that they struggled in school. Several different participants said that they did not like rote memorization, and the school system, especially early on, required that sort of approach to succeed. Svetlana remarked that she learned best when a teacher would treat her as an equal and be more conversational in class. Several participants said that for them to learn information, it needs to make sense, and that teachers need to be able to explain why something is true, or why something is the best way, instead of just saying it has always been done that way. In other words, the logic of why something was being taught to them was important to be included as part of their schooling. Caroline said that some of her teachers were "put off" by her pursuit of artistic hobbies when they felt she should be focusing more on math. But mostly, teachers were a positive factor in some students developing into polymaths.

Trinity, who was a very talented student, was invited to join a specialized high school where she would have had to pick a track such as math and begin specializing at a young age; because it would have forced early specialization, her mother did not allow her to go. Trinity is still sure not right if that was the right decision or not, even now. She said,

> And you have to choose a track when you go there, choose art or math or whatever but I was asked to go to the academy and I really wanted to go, I felt like it would be where I would be challenged by my peers. That's the other thing, I had no peers to challenge me. In art I did actually, fantastic artists who pushed me. In math and science I really had no one to push me. My mother refused, didn't want me pigeoned into one track. She wanted me to grow my social skills. She was always very nervous about me becoming so intellectual I couldn't deal with other people…from her working with surgeons and doctors and seeing poor bedside manner and having to fill those gaps as a nurse. She said no, I want you to experience life from your age group and have all of those firsts. She saw [a specialized school] more as an intellectual farm being farmed for something. We fought on that because I wanted to go, I saw it as an opportunity…I still don't know who is right…if my kid was in that situation I don't know what I would do. I'm grateful to my mom I could very easily have become…I'm naturally…proclivity towards introversion and I could have easily become the awkward shy introvert brain that doesn't know how to speak up and take charge, those are all skills we need right now. You need both. I'm grateful but still don't know if it was the right decision now.

Perhaps if there was a special high school for gifted and talented youth that did not require early specialization, Trinity's choices and experiences might have been different.

A college-level liberal arts education was mentioned several times as something that helped expose people to a variety of different fields, which was appreciated, although specialization (a major) was still required. One participant suggested that the school system become more interdisciplinary in the future, making connections between fields more, to encourage polymathic thinking in students. Even though students at a liberal arts college may get to sample many different subjects, the linkages between the subjects appears mostly absent, or up to the student to figure out on their own. Several participants noted that multi-disciplinary exploration was encouraged in school up to a certain extent, then specialization was expected—and that this change was jarring and hard to understand.

For a polymathic child who is very good in a lot of areas but who does not excel in one more than others, it can be challenging to figure out one's sense of place in the school system. Svetlana shared, "I felt very much in school, throughout even elementary school, middle school and high school, that I was trying very hard to do this thing of prove myself in this one place and be like, 'I'm smart, look at me.' But constantly being torn down, because I wasn't naturally good at one thing, I was kind of pretty great at many things. And there wasn't quite a place to put me in the educational system that I went through."

One participant opted not to go to college, precisely because he felt that college-level education was too narrow. Karl shared, "I had the choice either to go to the art school, but at that time there was no computers involved at all, and I'm really not good at painting manually. I would have to deliver something like a portfolio. That didn't work for me. Or I had the choice to study computer science, which totally did not cover the art aspect. That's why I didn't study anything [in college]."

However, having access to education is obviously a huge part of what supports the development of host polymaths. Trinity shared, "A good school system was a huge plus. I had access to things people in other school systems didn't have, things others didn't…Access to learning definitely was huge." Sebastian stressed that his quality education came from having male, white privilege, and that his parents had or could find the money to pay for his schooling, which included attending an arts boarding school and top-tier universities. For him, it was hard to separate his polymathy from his privilege. The type of access to schooling depends on financial resources to a large extent.

Overall, most participants credited their polymathy to some degree from having an education, having been exposed to various subjects, having teachers and mentors who helped them learn about different fields, although in some instances the school system was a hindrance as well. Several participants said that there might be more polymaths if they were encouraged to develop more disparate skills, to gather a toolkit of various capabilities, and the educational system should be a part of that equation.

Self-directed Learning: Polymaths exhibit, overall, a deep curiosity and love of learning; much of this learning was self-directed. In fact, every participant thought of themselves as a self-directed learner at least to some degree. Wendy said, "Certainly, post-formal education, I engage in a huge amount of self-directed learning, continually." Polymaths exhibit a "can do" attitude as it pertains to their ability to learn, and a deep confidence in their ability to figure out whatever it is they desire (even in some cases if figuring it out meant asking someone else to help them do so). Dianna shared, "I know that if I don't know something, I can learn it because I have time and again." Svetlana said, "I want to figure things out. I want to understand them I want to connect them to other things. And I want to draw logical conclusions for myself." But more than just a noteworthy ability to learn well, most polymaths have a real appetite for learning which frequently gets quenched through self-directed learning. Kevin said, "Self-directed learning is, in some respects, is a core value for living life in my mind."

Polymathy and learning are inseparable. And most of the time, there was no one to tell a polymath – especially as an adult—what to learn or how to learn it. This was something they each figured out for themselves, and which resulted in singularly unique career paths, unique combinations of interests, and unique learning trajectories for each person.

Interestingly, several polymaths mentioned that they like to figure things out for themselves best, rather than someone "teaching" them about something. Caroline said, "I really don't like being told things. I especially don't like being told things if I could have worked them out for myself because I find that really patronizing. It's like someone is telling me that they think I'm stupid.... I prefer learning things myself. I would much rather work everything else out for myself, and then only ask when I've really got stuck... I also like being self-taught because I've usually felt that no one understands me as well as I understand myself, and that if you don't understand someone, it's very difficult to help them. There are very few people who've succeeded in really understanding me." A couple of participants also said that a teacher using their authority as leverage was a huge turn-off: Karl shared, "I want to find it out myself and not be told how it is. Again, 'We have always done it like that way," that doesn't work with me, the authority way."

As it relates, several participants talked about the impact that the internet has had on their self-directed learning, namely, that it makes it even more possible to figure out whatever information they need on their own. Svetlana shared, "I would say, I am a self-directed learner. And in this day and age with the internet at the palm of your hand I think I have to almost control what I do and when I do it because I can become a little bit overwhelmed with information at times." Henry attributed his self-directed learning tendency towards his strong introversion, although not all participants in the study identified as being introverted.

For Wendy, though, her experience early on of developing her talents in math was almost entirely on a self-directed basis. Her mathematical talent was identified at a young age (pre-school or kindergarten); she was very advanced for her age. Instead of putting her in math class with the other students her age, her school had her teach herself math out of text books and just take exams as she was ready. They even had her tutor other older students who were struggling with math. She had very little teacher-based support in math but was still able to thrive in terms of learning it.

Hunter gave an example of being a self-directed learner as well. He was thinking about getting a Master's degree in music, but first did some research to learn from other people in those kinds of programs and find out what their experiences were like. He found out much of the program revolved around actually getting music gigs. He decided to—in a way—make his own Master's degree program in music. He opted to do some reading on the side, particularly about how to practice well. He continued pursuing music gigs on his own. He applied what he learned and continued with "deliberate practice," and this helped him going from feeling behind the curve to instead "accelerating in front of the curve" by "rolling my own graduate music experience program." This is an example of a big, ongoing self-directed learning project.

Alternatively, Levi viewed himself as being a self-directed learner, but also acknowledged the role that having a good teacher or mentor plays in helping to grow one's skillset and knowledge base. He said, it is "just much easier when I have a teacher to start with. I will easily pick what I want to learn, and I will decide what I want to do, but boy. And I spoke to Dr. [Jones] when I was learning magic. Oh my God. I would not be the magician I am right now. I would not be a professional without him starting me. And just in school in general. My parents… and then all my teachers....So I mean, yes, I'm self-directed. I do find things I like on my own. I do dictate my own interests… I also am wise enough to seek out a good teacher." Dianna talked about surrounding herself with people who can help her figure out the solutions to problems when she cannot on her own.

On the whole, all the polymaths interviewed for this research felt that they were self-directed in their learning, to some degree. How that shows up exactly—whether looking something up on the internet, experimenting to figure out a solution by trial and error, reading a book, seeking out a teacher or mentor, or asking family or peers for help—varied from person to person. But each person did take some level of ownership over their own learning journey; this is a key trademark of polymathy.

Curiosity: As it relates with self-directed learning, curiosity also came up in a number of different interviews as a trait of a polymath. Self-directed learning and curiosity are related, but distinct concepts; self-directed learning involves identifying what to learn and pursuing it by oneself , whereas curiosity is a state or being that might or might not lead to self-directed learning. Could a person ever even become a polymath without being curious? It seems unlikely. Felicity shared, "If it's just me, I feel like I'm always thinking. The brain never turns off. Curiosity drives my life, personally. Curiosity about any particular subject. And I guess that would be how I define myself as a polymath is that I'm endlessly curious about science or art or whatever. I'm going to find something and dig into it." Levi said, "I love seeing the layers in things, and I love to learn about the layers… to know the world in very different ways."

Many of the polymaths interviewed gave the impression that they are voracious learners—very curious people with an apparent never-ending hunger for a variety of growth experiences. Trinity said, "I definitely consider myself a self-directed learner…because I'm curious about everything." Karl said, "For me, every field is interesting...I'm interested in understanding how things work. As a child, I took apart everything to see what makes it tick." Svetlana described it as a "thirst for learning." Svetlana's curiosity shows up, frequently, in being interested in people. She said, "I'm also a very social person and I'm very interested in learning more about people. I will sit there and I will ask a million questions because I'm kind of just fascinated with the way humans work and the human condition in general. I myself find myself to be, I think that's maybe a thirst for learning, I'm not sure if that has to do with being a person that is polymathic, but I do have this thirst for knowledge constantly all the time."

Sebastian commented that if something is out of bounds—not possible—for him to do, it loses a sense of interest, and his curiosity wanes, because he knows pursuing that thing would not be possible. He said, "Some problems are more or less interesting to me...my inability to choreograph in New York City because I don't live in New York City is not something I have a choice about, really. So I moved to Rhode Island. My inability to take on commissions because I can't be away from my family for three weeks on end ... I can't do it, and so it stops being interesting....if I sense that I'm not going to be able to solve a problem or become frustrated with a problem, I'm probably faster to move on than other folks. So that question of interest and attention cuts a couple ways."

The polymath's curiosity feels like a type of openness. Levi shared that he is very open-minded, even if that involves changing his opinion on something. He said,

> There's just something about learning that just, I enjoy sitting there, and it's like, 'This is new. I didn't know this. How could that possibly be?' And there's just something absolutely appealing to collecting new knowledge, I guess. I guess, to a point, I do enjoy challenging myself, seeing how far I can go, but that's definitely not the be all end all of why I like learning… I'm just happy to learn something new. There is something definitely exciting about it. No matter what it is, I'm happy to learn it. I see a lot of people seem to be afraid of new knowledge, when their worldview gets changed or challenged. You see that all the time now. So even if it hurts my worldview, it's like, 'Oh. Oh, there was a fact there. Okay, sure. I'll have to adjust.' And I'm happy to.

Most polymaths are open to experiences and open to learning, and this shows up in the form of curiosity. Caroline also believed that her curiosity and her polymathy are related: "Because I was curious, [my interests were] a range of things and not just one thing."

Reading: Polymaths enjoy learning, and a very common way that they do this is through reading. The interview protocol for this research did not ask any questions about reading, yet it was a subject that came up at least to some degree with 11 out of the 13 interviewees. It seems most polymaths are avid readers, and this is probably related to (1) their curiosity and (2) their tendency towards self-directed learning. In fact, Svetlana linked her tendency towards self-directed learning with her reading abilities: "I do think I'm a self-directed learner and I think that came through being super comfortable with being a super strong reader...I was just very much into consuming a lot of books, it didn't really matter what they were. At one point when I was a kid it was just like constant. Or I would just like read encyclopedias."

It makes sense, given reading is a primary avenue to learning. However, the reading polymaths consume may or may not be related to curriculum presented to them in their formal education. Wendy said, "Reading, of course. I mean, I love reading. I was a big, avid reader in high school, and at about that time, I was like, 'Oh man…You mean there's books out there that they don't make you read that are actually well-written and are enjoyable? That's great. To hell with the curriculum. I'm reading things I like.'" Henry shared that his family was supportive of him reading from an early age: "I was encouraged to read, and that as a kid I was read to." Trinity said, "My mom had a deal worked out with librarian, I could take out 21 books not 14. Every week I would get 21 new books and I read myself through the entire library, I was voracious." Caroline said, "I'm just a very fast reader." Alternatively, Karl remarked that books might provide one explanation to a problem whereas, so it was worth considering, but also worth exploring on his own to find solutions. What is clear is that all polymaths read to some extent—though most are avid, quick, capable readers, and this is part of their ability to engage in self-directed learning and to quench their curiosity.

Change and Newness: Eight of the thirteen interviewees talked about liking change and/or newness, even though there were no explicit questions asked around that topic. While on one hand, polymaths might, by and large, be a very curious group, they may also become bored if not intellectually stimulated enough. This is not to say that they are easily bored, although one participant, Sebastian, did say exactly that: "I'm bored easily." On the other hand, another participant, Wendy, said "I'm never bored. Ever." Dianna said, "It's not that I get bored easily…it's that there's a lot of cool things to try in the world and I want to try all of them." Despite this contradiction in the experience of different polymaths, it seemed, overall, though, that polymaths enjoyed change and newness; they were not averse to it, as some other people may be, and could derive pleasure from learning something new or trying something different for the sake of change or variety. Having a full breadth of experiences and a large base of knowledge is something that polymaths value.

Other comments participants made alluded to change and/or newness being "exciting," including professional changes or challenges. Henry shared, "There is this sort of unsettled component, and then a very excited, exhilarating component with learning new things, achieving new goals… Just the thrill of taking on a brand-new challenge, even a challenge that most people think, 'What?' … The accomplishments and the satisfactions that come from the learning, and the discovery, and the newness… I really think it's the learning, the novelty of things, that keeps me most engaged."

In fact, several different interviewees said that staying in the job their whole career would never be something they would want to do. Participants seem to like change overall. Karl said, "I want change. I want new things to happen… I see interesting things everywhere...There's always new ideas coming up." Dianna said "It's exciting to try new things." Certainly, the fact that a polymath is interested in and capable of doing many things feeds into their ability to switch between tasks in order to create a sense of change and variety. Trinity said "Never being bored. I can't remember the last time I was bored. This might be my personal way of being a polymath, there's always something unfinished I'm working on. I like to switch gears."

The idea of not having newness, change, and variety in the life of a polymath is unpleasant. Sarah shared, "I just felt this pit in my stomach like, 'Is this it? Am I going to be doing this forever? Like just this?' …. But only doing that forever because in order to be, to really make any money at it and to be the level that I was interested in being at, you just have to be completely, singularly focused." Similarly, anything that is extremely repetitive is likely to be unappealing to a polymath. Karl shared, "Anything that's a repetitive task, I really don't like."

In a way, learning is a kind of change because it is adding information to the knowledge repository a person has at their command, so it is not surprising necessarily that polymaths—voracious learners—enjoy change and newness, since learning itself represents a sort of activity involving these components of change and newness. Sarah shared, "I don't think that necessarily all of my choices are related to the fact that I have multiple interests. I think a lot of it is probably related to the fact that I also really like change." Levi said, "I don't know how anybody couldn't want a new experience or new information, especially, especially when they know it's going to benefit them. And generally speaking, I think there's very little information out there that can't benefit someone."

Some participants said that once they really mastered a hobby or a job and were not learning or growing anymore, that is when they knew it was time to move on to something different. For example, Henry said that his way of pursuing hobbies includes "chewing up this hobby and then spitting it out and picking something else."

There is also an element with some polymaths, though not all, of starting hobbies or interest but not pursuing them long-term. Karl said that he is good at short-term, quick ideas, but that he is "really bad" at long-term projects and finishing them. He said he is "more a sprinter than a marathoner," partially because he desires change and newness to be happy. He went on to say, "I know that after a while I like to start things, and I like to pioneer things, but I don't like to maintain things."

Theme Seven Summary: Polymaths are voracious learners. In this section, a variety of aspects of this reality were discussed, including the role that formal education and self-directed learning play in the development of polymaths. This section also addressed polymath curiosity and how reading plays into their appetite for learning. This section also covered the preference polymaths have for change, newness, and variety. Polymaths and learning are inseparable.

Theme Eight: Polymaths are Quite Confident but May Also Experience "Imposter Syndrome"

Throughout many interviews, it became clear that the polymaths, on the whole, had a great deal of confidence in themselves, their abilities—especially in their ability to learn. On the other hand, one attendee who had a number of previous jobs he considered unimpressive said that it can be hard to dis-identify with having those sorts of roles. Polymaths may feel a mix of being very confident but also somewhat insecure in some ways, at times, depending on the person. But overall, the sense that interviewees gave is that they are quite confident individuals. Caroline shared, "The belief that I can do anything so that I won't be daunted if I want to do something. I'll figure out how to do it and believe that it probably is possible." Karl said "I think I can do anything. In a way, that's the thing I always believed. I can learn anything... I thought I could do everything, anything. I have to quiet some confidence in my abilities. I didn't think I wanted to be an assistant to anybody. That didn't work."

Polymaths must have confidence in order to try new things to the extent that they do. Dianna shared,

> There's a cool thing and I want to go try it. And even if I wasn't fully qualified or had any business saying yes to trying something, the opportunity was there and it was offered to me, so of course I said yes... [My friend observed that] many of us are presented interesting opportunities, 'You [Dianna] say yes. And you think to go after things that none of us would ever even consider going after because we wouldn't think we could get it.' He's like, 'But that filter's not there for you.' I've always said yes to opportunities that have come my way. I make my own opportunities. I don't wait for other people to do that for me. I'm not going to be stymied by some artificial, arbitrary thing that you must do according to society. It's because of [my mother], it never occurred to me that I couldn't do or be anything I set my mind to... I like who I am.

Dianna shared that she got much of her confidence from her mother. The relationship between polymath confidence and secure attachment as a child is an area for further exploration.

That said, the directionality of being a polymath and having high confidence (for the most part) is not clear, however. Having a sense of high confidence might encourage people to be more open to having various experiences, and thus become a polymath over time. Or being a polymath might foster a person's sense of confidence since it makes them capable across different areas. Regardless of the directionality of this relationship, it does appear, overall, that polymaths tend to be quite a confident group; in other words, polymathy and confidence do appear to frequently co-exist. For people who like learning new things and having a variety of experiences, it is not really surprising; it would be quite difficult for a person to go in the world, sampling new things, having adventures, if they did not have the underlying confidence to support that kind of exploration.

Various examples were given to show this sort of confidence. For Svetlana, an example of confidence was a willingness to try something new and risk failure. For Wendy, it was the courage to decide to and then actually complete a marathon:

> And I was like, 'Okay…you guys are not that special. So, if you can do these things [like run marathons] then clearly they're doable.' Because in my head these were not achievable activities, they seemed like super-human feats. And so it was almost like an, 'Okay, how hard are these things actually?' If you keep going long enough, you too will cross that finish line and so it was almost like a challenge to myself to be like…'Okay, what level of persistence is required to achieve these things that seem super human?' And it turns out, you just have to keep putting one foot in front of the other and you too can achieve super human things, right? So like I do all the athletics partially because I like to eat pizza [laughter] and partially because like I almost wanted to prove to myself that there isn't some tier of super humans out there that I will never be a part of; it's literally just a matter of persistence.

Deciding to travel by herself was another way that Wendy developed an increased sense of confidence. She shared the following vignette about how solo international travel helped her build a level of comfort with the unknown:

> Like, I'm good at managing the known. But the unknown really terrified me. And I didn't know how to succeed against the unknown. And traveling by myself all around the world without really an itinerary…I sort of picked a country…and like knew how long I was going to be there and that was it. I like showed up and like…figured it out as I went…that trained me in like getting comfortable being uncomfortable and gave me the confidence that even if I didn't know what I was about to step into, I'm strong enough and smart enough that I'll figure it out. And I think without that experience and that training, there's no way I could be doing what I'm doing right now in that I'm kind of crafting a career and like pieces of a life together in a world that ...like…what I want to do doesn't exist. Right? And I think that's probably true for a lot of polymaths who succeed at keeping those things in their lives, there isn't an obvious path to follow – you have to make it yourself. And that requires kind of a perspective and a …self-confidence that you can do that. So that requires building that experience to say I have the ability to do this, even if I don't know what that next step is going to look like.

For some, a sense of confidence came across in starting entrepreneurial ventures which are fraught with risk. Indeed, confidence to continually learn and bravely explore are part of what makes a polymath a polymath.

Once a sense of confidence and courage are developed in a polymathy, it facilitates even more exploration. Dianna said, "You [as a polymath] have the courage to say yes to so many more things because they're either interesting to you, or you make yourself open to the possibility of them existing, or even happening. The benefit is you get to experience a lot of cool things if you have the courage to step up and say yes, right, or I want to."

Sebastian shared that he considered himself an expert in fields perhaps quicker than others might have. This was due, in part, to his ability to learn very quickly. He said, "Even not really knowing what I was talking about, I could call myself an expert….there's this moment where I'm like, 'Oh, I could make money with this,' or, 'Oh, this would really make me feel good to be an expert in this thing, because I did a fraction of the work of other people and I'm getting all the much more attention and money for it.' [I could] learn about it sufficiently."

Sebastian also said that his polymathy enables him to make the most out of any given situation, and that this is related to his confidence. He shared, "There's a kind of faith and trust in that, maybe, which ... a kind of trusting the process…It's kind of the inverse of the imposter syndrome. I can enter a room where I have no credible expertise but have faith that I will be able to garner some value from it, even if I won't, at that moment, know what that value is… I can walk into cocktail parties and not be afraid." In fact, several polymaths talked about trying to extract value whenever possible. Wendy shared that her polymathy

> Allows me to play the best card in my hand...right.... depending on what the situation is. It certainly...I think it gives me a larger hand of cards, if we're extending this analogy...in the you know if the tools that I learned in business school aren't really working in this particular situation I can go pull something out of my classical music training or I can go and look at my mathematical skillset or my coding skillset and be like, 'Well, is there an analogy or framework or an approach to the work that I've used there that I might be willing to use here?' So there's a lot of kind of diagonal association and connection that just gives me a larger kind of toolkit to work off of than someone who has only pursued one path. The toolkit that I bring to any kind of problem solving situation is quite a bit larger than usually the other people in the room... Creative problem solving is probably one of the things that I do best.

Despite having such high confidence, for some polymaths, the desire to achieve may be driven in part by past hurts. For instance, Sebastian shared that he was bullied in his youth, and his way of getting revenge against those who hurt him was to achieve excellence. He said, "I don't want to be bullied or intimidated, so I'm going to go to a fucking Ivy League school and I'm going to get a piece of paper that says I'm literally smarter than [my bullies]." Polymathy on the whole is experienced positively by participants but may have some ties to negative experiences for some.

As it relates, six out of the thirteen interviewees talked about feeling like a "poser" or having "imposter syndrome" at times. Henry shared,

> The number of times I have felt like an imposter because I knew I was really not as good as other people who had truly learned the ropes and things and spent a lot more time specializing in certain areas...When I'm feeling not so good about what I'm doing, I feel like a fake. I feel like somebody who holds a job that they don't deserve, and that they are really just sort of playing the role of somebody who understands much less than they seem like they understand. For instance, I have a staff who are much better informed, much more expert in what they do, than what I am, and I end up telling them what to do all the time. There's a term, The Imposter Complex or something like that? That is something that I struggle with a lot.

Despite being quite a confident bunch on one hand, polymaths may also have a level of insecurity as well. Kevin shared, “I guess I do harbor sort of a latent concern on some of this stuff. You spend enough time in it, you start hanging around people who really that's the focus of what they do and are you kind of a poser because you're not committed to this one thing? The thought occurs to me but it's never been an issue.” Sebastian said, “There's a certain imposter syndrome that just never goes away.”

No matter the career successes they have had, in comparison to deep specialists, polymaths shared that sometimes they feel “imposter syndrome.” This is certainly an interesting finding, juxtaposed with the fact that many polymaths appear to be quite confident. In other words, on one hand polymaths frequently feel confident in themselves and their abilities, but on the other hand, they feel somewhat insecure about not being a specialist expert. This is not necessarily a surprising finding, but it is an important aspect to consider when trying to understand the experience of modern day polymaths.

A couple polymaths also talked about wondering what life might have been like if they picked a different path—or feeling like perhaps they could be doing something better if they were narrow specialists. Karl shared that he wonders if other people view him more negatively, as not as qualified as some others, because he is not a narrow specialist: “I guess, that's again the thing where people cannot put you in a drawer and then they might think you are not qualified enough for that. Again, like somebody else who has studied it might appear a better candidate for certain things.”

Karl also made note of this paradox of polymathy—of being confident and perhaps a little insecure at the same time. He shared, “I always have the imposter syndrome as well. That's the typical thing. I always think I know much less than other people or …in a way I'm over confident and also have an inferiority complex that I think everybody else knows more than me about something because they are expert in that field. There's always that conflict."

Another challenge polymaths have, despite their apparent high level of confidence in their abilities, is wondering if they could be doing their work better if they were narrow specialists instead. Trinity shared,

> Always feeling like you could be doing it better…There's always going to be someone who that's their pure passion and they might do it quote unquote better from an objective standpoint. There's only so many minutes in the day and if you're splitting it the less you feel you're able to fully do something. Maybe it's part of being female and the mom stuff, I feel like I could be doing better work. I'm not a specialist, I'm not only one thing... I have a hard time owning my own knowledge because it's disparate.

In a similar vein, Sebastian shared he often wonders what life would have been like if he had made different choices. "What that means is that there's a certain level of haunting. There's a certain level of, 'What could have been if,' for example, 'I had stayed in New York and had the artistic career that I could have had if I was based in New York?' I'm pretty sure I would've been miserable, and I'm pretty sure it wouldn't have gone very well. But there's no way of knowing, and that, on some kind of level, tortures me." Kevin shared in these sentiments: "Is there maybe a deeper fulfillment out there behind that somewhere or a deeper knowledge that you can get? By having disparate interests, the other side of it is you can't be obsessively focused on one or two things. I have wondered if there's something that you miss as a result of that. I'm not convinced that the answer is yes, but I have wondered that."

Taken together, polymaths on the whole seem to exhibit a unique mix of confidence and insecurity at the same time. They are confident in their abilities and their skills particularly around learning but are also somewhat insecure given they did not specialize. Compared to specialists, they may feel "imposter syndrome" despite coming across as very confident individuals.

Theme Nine: Polymaths Self-Identify as Highly Creative

Twelve out of thirteen participants involved in this research said that they believe their polymathy makes them more creative and/or better at problem solving. For instance, Caroline, a mathematician, believed this relationship existed but was not sure about the specifics of the relationship—i.e., if being polymathic spurred on her creativity, or if the two were just correlated without a causal relationship. Nevertheless, most participants reported that what they do best as polymaths is precisely creative problem solving, although two participants pointed out that non-polymaths, deep specialist, can also be creative and good at problem solving, too.

On that note, a few respondents talked specifically about the need in society and the important role for specialist monomaths, but also acknowledge the strength that a polymath can bring to solve particularly complex, multi-dimensional challenges. Felicity pointed out that narrow specialists could also be creative. She said that because they are such deep experts, they know so much about the field, and as a result they can come up with novel solutions that way. She said, "A true scientist who has only that part of them, they're very creative. They have to think of very creative solutions to problems. They're solving things that nobody else has ever solved. I will say that having the artistic side of me, or the other side, helps with that, but I wouldn't say that it's an exclusive benefit to being a polymath. I would say they're perfectly capable and very creative in their thinking." Most polymaths, however, felt that polymaths are in a better position for creativity to emerge than narrow specialists are in a position for. Of course, creativity is not a skill that only polymaths have, but it is a great strength that they possess given the breadth of experiences and knowledge they can bring to bear when solving challenges.

The concept of having a large "toolkit" or a "broader lens" was mentioned by several attendees as something that goes together with their polymathy. Being able to understand multiple points of view more than the average person was also mentioned. Regardless of these minor permutations, what was conveyed loud and clear is that polymathy and creative problem solving are absolutely related. Levi said, "I will process the same bit of information in three or four different ways all at the same time...The minute you have a background in some kind of scientific field and some artistic field, you immediately can look at things and process them in multiple ways, and to be able to realize that things don't just fit in the one box is a huge advantage...having a varied background is super useful. It really does help you process the world and make sense of it...Any time you have more than one approach, I think you're doing yourself a service. I think it really helps."

Sarah shared why she thinks polymaths are in a good position to bring creativity to their work and perspectives:

> The benefit that polymaths kind of bring to the world at large is this ability to make connections between different types of people and different perspectives and industries…Being able to approach things from different perspectives. Then also just from a practical standpoint, because I've just tried a bunch of different things and worked with a bunch of different types of people, I'm just able to bring more kind of ... There's just more experience that I can draw on [than some] other people.

This was a major recurrent theme from many respondents across all interviews.

Specifically, many of the respondents talked about "connecting the dots," looking at the larger system when trying to solve problems. What's more, participants gave the sense that they truly enjoy solving problems; instead of being fatigued or discouraged by problems, they frequently saw it as an opportunity to use their problem-solving talents in creative ways.

Polymathy allows individuals to see issues from multiple perspectives at once, which can be very useful, especially in understanding other people's perspectives. Caroline, a professor, shared this idea:

> I think I'm good at analyzing, understanding different points of view and seeing why people are disagreeing with each other, which is something that helps me a lot when I'm teaching. If someone has an opinion, I'm quite good at understanding why they have that opinion and tracing back their thought process, even if it's extremely different from my thought process, which doesn't mean I agree with them at all, but it means that I can see where they're coming from. I think that that's a skill I value a lot that I don't see a lot in other people all the time.

Caroline also said that the way her mind works, she is constantly finding connections between things. She said, "My brain connects everything to everything else. No matter what I'm doing, I will make some kind of connection with it to something else." This is particularly useful in her job as a math professor, because it allows for her to provide real-world examples to her students to aid them in understanding mathematical concepts.

Sarah talked about being a big picture thinker who can think across disparate disciplines. She said, "I feel like [my polymathy] makes me more of a big picture thinker, a vision person, and an idea person, maybe than others who might focus because I'm able to see across multiple different sectors and multiple different perspectives, and people's needs and stuff like that. I like that about myself. And I like coming up with ideas. That makes me feel accomplished and good." In this way, polymathic thinking is very similar to systems thinking. The noteworthy consideration, however, is that polymaths are able to use a sort of system thinking approach without reliance on others through language as a filter. They personify systems thinking within one person, given their broad experiences on which they can draw.

Polymathic approaches may also feel like design thinking, though. Trinity said she loves problem solving because it allows a chance for design: "I love solving problems…. it's the untangling…I get to…it feels like play…to solve a problem because if there's a problem, normally any problem is a chance for design… Not to be like woo woo spiritual, but I feel connected….I feel like I can see the connections, the whole concept of everything is connection. Everything IS connected." Indeed, seeing connections between things (when others do not) is a real hallmark of a polymath.

Similarly, polymaths may be able to distill complex relationships into simpler and easier to understand ideas. Henry said this is one of his greatest strengths: "I think that one of the things that I am best at is distilling complex relationships and articulate those things in a much more simple and straightforward fashion. I think I am good at connecting a lot of dots and saying, 'All right, given all these things, this is really what all these things are telling us.' And I think I'm fairly good at that."

Karl talked specifically about using information and approaches in one discipline and applying them in other areas in order to come up with innovations. He said,

> That's what I enjoy most. For me, creativity is the whole point of recombining existing concepts; taking existing knowledge but finding a new combination between it. Creativity is not really about creating something new from scratch, because that isn't possible. You can only work from what you know. In a way,

> that's like my core thing, that you cannot imagine something absolutely that you have never seen. You can only recombine or extrapolate a little bit. That's why I think having a knowledge of as many different concepts, ideas, things, in your head, is the best base of actually creating something new. Because if you just know things about one field, you can only play with these Lego bricks, in a way. Having different colored ones from a different field, or differently assembled ones, allows you to create something different, new in that field. You take something from the other field, a structure, and apply it to this field. In this field, it's new, even though the way it is being stacked together has already been done somewhere else. For me, it's of the essence to be creative, to have these multiple interests and be widely interested in everything...Looking outside your field and trying to see patterns that could be applied to something else, it works. I always think that you do not find the interesting inspirations for something you're doing in your own field. [It] pretty much has been explored already. You have to look outside. To create art, I look at mathematics, I look in biology. I look in whatever to find some inspiration... In general, the theme [in my career] is somehow creative, being creative.

This appears to be the unique strength of the polymath: the ability to forge connections across disparate domains for the sake of innovation and creativity; this is something that single-domain specialists are not in a good position to be able to do. This is the great power of the polymath: their creativity.

Theme Ten: Polymaths Cannot Be Happy as Narrow Specialists

Throughout the interviews, the idea of happiness came up quite a few times—though this was not something asked about directly. What was very clear is that a polymath cannot be happy living life as a narrow, focused specialist—at least not for long. Karl shared that freedom is at the heart of his polymathy: "Freedom is probably at the core, freedom in my decisions, freedom in what I want to pursue, is definitely a core value there, or core component that is super important." Several participants talked about needing an artistic outlet – a balance of scientific and artistic pursuits—to feel happy and comfortable. Participants also said that having to focus on one thing would be a certain path to unhappiness. For instance, Hunter shared, "It just wasn't making me happy to focus. I felt like I was missing a piece of myself every time I tried to focus. If I did have to sort of live and exist in a very narrow niche, I don't think I could be happy doing that."

Caroline shared that the way she achieved happiness in her career was by combining her interests into a unique career:

> I realized that it wasn't enough for me to be a math professor as my profession and do everything else as a hobby. I needed to get everything else back on more of an even footing, or more really taking part in my career… It gradually dawned on me. I was pushed because I was quite unhappy there. I sat down and analyzed why I was unhappy. It was a combination of things. It was partly because I didn't fit in very well in at [the university where I was working] and I felt that I was bullied and underappreciated. When it came down to it, what really happened was that I wrote a list of all the things I think I'm good at, and I realized how wide of a variety it was. Then I crosschecked it against the list of all the things that I was actually making use of in my life, and it was tiny. Then I realized that that was really not only making me unhappy but also that I wasn't making as good a contribution to the world as I could, if I made use of all the things that I'm good at. That's when I started really thinking about how to bring all of that back.

However, not all polymaths are able to find a way to combine interests the way she did—some have to juggle their distinct passions separately, but at the same time, which can be difficult.

There is also a simple joy that a polymath who enjoys learning can experience in that process. Polymaths generally like to learn and so when they are learning, it brings them a sense of happiness. Levi shared, "I'm actually happiest when I'm learning…. I'm happy because I'm learning." Levi shared that he struggles sometimes with depression, and that learning is actually what staves off feelings of depression in him.

> I mean, my depression holds me back every now and then. What's funny is I ... I've been very depressed at various points in my life, and it's always kind of lurking back there... And there are still days where I shut down... With my Sundays, when I don't have a commitment, and I cannot get out of bed, I'll just sit for a long time. ...It hurts. I've talked to therapists and everything, and the funny thing is, I've found that the thing that keeps me going is learning. I find that I'm actually happiest when I'm learning.... I'm happy, because I'm learning. I'm happy

> because I'm in shape, and I can feel it. I'm happy because of the many more people that I know and I can relate to on a different level.

Felicity shared a similar comment regarding being very unhappy if she cuts off a part of herself. She said, "When I tried not to be a polymath, when I tried to focus only on med school, that's when I was most unhappy and had to step back and be like 'Why am I unhappy?' Oh, it's because I'm not acknowledging this other half of me." If a polymath ignores a part of themselves, an area that they enjoy pursuing, it appears to create a sense of imbalance, a sense that something is missing, and that may make them feel depressed or, at a minimum, uncomfortable.

Polymaths may also have to change their pursuits as needed in order to stay happy as well. Henry said, "I mean, from my perspective there's a great deal of discontentedness that comes along with polymathy because one never truly settles into like, 'Well, this is what I know I want to do for the rest of my life.' Instead it's, 'I hope I can stay happy doing this for the next five years.' That's not an impediment, but it's an irritant, or it's a little bit of a cloud that one lives under, I would say." And reinventing oneself, as several polymaths shared that they have done before, could lead to tremendous happiness. Henry shared, "To completely reinvent my career…or really who I am…and to develop a much broader network of colleagues than I would have ever developed had I stayed in that private sector job. And so, I guess being able to make that big a change in my late 40's, early 50's was, I feel, in some respects, sort of saved my happiness, it really gave me a second lease on life."

Worth noting is that there is a joy that comes from having a sense that what they are doing in the world is helpful. Of course, helping other people makes most people feel good; making an impact feels rewarding and creates a sense of happiness. A number of different polymaths shared that they are happiest when they are contributing to the world or having some sort of impact through their work or helping other people. Felicity said, "I'm most happy when I feel like I'm making a contribution to the world." Svetlana shared, "Right when I started my career my measure of success has been how many people outside of my world I can touch in a way that kind of is better for the world. So kind of creating things and content and disseminating things in a way that is interesting and different and allows people to either learn something or helps better some part of the world." This is probably not a unique characteristic of a polymath but is worth considering when trying to understand the experience of modern day polymaths.

The big takeaway for this section, though, is simply that a polymath made to exist as a monomath will find it difficult to be happy. For someone whose nature is to experience life broadly, forcing a narrowness to their experience will feel stifling; a polymath cannot maintain life as a monomath for long and stay happy.

Theme Eleven: Effective Polymaths are Effective Time Managers

Ten out of thirteen interviewees brought up the issue of time management as a polymath; this was not asked about specifically, but it was something that they raised on their own as a real issue they face. Being a polymath—someone with lots of interests—tends to mean that the person is busy. Literal time management, and relationships to time, as someone who has a lot going on in their lives, is something that polymaths have to navigate and juggle. Karl shared, "Time is kind of an important thing. Time is actually the most valuable resource. I try to optimize everything, so I can maximize the time for experimentation or artistic exploration. Anything that wastes my time is kind of the worst."

For a polymath to be able to pursue everything they want to, they need to be able to manage time effectively. Levi shared "I am hyper organized." Being a polymath may also mean, as Henry shared, having internal conflicts about the best way to spend one's time: "The way [polymathy] affects my day-to-day life is there are times, like some pretty severe conflicts between how I would like to spend my time."

Wendy shared a distinction between managing time well and being disciplined, and also talked about being compelled to constantly be productive with little down time:

> I am a master of time management and I'm still not sure how I get it all done….. Certainly, time management is crucial as a polymath. I think it fits in with discipline, but it is very specific. I know plenty of musicians that have discipline and like can't fucking manage their schedule to save their lives, so time management is a huge part of it because you have to piece together your schedule. No one, no one person is doing it for you… I work seven days a week. So, it is it is…hard to actually ever have true time off. So actually, ever having time off is zero. Part of the joy of being a polymath is I would still choose to do the things that I do…right? So it's not that I have a never ending to do list. I do. But like if I had the whole day free, you know like, you can do whatever you want today, I would do like at least half of the things that I'm already doing. I mean like the notion of sitting on a beach and doing nothing really stresses me out.

What is interesting here is that for Wendy, she feels uncomfortable doing nothing. Polymaths seem to have a drive to be productive and stay busy, filling in "free" time on their calendar with their various pursuits. Yet, as Wendy shared, "It feels like there's never enough time," which can feel stressful. Wendy went on to say:

> It feels like you can never turn your brain off. It feels like no matter what you're doing in any of the worlds that I live in, I will get this kind of jolt of connection and be like, 'Oh this would make so much sense over there.' This is sort of where you don't really have time off either right, because your brain is like kind of always making those connections and always kind of zig zagging there. So I …it's not burn-out so much as just like, there are moments of real like

> intellectual exhaustion and I have not yet developed a great set of skills to recover from that. Because of all of the different things I do, there's never that moment of like, 'Ah, I've accomplished it and now I get a little break.' The ebbs and flows … cancel each other out.

Similarly, Caroline said that "I definitely always feel mentally active so there's always some 25 plots in my head that I'm planning." Kevin shared that he likes to find time each day to mix in a variety of his interests. He said, "I've structured my life so that I have opportunities every day to indulge in a range of interests...That's all part of the rich tapestry." Svetlana shared she has to work at getting the right balance of her various interests and obligations:

> It's a challenge in terms of work life balance and life-life balance I should say, because if I am too focused on one thing then I feel like I'm letting other things fall by the wayside. Let's say it be something like music and then I'll become very stressed out about this idea where I'm like 'Oh I'm doing one thing too much, how do I balance it out with this other thing?' And I almost have this like internal kind of brain meter that's like, 'Okay, [Svetlana], you have to focus on this thing now.' Because if you don't I can almost see the meter running and I need to re-up on that. So it can be a little bit a challenge in terms of the week to week work life balance especially. So that would be I would say definitely a realistic thing.

Unexpectedly, though related, sleep came up as a topic from four different participants, though there was no unifying theme among the comments they made about it. Some commented about how well they can function with very little sleep, while another said they prioritize getting enough sleep. Wendy was one who likes sleep: "I believe in sleep. I need sleep. I sleep seven hours a night at a minimum. I sleep really well – I'm a great sleeper. But like…there are moments where you look at your calendar, your week and you're like, 'There is literally just not enough time.'" Trinity was one who can get by with less sleep: "Do polymaths sleep? I don't. I get up early I go to bed late. There were times when I was building things in my career when I didn't sleep….it's not a problem for me." The important point was that as a busy person, sleep as a form of self-care is something that takes up time and something they must consider while also juggling their various commitments and interests.

Theme Twelve: Polymathy is Due to Both Nature and Nurture but Polymathic Excellence Requires a Level of Effort and Attention

One of the questions asked in all the interviews was whether the participant believed their polymathy was due more to nature or nurture. Of course, their opinions about what impacted the development of their polymathy more does not constitute proof of nature or nurture (either one) being the true, sole source of their polymathy, but it is interesting to consider what polymaths think of their own development in this regard. Overall, participants reported, mostly, that they think both nature (genetics, biology, etc.) are involved to some degree, but so is nurture (environment, resources, family, social factors, educational variables, etc.).

First, for participants who credited it slightly more to being genetic, they mostly cited having relatives who are polymathic, or just always being polymathic from a very early age, or because of having a sibling raised in the same household who is not polymathic. For instance, Caroline shared that she believes she is polymathic partly because her parents are so different:

> Well, I'm going to have to say both. I mean, who knows? It's the big question about nature and nurture. I think that genes do do something. Environment does a lot of things as well. My parents are very different from each other. I think that as far as genetics and upbringing, both go, that is a contribution because if your parents are very similar, then maybe you'll go down a similar route. My mother's very, very logical, mathematical, organized, very clear thinking, very rigorous. My father is extremely lateral. He's very intuitive and on the face of it disorganized and empathetic, and apparently random at times. I think that I'm a combination of those things.

Similarly, Sarah also shared, "I mean, because it kind of runs in my family, it's got to be both. I mean, because I assume it's both. Because my parents are basically polymath[ic]." Similarly, Trinity felt in her case, it was more nature:

> I think I definitely was born to be a polymath and I say that because I feel I would have come to it naturally regardless of the nurture. There were periods of my life where there was no nurture and I was on my own and I still found it and sought it out. However, I think having parents for all their flaws that interacted with the world in the way they did certainly propelled me to be comfortable with it and explore both sides constantly...So I think it was nature, not nurture. Because my brother, same parents…definitely not the same…he's not a polymath at all…he's very much one sided. He's got the math side…. very tangible math side, ….his only interest in the arts is to talk to people and seem cultured, a strategic interest. Consumer totally.

Likewise, Wendy shared that she felt she was born polymathic because mathematical talent like she had was not found in previous generations of her family:

> I honestly think I was born with this. Neither of those two things [mathematical or musical talent] really exist in our family history. [My father's] side of the family is very musical so I can see some of that coming through, maybe, but like…if you would have picked any family ever to have two little math/music polymaths, this is not the family you would have ever expected, but we both [my sister and I] had this from the very beginning, and I think we were just very lucky in that our…my grandmother…wanted that musical talent to be supported and like poured a ton of time and money and effort in ensuring that was the case. Uhm…but it was always there.

Some respondents leaned more towards environment impacting their polymathy. For instance, Kevin shared that he was raised to believe he could accomplish anything he wanted to, and this may have played into his polymathy: "The environment that I grew up in always felt limitless and unbounded in terms of what you could accomplish. Between the school environment, the home environment, I'm sure all that nurtured this idea that you could do anything, and it felt very genuine to me." Slightly more participants did lean more towards crediting their polymathy to nurture, or environmental factors. In fact, several participants said that polymathy can be taught. Henry said he thinks the environment is a huge factor: "I do think that a lot of it was environment. I don't necessarily think that they are mutually exclusive, but it is difficult for me to overlook, or to downplay the impact that the way I was raised had on my development, both in positive ways like the fact that I was encouraged to read, and that as a kid I was read to." Felicity had a more nuanced answer, which was "I think maybe the artistic side is maybe nature and developing the science part was more nurture for me."

Levi shared his belief that polymathy is teachable, which would mean it is more affected by environment—or at least requires the right environment to surface it. He said, "They could learn any number of things, and work towards being a polymath. But I don't think I'm special. I think it's learnable." Dianna also shared this belief. She said, "How many polymaths are we potentially missing out on because of their life circumstances? Like even if you think about piano prodigies, or child prodigies, like God, I'd imagine we have some in like, I don't know, middle America, but they never had a piano so we never would know that, and same with polymaths. There might be people who are, and who's to say something like ADHD isn't a polymath, but we put them under medicine so, because they weren't focused enough?"

Several interviewees voiced their opinion that it must require both nature and nurture to support the development of a polymath. Hunter pointed out that a genetic propensity towards polymathy is not enough—it requires environmental support too.

> I don't know to what extent this kind of personality or temperament or anything else, is genetic or not. But, if it is genetic, it's definitely not sufficient. It definitely requires a kind of environment and really good teachers and supportive parents and all this stuff, over a very long time. And if you don't have that, I think it probably is pretty easily quashed. And on the flip side, you might not be born

> with it exactly, but it might easily develop if you're in the kind of environment that has a lot of people who are interested in doing a lot of different things.

Felicity felt the same, saying, "I think it's a little bit of both." Dianna felt that in her case, it was half nature and half nurture, why she became a polymath: "I think half of it was innate. I think that is who I am... So that's where I think the nurture comes in right, like where life gives you a situation. For me in particular though, I think it's half and half."

Similarly, every interviewee was asked a question regarding whether their polymathy was easy or if it was something that took work to achieve. The answers were mostly alluding to the fact that they are naturally, easily interested in various subjects, but to achieve excellence in a discipline, it usually takes some amount of effort and practice. Most polymaths felt that they had to work hard to achieve their current career status, but one interviewee said it came quite easily to him. Karl said, "Some of the things that I do are, I think, quite good. That's the funny thing, I never really have to work for that."

Several participants pointed out that it was relatively easy to become fairly adept in certain areas, but to achieve higher levels of excellence, it requires effort and work. Sarah said, "I've just always been able to do many different things pretty well. I'm not completely world class in anything, of course. I think that's probably the case I imagine for most polymaths. That you're able to pretty easily, without a ton of hard work, operate at a semi-high level in a couple of different sectors. But then, to really move beyond that level then you really do have to put in the work and you have to really focus on one thing." Similarly, Levi shared,

> I do seem to be able to pick up on things very rapidly. Like, I can become mediocre at a thing without trying. It does not seem to matter what, thus far in my life, but mediocrity is immediately attainable for me…It's just rapid learning curve, where I pick up on things very fast. But I mean, once I get past that initial comfort zone and that initial mediocrity, then the effort kicks in, and then I have

> to choose whether or not I want to keep going and keep getting better, or whether I want to be okay at being okay...So I mean, things tend to come easy at first, to become proficient, but then it gets harder, and then I have to put in the effort.

Likewise, Henry said, "I am able to get a very little bit of information and turn around and sound like an expert on it because I can process the information and really understand it and start to actually articulate ideas about that. I think the ability to become functional within an area with relatively little experience or information is either basically good acting, or just very efficient use of information." It seems polymaths can achieve a level of understanding and accomplishment very quickly, i.e. learn the basics, but to develop more refined skills, then it took additional effort.

Alternatively, several polymaths pointed out that they worked very hard to achieve the level of success, professionally, that they had. It appears that there was a level of openness to experience that is required to become a polymath, but there is also a level of *willingness* to work that is required to achieve excellence. Dianna said it succinctly: "I'm fortunate to have had the experiences I did but it's because I busted my ass and worked hard." Hunter made an astute distinction: he said he never had to work at being interested, but he did have to work to achieve excellence. "Yes, it's something I had to work at. I didn't have to work at being interested in things. For most of the stuff I've ever been interested in, I had to work at it. And there weren't a ton of things where I'm like, 'Oh, I just started doing this and now I can do this at a really high level and it's effortless.'" It was through deliberate practice that he was able to achieve excellence in his fields.

However, most of the time, it did not feel like work if the polymath was pursuing something that they were interested in deeply—otherwise they would have stopped.

Caroline shared, "I really, really spent all my time from the age of three working hard at things because I was practicing the piano for hours a day from that age onwards, and reading tons and tons of books…I must have been born with some ability to do some things but spending loads of hours doing it, I think, really makes a difference." At the same time, however, Caroline said that she only pursued things with a high level of effort that she truly enjoyed: "It never felt like work. When things did feel like work, I just didn't do them…It doesn't feel like work all of it because it's something that I just wanted to do. For me, for example practicing the piano isn't work. I just get obsessed with the piece of music and I don't stop until I can play it and make it sound like the way I want it to. The reason I don't stop is because I'm enjoying doing it so much. To me, it's not work. It's really indulgence."

Growth Mindset and Self-Actualization: One of the defining traits of a polymath is a desire to keep learning; this could be considered a growth mindset. This also relates to the idea of polymathy requiring a level of effort to achieve excellence. Accordingly, one of the questions asked of the thirteen participants revolved around whether their polymathy in any way related to an effort to become the best version of themselves. In other words, is their polymathy in any way related to the idea of self-actualization? Most respondents answered yes to this question. For instance, Caroline shared, "I feel like I have been spending all of everyday improving myself in some way ever since I was three. That's a lot of hours to spend improving yourself…I've definitely always been taught and believed that it's important to become your best self and improve yourself all the time. I'm always seeking to do so." For Henry, "There's not really that much difference between my self-actualization and these polymathic traits because it's almost like one and the same." Likewise, Trinity shared, "Polymathy definitely plays into my quest for self-actualization."

For a few of the interviewees, self-actualization was not a goal they thought of as such, but they have an innate tendency towards self-improvement. Karl said, "It's not something like a goal I have, to become my best self. But I always want to have a perspective. Stagnation is probably the most horrible idea that I could imagine; not moving on, not being innovative anymore, not finding new things to do." Polymaths appear to have a drive not only to explore and to learn, but also to improve. Felicity said, "I am now continuously aiming to improve myself. ... I don't think you can reach your fullest potential in life if you just float along. I'm definitely my biggest pusher."

For a polymath who prefers variety, enjoys learning, and has a growth mindset, they cannot imagine becoming their best, truest self without exploring their varied, disparate interests. That said, this does not mean—as Kevin pointed out—that polymathy is the only path towards self-actualization. Non-polymaths may find self-actualization through other approaches, including being narrowly focused in their interests and pursuits. But for a polymath, becoming one's best self very much requires feeding their polymathic appetites to grow in knowledge and experience, and to feel a sense of continual improvement.

Summary of Section One

Section One in this chapter summarizes findings from individual interviews with thirteen polymaths using Identity Theory as a framework for understanding. The key findings from this research have attempted to explore what the real, lived experience of being a polymath is like. Polymaths from this study share a common experience of liking their polymathy for the many strengths it brings to their careers and personal lives, but also having to navigate the challenges involved with it. The 12 themes that surfaced from the 13 interviews are as follows:

1. Theme One: Polymaths Define Themselves as Experts Across Disparate Disciplines
2. Theme Two: Polymath Identity Emerges from Not Fitting in A Box
3. Theme Three: Being Polymathic Impacts One's Social Experiences
4. Theme Four: Polymaths Have Difficult Career Choices
5. Theme Five: Financial Resources Can Both Hinder and Promote Polymathy
6. Theme Six: Polymaths are Shaped by Their Families
7. Theme Seven: Polymaths Are Voracious Learners
8. Theme Eight: Polymaths are Quite Confident but May Also Experience "Imposter Syndrome"
9. Theme Nine: Polymaths Self-Identify as Highly Creative
10. Theme Ten: Polymaths Cannot Be Happy as Narrow Specialists
11. Theme Eleven: Effective Polymaths are Effective Time Managers
12. Theme Twelve: Polymathy is Due to Both Nature and Nurture but Polymathic Excellence Requires a Level of Effort and Attention

Section Two: Moustakas's (1994) Phenomenological Method

Section Two presents findings using Moustakas' (1994) phenomenological methodology to look at the experience of modern day polymaths. There were not any predetermined notions to be examined. A total of thirteen individual 90-minute interviews were conducted; an inductive approach was used for the purposes of studying the phenomenon of polymathy. The intent was for this researcher to be open and allow the essence of experiences to emerge. These experiences emerged through in-depth, semi-structured interviews of 13 accomplished polymaths. This resulted in approximately 500 pages of interview transcripts. Each transcript was read several times to ensure understanding and support interpretation. While each polymath was unique in his or her experiences, there were invariant experiences that transcended their individual experiences.

This researcher employed epoche to bracket any preconceived notions regarding the lived experiences of polymaths. Raw data were gathered through thorough interviews with polymaths who met pre-determined selection criteria. This raw data was divided into statements, or horizonalizations. These horizonalizations were then grouped into clusters of meanings that make up the invariant meaning horizons and themes. Lastly, the invariant horizons were combined to create the textural description of what polymaths have experienced and the structural description of how they were experienced. These textural and structural descriptions were then integrated to describe the invariant structure or true essence of the experience of being a polymath. As recommended by Moustakas (1994), examples of each of these elements of data analysis are provided herein: epoche, horizonalization, invariant constitutents and themes, individual textural and structural descriptions, and also composite textural/structural descriptions.

Epoche

Epoche comes from the Greek language and means to stay away or abstain. In the phenomenological research tradition, it is also called bracketing; phenomenological researchers use this technique to set aside any preconceived notions, biases, prejudgments, or ideas in order to best understand the phenomena at hand. The goal is to let the participants and the data speak for themselves (Moustakas, 1994).

This researcher employed epoche by stating up front at the beginning of each interview that there were no right or wrong, desirable or undesirable answers, and that all that was desired was for the interviewee to feel comfortable sharing their actual experience—their truth. This was a way that this researcher bracketed any preconceived ideas about polymathy to try understand it through the eyes of the participants. This researcher asked open-ended questions (with follow-ups to ensure understanding, as needed) so that participants could share their truths. At times, there were statements made that this researcher did not expect—and it was at those times that follow-up questions were asked even further, to ensure full understanding of any unexpected statements. This researcher would "mirror back" what was heard to make sure it was accurately received, and to allow the interviewee to make any corrections.

Horizonalization

This researcher gave equal consideration to all the statements made in the verbatim transcript from each participant interview so that all statements could be examined equally regarding their experience of being polymaths. Each horizon, or statement, contributes towards understanding of the experience of polymaths. These horizons helped to inform the invariant horizons, as well as the textural and structural descriptions, and also the composite textural/structural descriptions. The process of horizonalization helped aggregate the raw data for analysis. In the following subsections, quotes from some of the interview transcripts of three participants provide examples of horizons.

Horizonalization Excerpts: Caroline's Interview

1. "I was pushed because I was quite unhappy…I sat down and analyzed why I was unhappy. It was a combination of things. It was partly because I didn't fit in very well [at that organization] …when it came down to it, what really happened was that I wrote a list of all the things I think I'm good at, and I realized how wide of a variety it was. Then I crosschecked it against the list of all the things that I was actually making use of in my life, and it was tiny. Then I realized that that was really not only making me unhappy but also that I wasn't making as good a contribution to the world as I could, if I made use of all the things that I'm good at. That's when I started really thinking about how to bring all of that back."
2. "I'm just a very fast reader."
3. "I think I'm good at analyzing, understanding different points of view and seeing why people are disagreeing with each other, which is something that helps me a lot when I'm teaching. If someone has an opinion, I'm quite good at understanding why they have that opinion and tracing back their thought process, even if it's extremely different from my thought process, which doesn't mean I agree with them at all, but it means that I can see where they're coming from. I think that that's a skill I value a lot that I don't see a lot in other people all the time."
4. "I define success by how much I've helped other people."
5. "There's that curiosity but there's also the fact that they [my parents] instilled in me right from the start a very, very strong work ethic."

6. "I feel like I have been spending all of everyday improving myself in some way ever since I was three. That's a lot of hours to spend improving yourself…I must have been born with some ability to do some things but spending loads of hours doing it, I think, really makes a difference."
7. "It doesn't feel like work, all of it, because it's something that I just wanted to do. For me, for example, practicing the piano isn't work. I just get obsessed with the piece of music and I don't stop until I can play it and make it sound like the way I want it to. The reason I don't stop is because I'm enjoying doing it so much. To me, it's not work, it's really indulgence…When things did feel like work, I just didn't do them."
8. "I think that having an older sister definitely helped me want to get better at things because I didn't want to lag behind her all the time."
9. "I don't like being told things. I especially don't like being told things if I could have worked them out for myself because I find that really patronizing. It's like someone is telling me that they think I'm stupid…I prefer learning things myself…I would much rather work everything else out for myself, and then only ask when I've really got stuck."
10. "That is an issue—just the different pulls on my time from different directions."
11. "I think that in building my career, I had to think much harder about how to get a career that was going to be fulfilling for me. I think my greatest personal success, I still view it that my greatest personal success, is in succeeding in doing that, and not just languishing in the standard career that I started with because it would

have been easy to just go with that because there was a blueprint and because it was safe."

12. "It's quite intense. Intense is a word I've used to describe how I feel ever since I was very small. I think it's because I don't often have downtime. Instead of having downtime, I switch from one thing to another. I don't have a break from writing to do nothing. I have a break from writing by practicing the piano. Then I'll break from that by doing some research. I'll break from that by baking something. I switch between things, rather than just doing nothing, which means that I'm continuously on the go all the time."
13. "I definitely always feel mentally active so there's always some 25 plots in my head that I'm planning."
14. "I feel different all the time. I don't really mind feeling different."
15. "I've definitely always been taught and believed that it's important to become your best self and improve yourself all the time. I'm always seeking to do so."
16. "My brain connects everything to everything else. No matter what I'm doing, I will make some kind of connection with it to something else."

Horizonalization Excerpts: Wendy's Interview

1. "Growing up without much money…it forces you to be scrappy and creative and like get comfortable without much of a safety net. I think the forcing function of not having a ton of resources at each of these stages was a great blessing in disguise that forced me to say, 'What do you have?' And 'Where is your scrappiness, your creativeness, your network? Okay, get back in the game. And build that resilience a lot faster."

2. "They just handed me a text book and I taught myself in a corner for my entire mathematical education until my junior year of high school."
3. And so, at an art school, I found this identity as a mathematician which became very clear to me, that yes I am both and, and those are not inconsistent."
4. I wasn't the only one, there were plenty of us there that said I am an artist, but I am also this other thing. And I need both of those things to be happy.
5. "I honestly think I was born with this."
6. "The early acceptance that I would never fit in and so that was not a thing I ever aspired to…the earlier you accept that you're not like other people, the faster you can go and become who you're supposed to be, which is really freeing."
7. "I probably played up my opposition to the group more than I necessarily felt in the moment because that's what set me apart. And that's also what helped me develop my brand, so to speak. But by choosing to stand out versus blend in and find what I had in common, I think that allowed me to develop very specific identities that set me apart and kind of embrace that differentness."
8. Certainly, time management is crucial as a polymath. I think it fits in with discipline but it's very specific. I know plenty of musicians that have discipline and can't…manage their schedule to save their lives. So time management is a huge part of it because you have to piece together your schedule; no one, no one person is doing it for you."
9. "I work seven days a week. So, it is…hard to actually ever have true time off. So actually, ever having time off is zero. Part of the joy of being a polymath is I would still choose to do the things that I do. So, it's not that I have a never

ending to do list. I do. But if I had the whole day free, you know like, you can do whatever you want today, I would do like at least half of the things that I'm already doing. I mean like the notion of sitting on a beach and doing nothing really stresses me out."

10. "In any group of people in any setting, I can find a thing to talk about. I can find a way to connect with literally anyone."
11. "I have like seven different sources of income. My financial planner loves me. But it's a meaningful amount, it's like 30% of my income comes from these so-called side-hustles, which is nice to have, kind of a diversification of income streams, should anything happen."
12. "The stress level is pretty high."
13. "I'm never bored. Ever."
14. "It has made my professional life richer and more complicated."
15. "My employers distinctly have not known how to leverage my skillsets which is why I became an entrepreneur."

Horizonalization Excerpts: Levi's Interview

1. "I actually have told people, when I introduce myself to them, and they're like, 'Well, what do you do?' And I go, 'I'm complicated,' is usually my answer."
2. "Accident, pure accident: all of these things that I've gotten into randomly…And all these little things that I've done, just luck—and just willing and wanting to take that chance when the opportunity presents itself."

3. "I think a lot of it did have to do with my parents always taking care of me and giving me the chance to be whatever I wanted to be. They were pretty non-judgmental."
4. "I do seem to be able to pick up on things very rapidly. Like, I can become mediocre at a thing without trying. It does not seem to matter what, thus far in my life, but mediocrity is immediately attainable for me…it's just a rapid learning curve, where I pick up on things very fast. But I mean, once I get past that initial comfort zone and that initial mediocrity, then the effort kicks in, and then I have to choose whether or not I want to keep going and keep getting better, or whether I want to be okay at being okay…So I mean, things tend to come easy at first, to become proficient, but then it gets weirder, and then I have to put in the effort."
5. "I will easily pick what I want to learn, and I will decide what I want to do, but boy….and I spoke to Dr. [Jones] when I was learning magic. Oh my God. I would not be the magician I am right now, I would not be the professional, without him starting me. And just in school in general…my parents…and then…all of my teachers…so I mean yes, I'm self-directed, I do find things I like on my own. I do dictate my own interests. I do pick what I want. I do pass up opportunities. I also am wise enough to seek out a good teacher."
6. "Time is always the biggest thing. Still is. Its time is the thing that kills me the most."
7. "I mean, I guess maybe this is where money becomes a limiter, because, you know, could I go and do more magic? Yes. How would I do that? I would buy

more books. I would go to more lectures. I would travel around the world to study with people I've met only briefly."

8. "I mean, my depression holds me back every now and then. What's funny is I…I've been very depressed at various points in my life, and it's always kind of lurking back there…it hurts. I've talked to therapists and everything, and the funny thing is, I've found that the thing that keeps me going is learning. I find that I'm actually happiest when I'm learning. I'm happy because I'm learning."
9. "Revenge is a big self-motivator. Whenever I'm like, 'I don't like you. I'm going to be better than you at this."
10. "There's just something about learning that just…something absolutely appealing to collecting new knowledge…I'm just happy to learn something new. There is something definitely exciting about it. No matter what it is, I'm happy to learn it."
11. "I know when I meet someone, I need to be careful about the [Levi] that I show them, and then once we become friends, then they can learn all of the weird shit….People will get to know me over time…they will create a new box that is labeled [Levi], and I will be in that box, and they accept the whole thing."
12. "I have to be organized to do what I do…I'm pretty hyper-organized."
13. "Sometimes it's frustrating, because I see things in ways people don't, and to me, certain things are obvious, and I get frustrated when people don't see them."
14. "Sometimes I have to shut it down and sit in a quiet room and just listen to music on my own, because I take in so much, so fast sometimes. Because I see all these layers. Sometimes it gets unnerving. Sometimes, my brain starts to hurt, and I'm

just seeing too much right now. Overload can be a problem when you process it on a bunch of levels. Occasionally, if I'm left to my own devices, I start to process everything around me that way, and it just gets to be overload, where you just take in so much information, which I think is why I like some of the hobbies I do – they force me to focus."

15. "I don't think anybody knows what my full skillset is."

Invariant Meaning Horizons and Themes

Of course, each interviewee had a unique experience regarding what it is like to be a polymath, and each made sense of their experiences in their own way. That said, there were some common experiences among the participants. The verbatim transcripts from each of the thirteen participants were analyzed using phenomenological reflection as well as imaginative variation to find the significant, relevant, and invariant meanings that all of the participants shared. A total of 60 constituents were clustered into 12 total themes. The themes which surfaced were checked against the individual horizons for validation. Each interviewee's horizon was examined to compare whether anything in the individual horizons was not accounted for in the clustered themes, and whether the themes contained topics that were not in the original horizons. The original horizons and themes showcase a deeper layer of nuance in the experiences that polymaths face.

Table 4-4: Invariant meaning horizons

Theme One: Polymaths Define Themselves as Experts Across Disparate Disciplines	Theme Two: Polymath Identity Emerges from Not Fitting in A Box	Theme Three: Being Polymathic Impacts One's Social Experiences	Theme Four: Polymaths Have Difficult Career Choices	Theme Five: Financial Resources Can Both Hinder and Promote Polymathy
Defining a polymath	Adventurous spirit	Bullying	Career Implications	Finances
	Being different	Discouragers & Obstacles	Leadership	Financial impact of being a polymath
	Go with the flow	Independent spirit	Narrowness Feels Stifling	Necessity for Polymathic Skills
	Identity	People Skills		
	External Opinions of Polymathy	Polymath Community		
	Luck/Chance	Privilege		
	Lucky	Social Considerations		
	Traits of a Polymath			

Theme Six: Polymaths are Shaped by Their Families	Difficult childhood	Family considerations	Major influencers to polymathy	Resilience						
Theme Seven: Polymaths Are Voracious Learners	Boredom	Liking change & newness	Curiosity	Education	Great ability to learn	Learning	Openness to Experiences	Reading	Self-Directed Learning	Travel
Theme Eight: Polymaths are Quite Confident but May Also Experience "Imposter Syndrome"	Liking a challenge	Competitive	Confidence	Imposter Syndrome	Pursuit of perfection and excellence					
Theme Nine: Polymaths Self-Identify as Highly Creative	Creativity	Problem Solving	Toolkit to Solve Problems							
Theme Ten: Polymaths Cannot Be Happy as Narrow Specialists	Feeling of being a polymath	Freedom	Happiness	Helping others	Life benefits					

Theme Eleven: Effective Polymaths are Effective Time Managers	Efficiency	No wasted time	Productivity	Sleep	Stress management	Switching	Time Management			
Theme Twelve: Polymathy is Due to Both Nature and Nurture but Polymathic Excellence Requires a Level of Effort and Attention	Growth mindset	Natural or Work at It	Nature Versus Nurture	Self-actualization						

Textural Descriptions

Individual Textural Descriptions

Creswell (2013) explained that a textural description is about the "what" of the appearing phenomenon; it describes in concrete, clear, thorough terms what composed the experience, including a full description of the participant's conscious experienced as explained to the researcher. This includes the thoughts, feelings, ideas, opinions, examples, and situations that composed the experience. The two textural descriptions provided below show that while elements are unique to each polymath experience, some other aspects are shared across all study participants. These common, shared elements constitute the composite textural description, which follows some sample individual textural descriptions.

Individual Textural Description: Hunter

Hunter thought of himself as being a self-directed learner and liked the term Renaissance Man over polymath to describe himself. For his undergraduate education, he double majored in physics and music, and later earned a Master's degree in electrical engineering. He first had a career working in the field of nano-technology and did quite well in that world, including getting over 15 academic articles published and creating several inventions with associated patents filed, in addition to working in his full-time job. While working in the field of nano-technology, he began pursuing music jobs on the side. Over time, he was able to get more music gigs while still maintaining his full-time job, until he landed a job as principal timpanist at a famous, prestigious opera house in the United States and became a professional, full-time musician (which is his current profession). In other words, he has been both an accomplished, professional scientist and an accomplished, professional musician. He is also a music professor. Due to his disparate career paths, he has both an arts resume and a science resume to showcase these different careers he has had.

Hunter's idea of what it means to be a polymath involves "not just being interested, but actually following through to some extent." He said, "I like to have a grounding in things that lets me do lots of different things and apply it, rather than learn one super specific, narrow, focused thing…If I did have to…live and exist in a very narrow niche, I don't' think I could be happy doing that." This value is evidenced by his career choices.

He credited his appreciation for this sort of "liberal artsy" approach in learning to his upbringing. He said that being a polymath

> Probably requires having parents that are very open to a lot of different things you want to do. They never really pushed me specifically to do anything. They also never discouraged me from specifically doing anything. It was just very much like, 'What are you interested in? Cool, we'll support that,' which certainly made it a lot easier to go off and do a lot of different things. It's interesting now, being in the field I am, I am surrounded by a lot of colleagues who had parents that were like, 'You know, from the age of four, you're going to start playing the violin, and that's all you're going to do.' And that's a very different experience growing up as a kid, you know? I know it definitely sucks some of the joy out of it. It's a whole lot different when you get to feel a sense of agency and autonomy over what you're exploring.

Hunter displayed a great deal of confidence at various times in his life, for example, in his willingness to continue to pursue music, despite many auditions that did not result in selection for the gigs. His view was that continuing to try would eventually pay off: "It will happen for you, if you just stick with it long enough. You know, you need to serve enough shots on goal to make it work." He also opted not to get a graduate degree in music, and instead design his own, self-directed music program based on deliberate practice, reading, pursuing jobs, performing, networking, etc. This is another example of how he showed confidence in himself as well as a high degree of self-directed learning because he determined his own learning journey to become a full-time, professional musician. As a music professor, he encourages his students to also be self-directed in their learning, as well.

Although Hunter had a natural interest in both the arts and the sciences from an early age, succeeding in both fields did take some amount of effort on his part. He said that his polymathy is "something I had to work at. I didn't have to work at being interested in things. For most of the stuff I've ever been interested in, I had to work at it. And there weren't a ton of things where I'm like, 'Oh, I just started doing this and now I can do this at a really high level and it's effortless.' He talked about the idea of deliberate practice to achieve a level of mastery.

Because of his experiences, he believes that his polymathy is due to a mixture of both nature and nurture. He said, "If it is genetic, it's definitely not sufficient. It definitely requires a kind of environment and really good teachers and supportive parents and all this stuff, over a very long time. And if you don't have that, I think it probably is pretty easily quashed. And on the flip side, you might not be born with it exactly, but it might easily develop if you're in the kind of environment that has a lot of people who are interested in doing a lot of different things."

Although his broad-mindedness is something he feels is an asset, it could also lead to situations sometimes that could be frustrating for him. "The day to day existence of being like this is cool and enriching. It's hard to imagine being any other way. Where it becomes a little more obvious that it's different than some other people's experiences is…where some conflict arises or misunderstanding, and then I'm like, 'Well, wait.'" He talked about the frustration he feels when dealing with "narrowly exposed people." He went on to explain, "There's the narrowness of experience, and then there's being narrow-minded. And there's not a perfect overlap, but there is some of that Venn diagram there, and I think it's generally super unhelpful." This is part of why he believes his mind is so broad—because he has also had broad experiences.

Worth noting is that Hunter believed that his polymathy makes him a better person: "Well, how one defines a good person or not is somewhat ambiguous. But, for me, it is like having a diverse set of interests that I find enriching in their own right, and it helps me be rewarded for it, more empathetic, more able to deal with the world. And then ultimately, hopefully impact it in some sort of positive way." He believes his rich experiences in different areas has informed and improved his work as a musician.

Individual Textural Description: Sarah

Sarah has been a voracious learner with a career spanning both the arts and STEM. She has three Master's degrees: one in business, one in architectural acoustics (a type of engineering), and one in vocal performance. She has been a CEO of a company that puts together conferences which explore the intersection of arts, technology, and entrepreneurship. She is an app developer. She has also been a professional opera singer. She defined polymathy as "an interest in multiple, different industries or sectors. And then, maybe I would add to that, actually taking action to develop expertise in them…Choosing to follow more than one path."

Sarah said several times in her interview how strange it was to her that growing up, the expectation is to try lots of different things—to try to express Renaissance ideals—and then later in life, you are expected to focus more narrowly:

> Our school system…trains people to be…polymathic during school, and then suddenly you're supposed to get one job that does one thing, like one very focused, specific thing. And it's like, that's crazy. You didn't prepare me to do one thing. In order to get into college, I had to have all these hobbies and stuff and now none of that's important anymore? And that was tough. It took me a couple of years to be like, 'Oh wait, no. I refuse. I shall not focus.' You know, I'm not going to do that. I'm going to do a bunch of different things and I'm going to figure out how to combine them if I need to.

She reiterated this point later in the interview, stating the same idea slightly differently:

> Our school system is set up for polymathy in that we're literally taking like History class and English class and Science class and whatever club. You're doing all these different things and then all of a sudden, it's different when you get into the real world and people are like, 'Well, it's different when you get into the real world,' and you're like, 'Well, why?' Why does school have to be so different from the real world? Why can't either school be modified to match the expectations of the real world, or why isn't it more acceptable to continue in the

> way that you did in school, in terms of all your different interests and abilities? It's just crazy to me.

Further, Sarah said when she tried to focus more narrowly in the past, she was unhappy. "It just wasn't making me happy to focus. I felt like I was missing a piece of myself every time I tried to focus." She realized "it wasn't just that I didn't like opera. It's a larger phenomenon with me. It wasn't that opera wasn't the thing and acoustics isn't the thing. It's that they're too focused." She also shared that if she completely cuts out an area of interests that she enjoys, she feels like something is missing in her life—that part of her identity is gone:

> I totally feel like I would be missing a big chunk of myself…even now, I'm not singing much right now and I really feel kind of discombobulated and out of sorts, and I think it's got to be related…because there's this thing that I've identified or rather has been a big part of my identity for so long, and then to not do it for a couple of years…at first you don't realize it, the effect that it's having, and then after a while you're like, 'Oh yeah, this thing I used to be really good at that people thought of me when they thought of this thing, or when people thought of me, they thought of this thing, if you're not doing it anymore, it kind of stops being a part of your identity and then it feels like you're missing something.

Sarah said that everyone in her family has polymathic tendencies, and in her youth, she was very much encouraged to be well-rounded and pursue different interests. As she grew into adulthood, though, her mother began critiquing her educational and career choices:

> My mother would say…she uses the word flighty, which I hate because…flighty implies that I'm flitting from one thing to another and I'm not really accomplishing anything. But I feel like, in each of these realms, I made a tiny difference. I did something in each of them and enjoyed myself and I learned something…I love my mother and she's been incredibly supportive. But I kind of wish she didn't tell me I needed structure. I mean, in a way, maybe I need structure, but I create the structure for myself. It's not like I'm lazy. I figure out what I'm going to do and then I go do it…I feel like I'm having to…even though my family, and even to some extent friends, you know—people that have chosen a path that's a little bit more traditional according to what society considers

> 'normal' in terms of career…I think it's hard for them to understand sometimes the well-rounded, polymathic choices. It's just hard. You have to craft a version of the story that can help them understand. Like, I couldn't just say, 'I'm just interested in tons of things and I want to try everything.' I think if I said that, they'd be like, 'Well, you can't try everything in life.' Something like that, which is kind of a downer. And my, I don't say this, but my actual response would be like, 'Why the hell not?' You know, I've got one life to live. But most people don't do that. And don't value that in life. That's just not one of their goals. Because yeah, I kind of want to try everything…But I feel like I'm constantly having to defend what I want to do.

This example speaks to a recurring theme for polymaths, which is that they must navigate the sensemaking others do surrounding their educational and career choices. Being a polymath, to some extent, involves coming up with a narrative about oneself that others can understand and support—otherwise the polymath feels not understood and not supported.

Regardless of these challenges, for Sarah, there was no choice; the idea of having a narrow, specialized career is not something she would have ever considered. "I just felt this pit in my stomach, like, 'Is this it? Am I going to be doing this forever? Like, just this?' But only doing that forever because in order to be…to really make any money at it and to be the level that I was interested in being at, you just have to be completely, singularly focused." She said sometimes she wished, though, that she could be a specialist. "Oh my God, I'm just not like those other people. You know, I wished I was like those other people. They ate and breathed singing and I just wasn't like that."

Eventually, Sarah realized that she might have to be an entrepreneur in order to be happy professionally. "This realization that like, 'Oh wait, I might have to make my own thing in order to pursue more of my interests, instead of just taking a job.'" Over time, she came to appreciate the idea of being an entrepreneur. "In general, I'm more interested in starting my own thing because I'm going to be more interested in it. It'll be a combination of my different skillsets, if not my different interests." To some extent, though, she felt once this decision was made in this way, there was no turning back. "Once you make the choice to do multiple things, it's pretty hard to get back into the workforce to do one thing."

Sarah said she believes that polymaths can add great value to organizations and to society, nonetheless. "The benefit that polymaths bring to the world at large is this ability to make connections between different types of people and different perspectives and industries." She said that "being able to approach things from different perspectives" is helpful. "Then also, just from a practical standpoint, because I've just tried a bunch of different things and worked with a bunch of different types of people, I'm just able to bring more kind of…there's just more experience that I can draw on."

Composite Textural Descriptions: Polymath Learning Experiences

Learning experiences are a huge part of the polymath experience. For instance, polymath learning appears to be highly self-directed (with support from family, teachers, their environment, etc. to some degree). In other words, polymaths decide on what they are interested in learning about without someone else directing them in this way, and then take the initiative to pursue what they are curious about (though their learning about various subjects may involve teachers, mentors, coaches, etc.). Without this key ability to self-direct their own unique learning paths, they likely would have never become polymaths. As it relates, curiosity is a hallmark of polymathy and another essential ingredient of polymathy; in fact, polymaths have not just a willingness or interest in learning, but rather a real hunger for learning due to their high levels of curiosity. In addition to formal education, another popular method through which many polymaths learn is by reading.

Another part of their learning journeys—aside from formal and informal education, and professional experiences that they learned from—includes learning about their identities. Self-categorization for a polymath is not easy; for some, polymath identity formation was realized early on in life, whereas for others, they were only becoming consciously cognizant of their polymath identity (particularly using that term) in recent times. Of course, polymath identities, like other identities, continue to evolve over time, and this is another kind of self-learning that is occurring. Polymaths must also learn to navigate their career paths in unique ways, since they do not "fit in a box" the way that narrower specialists do. They must learn to effectively tell the story of who they are and what they do in a way that others can both understand and support. Polymaths must also learn how to navigate a complex social world, which comes with certain advantages and disadvantages, given their unique multi-disciplinary identities. Polymaths also must learn to manage time differently than perhaps a monomath would have to, juggling their various polymathic commitments and interests. What is clear is at the heart of the polymath journey is continual, life-long learning, with all its challenges and benefits.

Structural Descriptions

Moustakas (1994) said that a structural description explains the "how" of a phenomenon, which in turn may be used to also understand the "what" of the experience to develop a deeper understanding of it. This researcher used imaginative variation to study the underlying structures of each polymath's experience. The textural descriptions of polymaths' learning—constructed from the phenomenological reduction process, including the various thoughts, feelings, ideas, examples, and situations that comprise the experience—were used to consider all possible meanings and divergent perspectives, to accommodate different frames of reference about the phenomenon of polymathy, and to build a description of polymath experiences. Below, two structural descriptions are provided to show some possible underlying and perhaps causal factors to become a polymath.

Individual Structural Description

Individual Structural Description: Trinity

The structures that facilitated Trinity's strong sense of polymath identity are rooted in several areas. First, she believes there is a strong genetic component. Second, she believes that access to learning (whether through good schools, library access, higher education, etc.) was critical. Third, she believes that her family's support of her polymathy also helped it to come to fruition. Fourth, financial considerations have, to some extent, encouraged the development of her polymathy. Each of these ideas will be discussed below further.

From a nature versus nurture standpoint, Trinity shared that she believes her polymathy was destined to emerge, regardless of her environment. She said,

> I think I definitely was born to be a polymath, and I say that because I feel I would have come to it naturally, regardless of the nurture. There were periods of my life where there was no nurture and I was on my own, and I still found it and sought it out. However, I think having parents, for all their flaws, that interacted with the world in the way they did, certainly propelled me to be comfortable with it and explore both sides constantly. So, I think it was nature, not nurture, because my brother—same parents—definitely not the same. He's not a polymath at all, he's very much one sided. He's got the math side, very tangible math side, but…his only interest in the arts is to talk to people and seem cultured---a strategic interest.

She said that her polymathy came quite naturally to her. "I definitely didn't need to work at it. I was the obnoxious kid that got A's without trying." In this way, an underlying structural component of her polymathy was genetic, in her opinion.

Access to learning opportunities was another crucial component underlying the development of her polymathy. She said that a "good school system was a huge plus. I had access to things people in other school systems didn't have...access to learning definitely was huge." Trinity shared that she had "a place with other kids that were equally as curious" which helped her in her learning journey. She also said that her "mom had a deal worked out with the librarian. I could take out 21 books, not 14. Every week I would get 21 new books and I read myself through the entire library, I was voracious." This example speaks to both the fact that Trinity had access to information, but also her mother's role in her development as a polymath.

Trinity's mother came up several times throughout the interview as being a major factor that supported her polymathy. Trinity's mother, who passed away a number of years ago, was a member of Mensa, the high IQ society, and worked as a nurse. Trinity said that her mother never truly reached her full potential, due mostly to economic reasons. She said, "economics and exposure are huge."

Nevertheless, Trinity's mom valued broad, diverse learning experiences, and wanted her daughter to have myriad opportunities. At one point, Trinity, who was a very talented student, was offered an opportunity to attend a special high school that required picking a track (i.e., math or art), but her mother refused to let her go:

> My mother…didn't want me pigeoned into one track…she also…wanted me to grow my social skills. She was always very nervous about me becoming so intellectual I couldn't deal with other people…. from her working with surgeons

> and doctors and seeing poor bedside manner and having to fill those gaps as a nurse, she said, 'No, I want you to experience life from your age group and have all those firsts.' She saw it more as an intellectual farm being farmed for something. We fought on that because I wanted to go. I saw it as an opportunity. I still don't know who is right. If my kid was in that situation, I don't know what I would do. I'm grateful to my mom. I could very easily have become…the awkward, shy introvert brain that doesn't know how to speak up and take charge. Those are all skills we need right now. You need both. I'm grateful, but still don't know if it was the right decision now.

Trinity summarized her mother's belief in a broad approach to learning by saying, "She was an advocate for balancing. Don't let your education get in the way of your education."

This next example is both an illustration of the impact her parents had on her polymathy, as well as financial considerations as it relates to polymathy. Trinity shared, "My parents made the conscious decision that was very painful for them to live as the poorest family in a wealthy neighborhood, so I could have the best schools." But growing up, she wanted to climb the ladder from a socioeconomic standpoint:

> I wanted out of blue collar world, I wanted out of the socioeconomic class my parents were in. I wanted out of a house that was rife with drug abuse. I wanted out of a house that was rife with domestic abuse. I wanted out of feeling less than everybody else. I wanted to feel like I fit in. I wanted to have things that were not knockoffs. I wanted to climb…I read Oliver Twist and Dickens and I saw myself in those characters and I was bound and determined to climb up out of it. I studied wealthy people, I would go the mall and people watch. That person has social status, how do they carry themselves? What are they wearing? It was scientific in the way I studied people because I wanted to fit in with a class of people…I went to a very wealthy college where I didn't fit in… It was never an option to me to not be able to climb socially. I feel like I haven't climbed to the point where I want to, no, I'm not there yet. But I have a map and I have a plan and I also…I know what's enough for me. And I'm not scared of being lower either…so I think that's freeing. Some people climb and climb and can't stop because it's never enough.

She shared that because, over the years, she has needed to earn money, she has had a broad array of experiences, doing many different kinds of work in order to support herself. Learning various kinds of jobs is very much in line with her polymathic nature, since she is curious about different fields. To some degree, her needing to do many different kinds of work and exploring all of those parts of herself was borne out of financial necessity, though. So, her polymathy was actually supported by financial struggles.

Individual Structural Description: Wendy

The underlying structural factors buttressing Wendy's development into a polymath are multi-faceted, including genetic, familial, educational, and financial considerations. To start, she believes that in her case, her polymathy is heavily rooted in her genetic inheritance. She shared, "I honestly think I was born with this." But at the same time, she said "if you would have picked any family ever to have little math/music polymaths, this is not the family you would have ever expected." Part of this may have been due to the role that Wendy's grandmother played in her upbringing.

Wendy's grandmother, who she and her sister grew up with, was a pivotal character in the development of her identity as a musician in particular. "My grandmother…wanted that musical talent to be supported and pored a ton of time and money and effort in ensuring that was the case…she paid for all of our music education basically. And we grew up with her. We had an environment that she instilled discipline and very much supported this world." More largely, Wendy's family environment may have impacted her polymathy as well. Wendy shared that she had a "pretty difficult childhood…but as a result of that, I think I developed a self-awareness and an understanding very, very early."

From an educational standpoint, her school environment was crucial to her identity as a polymath. Before eleventh grade, her schools did not have the proper staff to teach her at the level she was capable of, because she was advanced for her age, and so they had her teach herself. She shared,

> I went to a shitty private Christian school that didn't have teachers that were actually credentialed in what they were teaching, and they identified my mathematical talent in pre-school or kindergarten and just kept letting me run ahead with my own self to the point where I distinctly remember, fifth, sixth, seventh, eighth grade, I just took the textbook from two or three years ahead and I would just hit the library and I would teach myself, and I would say, 'Okay, I'm ready to take the next test.' And then I'd take the test and then…keep moving on. And then they would use the rest of my math period where I would be tutoring the high school basketball students who were about to get kicked off the team because they were behind on math. So, it really wasn't until my…calculus teacher in the eleventh grade when I actually had someone supporting that interest. That was all self-motivated.

Further, she said "at an art school, I found this identity as a mathematician, which became very clear to me, that yes, I am both and, and those are not inconsistent." So, it was a combination of the fact that her schooling up until eleventh grade forced her to become very self-driven in her mathematical education, until finally, at her arts high school, she had more support in this area. It is unclear if it is in spite of her schooling or because of it that she became so talented mathematically.

From a financial perspective, Wendy shared that she grew up without a lot of money, which spurred her polymathy on more. And even today, because she feels completely responsible for herself financially—there is no financial safety net in her family necessarily—her polymathy itself has become her safety net:

> Growing up without much money…it forces you to be scrappy and creative and get comfortable without much of a safety net. I think the forcing function of not having a ton of resources at each of these stages was a great blessing in disguise that forced me to say, 'What do you have? And where is your scrappiness, your creativeness, your network? Okay, get back in the game, and build that resilience

> a lot faster…I feel like I have more optionality and more kind of irons in the fire to do that should a life change happen, or should an economy change happen…I feel like I have a safety net in my polymath skills that maybe I didn't have or don't have from like a financial or family perspective. And quite honestly, that may have been what drove me to continue to develop multiple skill sets and multipole networks and multiple paths. I am never quite certain which came first, the chicken or the egg there.

Wendy's polymathy may be a result of financial struggles early in her life, although now her polymathy has led to great financial success. "I have like seven different sources of income," she said. "It's nice to have a diversification of income streams, should anything happen." All of these underlying structures impacted Wendy's growth into a polymath as well as her identification as such.

Composite Structural Description: Polymath Learning Experiences

The underlying structures that permeate polymath experiences are really focused on their need to continue learning and growing. This need is rooted in their deep curiosity and, for most polymaths, a strong desire for continual self-improvement. Many polymaths also like change, newness, and variety, which is related to their tendency to learn, since learning itself implies that something new is being taken in. This sort of variety of information helps to satiate the polymath's hunger for knowledge. Along these lines, another commonality amongst polymaths is that their polymathy is based in self-directed learning; no one laid out the path for them of what they should learn. What emerged for each was a unique combination of their own interests and self-expression. One method of self-directed learning that many polymaths spoke about was through reading; in fact, many participants described themselves as being voracious readers.

Because of this inherent appreciation for broad learning that exists in polymaths, learning about one subject is not enough—hence why polymathy often emerges for these individuals—because they want to learn about many different things. They prefer multi-disciplinary experiences and lessons as opposed to more narrow ones. Further, polymaths have a high level of openness to experience (even if experience shows up in wanting to learn about disparate subjects), as was anticipated. Although being a polymath has some challenges—whether they be career, social, or financial considerations—all polymaths liked this aspect of their identity; they appreciated their broadmindedness and accomplishments across disciplines, despite societal pressures to be more narrow, focused, and specialized. Continuous, life-long learning across domains is foundational to polymathy.

Textural-Structural Description of Essence

This research employed a phenomenological approach aimed at understanding the real, lived experiences of polymaths. This research systematically builds upon findings from thorough, step-by-step data analysis which has been presented in this section in an effort to produce the textural-structural description, or essence, of polymath experiences. This approach requires thoughtful consideration of all the data and an imaginative assessment of it. This allows for the real essence of the data and other related elements to rise to the surface and become distinct from the non-essential elements. The textural-structural synthesis is provided below as the "essence" of a person's experience being a modern-day polymath.

Textural-Structural Synthesis: Polymath Experience

Taken on the whole, being a modern-day polymath requires a certain type of free spirit, one that does not fit conveniently within a single box. A polymath is a person who loves to learn. A polymath values freedom, which shows up in the form of forging one's own singular path in life. A polymath is brave to explore his or her unique journey mostly on their own—so a polymath is someone who can pave his or her own way professionally and otherwise. A polymath is someone who is somewhat rebellious beneath the surface, refusing to live life as a narrow specialist as society might prefer for them to be. A polymath has a confidence to boldly explore the many, various parts of his or her personhood and the resilience to withstand the challenges involved in that endeavor.

A polymath may also experience a life with contradictions. A polymath may have career paths and/or hobbies that appear contradictory on the surface. A polymath is someone who gets their sense of identity as a polymath from *not* from fitting in, but by being different. A polymath is someone who can connect with almost anybody over myriad subjects and yet never truly feels like they fit in within any single group. A polymath is someone who is quite confident, but may feel "imposter syndrome" at times, yet does not allow that to stop them in their pursuit for internal diversification. A polymath is someone who seeks to deeply understand the world they live in but who rarely feels well understood by others in return. A polymath may obtain the most impactful parts of his or her education outside of formal schooling, as he or she self-directs their own learning journeys.

This is what it feels like to be a polymath. It is a rich experience, but it is hard at times, and it is full of contradictions. The true essence of a polymath is a desire to expand, never shrink. Polymathy is about fully savoring life with zest—wanting to make the most of this human experience in all its rich variations and striations—the good, the bad, all of it. Polymaths have an openness to experience—in fact, this is essentially an openness for life itself. They are self-directed learners committed to lifelong learning and personal growth. A polymath, in essence, strives for self-mastery, through various forms and combinations—each polymath unique in his or her own right.

Summary of Section Two

Section two of this chapter has utilized Moustakas's (1994) approach of presenting the findings from phenomenological data analysis. Before collecting data, this researcher engaged in epoche to suspend her personal opinions about the phenomenon of polymath experiences. The phenomenological approach entailed providing examples of the data analysis throughout each step of the process. The various examples showcased how this researcher derived the meaning and essence of polymath experiences based on the data itself. Samples from individual meaning horizons, invariant meaning horizons and themes, and individual textural and structural descriptions of polymath experiences were provided. Using Moustakas's (1994) method, this researcher attempted to understand the phenomenon with an unbiased attitude to the greatest extent possible. The textural-structural synthesis, or essence, of polymath experiences depicted polymaths as people who are brave adventurers of life, navigating and owning contradictions they face along the way in the pursuit of self-mastery through broad learning and experiences.

Chapter 5: Conclusions, Interpretations, and Recommendations

This last chapter discusses this researcher's conclusions, interpretations, and recommendations related to the phenomenological study of 13 people's experiences of polymathy. This chapter considers the scholarly literature reviewed as part of this effort as well as the findings in chapter 4, combined, when making these conclusions, interpretations, and recommendations.

This chapter is divided into five different sections. First, a brief *overview* of the study is provided. Second, an overview of the emergent *themes* is included. The third section includes *conclusions*. The fourth section provides *implications* for theory, practice, and research. Last, the fifth section provides *concluding remarks* as it relates to this study.

Overview of the Study

The overarching purpose of this study was to deeply understand the real, lived experiences of modern day polymaths; the reason for doing this phenomenological study was to help fill in the gap in the literature as it pertains to the experiences of polymaths in the 21st century. The intent was to understand how polymaths got to be adept in multiple, disparate areas—what motivated or led them to do so—and more generally what their experiences are of being this way.

This study used the phenomenological approach leveraging in-depth, one-on-one interviews with participants using a modified version of Seidman's (2013) approach. Given the busyness that many polymaths experience as they juggle their various commitments and pursuits, one interview was conducted rather than three but still covered each of these three critical components that Seidman (2013) advocated. Section one of the interview was about life history, section two was about details of the experience, and section three was about meaning making. Interviews ranged from 1 – 2 hours, though most were around 90 minutes long. The thirteen participants were found utilizing the snowball (also called chain or network) sampling methodology, taking into consideration the participation requirements that were previously set. A number of possible participants were excluded from being involved in the research since they did not fully meet all the criteria.

Using a phenomenological method for this research added great insights into understanding the phenomenon of polymathy. All thirteen participants were enthusiastic about participating in the study and each one was quite introspective and insightful into their experiences as polymaths. Some findings were anticipated while others were not. The research findings brought their experiences to the fore, shedding light on what life is really like for modern day Renaissance persons. Findings included both the benefits and challenges that they face as they navigate life as 21st century polymaths. Those themes are reviewed in the following section.

Overview of Themes

The overall research questions and associated subquestions for this research are as follows: *What is the lived experience of polymaths?* The subquestions were: *What is it like being a polymath? How does it feel? How does polymathy impact creativity and creative problem solving?* The other primary research question was: *How did polymaths come to be that way?* The associated subquestions were: *How did polymaths discover their identity? What in a polymaths' environment impacted them becoming a polymath?*

A total of 12 themes emerged based on the interview data to help answer these research questions:

1. Theme One: Polymaths Define Themselves as Experts Across Disparate Disciplines
2. Theme Two: Polymath Identity Emerges from Not Fitting in A Box
3. Theme Three: Being Polymathic Impacts One's Social Experiences
4. Theme Four: Polymaths Have Difficult Career Choices
5. Theme Five: Financial Resources Can Both Hinder and Promote Polymathy
6. Theme Six: Polymaths are Shaped by Their Families
7. Theme Seven: Polymaths Are Voracious Learners
8. Theme Eight: Polymaths are Quite Confident but May Also Experience "Imposter Syndrome"
9. Theme Nine: Polymaths Self-Identify as Highly Creative
10. Theme Ten: Polymaths Cannot Be Happy as Narrow Specialists
11. Theme Eleven: Effective Polymaths are Effective Time Managers
12. Theme Twelve: Polymathy is Due to Both Nature and Nurture but Polymathic Excellence Requires a Level of Effort and Attention

Throughout Chapter 4, examples were provided with thick, rich data, including showcasing individual meaning horizons, invariant meaning horizons and themes, as well as individual textural and structural descriptions of polymath experiences. The textural-structural synthesis, or essence, of polymath experiences depicted polymaths as people who are essentially brave adventurers of life, not only navigating but in fact owning the very contradictions they personify as they pursue self-mastery through broad learning and experiences.

Conclusions

When taking into consideration these themes as well as the relevant literature, the following synthesized conclusions can be drawn, each of which answers one of the research questions:

1. **Conclusion 1: To be a polymath, one must accept not fitting in a typical box and perhaps even embodying apparent contradictions; polymathy is being intrapersonally diverse.** In answering the question, "What is the lived experience of polymaths?" a succinct answer is that they may embody a life of contradictions given their unique, intrapersonal diversity. For example, a polymath may have career paths and/or hobbies that actually appear to an outside onlooker to be contradictory on the surface. There are other contradictions that a polymath may embody as well. For instance, a polymath is someone who can talk with almost anybody over myriad subjects and yet never truly feels like they fit in within any single group. A polymath is someone who seems very confident, but still may feel "imposter syndrome" at times. A polymath is someone who seeks to deeply understand the world they live in but may not feel very well understood in return. A polymath may be very educated, but much of their education may have been through informal, lifelong, self-directed learning. The lived experience of polymaths is rich and rewarding, but it is also quite complicated.

   Polymaths also are not able to be a part of an in-group of other polymaths, so a polymath may develop their sense of identity as a polymath from not from fitting in, but by being different. According to Social Identity Theory, people typically forge their identity first and foremost by where they do fit in; social identity is "a person's knowledge that he or she belongs to a social category or group" (Stets & Burke, 2000, p. 225). A polymath does not have an in-group of polymaths to be a part of, and they tend to not "fit in a box," so they must navigate their polymath identity mostly by themselves.

The lived experience of a polymath also entails having a high degree of intrapersonal diversity. The current scholarly literature on intrapersonal diversity focuses on functional intrapersonal diversity, which has to do with someone's professional experience—specifically, how much they are either a narrow specialist with limited experience in a small range of functions versus a broad generalist whose prior work experience spans a number of functional areas (Bunderson and Sutcliffe, 2002). The polymath participants in this study could all be considered intrapersonally diverse from a functional perspective because someone who is functionally intrapersonally diverse has a wide "breadth of functional experiences" (Bunderson and Sutcliffe, 2002, p. 875). Becoming intrapersonally diverse is seen by polymaths as a way of maximizing their potential and making their lives more interesting. Based on this study, it is safe to say that polymathy and intrapersonal diversity coexist. This research adds to the existing scholarly literature by forging a connection between these two constructs.

2. **Conclusion 2: Polymaths are exposed broadly, think creatively and strategically, and juggle their many interests and obligations through effective time management.** In answering the question, "What is it like to be a

polymath?" one must take into consideration how polymaths define their own polymathy and how they manage it on a day to day basis. Based on the interviews, being a polymath means that someone is adept, skilled, and even expert across disparate disciplines; the way polymaths from this research think of themselves is supported by scholarly definitions of polymathy in the literature. For example, according to MacLachlan (2009), the term "polymath" refers to very well-educated people who were distinguished not only by their unique strengths and capabilities in particular fields of interest, but also by their noteworthy ability to traverse different fields of specialization and to sometimes see their interconnections. Scholarly definitions of polymathy are similar to the explanations that individual polymaths in this research provided.

Indeed, polymaths are uniquely situated to be able to forge connections between the disciplines, or to have unique insights as a result of their multidisciplinary experiences. This idea is also in line with the literature on the topic. For example, a number of studies have shown that creative people are more broadly trained, have more avocational interests, and show increased abilities in those interests than the average individual does (Root-Bernstein, 2015). Creativity scholars refer to polymaths as being highly creative people (Root-Bernstein, et al., 2008, Kaufman, et al., 2010) who are able to experience a broad array of disparate and unrelated—even paradoxical—activities. These people are open to novel experiences whether professionally or through hobbies (Csikszentmihalyi, 1996). Highly curious people, such as polymaths, also have higher employability and many become entrepreneurs (Chamorro-Premuzic,

2014) which is also the case for polymaths. Both the scholarly literature as well as this research points to the fact that because polymaths are highly curious, they choose to become exposed broadly and that they think creatively and strategically as a result.

On a practical level, the experience of polymaths is also typically very full and busy simply from a schedule perspective. A typical polymath has a lot going on in his or her life, usually, and managing all their interests requires that they manage their time well in order to accommodate those pursuits. Polymaths tend to be busy people. Someone who cannot juggle many different projects, interests, responsibilities, and demands is unlikely to develop into an accomplished polymath.

3. **Conclusion 3: Being a polymath can make life richer, but it can also be quite difficult.** In answering the question, "How does being a polymath feel?" given this research, the best answer is probably that it feels wonderful and hard at the same time. Almost all polymaths interviewed for this research felt that their polymathy is something they like about themselves (only one interviewee, Sebastian, was not sure). Participants believed it makes their life richer as they are more broadly exposed to life itself.

   But polymathy also comes with quite a lot of downsides, such having challenges in the workplace especially when jobs may feel stifling and narrow. This is in line with what De Jong, et al., (2001) found, which is that individuals high in openness to experiences, such as polymaths, tend to be dissatisfied in jobs low in skill variety; they become dissatisfied and frustrated if jobs are mechanical or unchallenging. Being a polymath means that making career decisions can be quite difficult and then even once career choices are made, many jobs frequently require a kind of focus and narrowness which does not work well for a polymath who prefers variety, novelty, and continued learning.

There are other downsides to being a polymath. For instance, polymaths may not feel well understood by others. Being a polymath can even make dating and finding a mate more challenging. Being a polymath may be jarring to friendships if a friend expects one sort of personality from the polymath and then the polymath changes as their interests evolve over time. Some polymaths become entrepreneurs to try to customize the ideal career, but that path comes with its own challenges, difficult demands, and risks. Polymaths also do not settle into careers the way monomaths do so a polymath's career may have periods of relative stability interrupted by occasional upheaval as the polymath makes big jumps into different disciplines professionally.

All of these factors can make telling the story of one's career very difficult and one's personal brand somewhat messy. Being a polymath can feel like your brain is always turned on and it's hard to slow it down and relax; being quite productive and efficient, always looking for value in any situation, is the modus operandi of many polymaths. It can feel like there is never enough time to pursue all of one's interests or complete everything on the to do list. Polymaths may not be appreciated by others, let alone understood by them. Lastly, polymaths may lack a sense of place and a sense of community, as they have no defined "in-group" (per Identity Theory and Social Identity Theory) that they can join (at least not currently and not formally at the current time).

Being a polymath is both an enriching experience as well as, at times, a challenging one. Based on this research, it appears that polymaths truly enjoy their own polymathy and would not want to be any other way. That said, navigating life as a polymath in a world that mostly prefers people to function more narrowly is challenging at times; we certainly live in a society and time where the major paradigm is that of specialization (Shavinina, 2013). Disciplinary specialization is common in our time (Ross, 2011) and it is seen as a requirement for adult success (Shavinina, 2013). Because of that, polymaths usually do not feel well understood by others, and are frequently not fully appreciated. This is the case despite the fact that specialization also has downsides: the problem with deep specialization is that those specialists may get entrenched in their own, limited points of view which negative impacts creativity and innovation (Wiens, 2012). Along with all these considerations, we must also consider that polymaths do not have a sense of "place" with regard to their polymath identity. Even some highly qualified polymaths struggle with their identity as a polymath, in fact.

Living life as a polymath has some burdens and some benefits—it is wonderful and complicated and difficult all at the same time. But for a polymath with divergent interests and an insatiable desire to explore, learn, grow, and improve, there is no other choice; they must be who they are in all its broadness, otherwise that person will not be happy. Being happy as a polymath requires thoughtful consideration for how to curate one's own life in a way that will satiate the various appetites that a polymath has, while also navigating the larger society's expectations and preferences for narrow expertise. This is a difficult journey to navigate. So, in some ways, polymathy "may be a vice as much as a virtue in this age of specialization" (Robinson, 2006, p. 409).

4. **Conclusion 4: Polymaths are excellent at being creative and solving problems creatively.** In answering the question, "How does polymathy impact creativity and creative problem solving?" the answer is, it makes those skills considerably better. Creative problem solving involves coming up with approaches and solutions that are new to the solver or even new in the context of history (Boden, 2004). For a solution to be considered creative, it must be useful, correct, and valuable (Amabile, 1983). Many interviewees said that because of their broad exposure and experiences, they have more "tools in the toolkit" with which to solve work or life challenges in novel and useful ways. Further, polymaths are voracious learners, constantly looking for new information to absorb and integrate, thus making their ability to innovate even stronger and more well-informed. Creativity and being able to creatively solve problems is a very valuable skill because it is one of the most important factors affecting individual performance in various domains of work (Sung and Choi, 2009). In fact, "considerable evidence demonstrates that creativity promotes individual task performance" (Sung and Choi, 2009, p. 941), which in turn impacts organizational innovation and effectiveness (Amabile, 1996; Scott and Bruce, 1994). Polymaths are uniquely situated at the intersection of disparate disciplines

and are capable of seeing connections in the way that single-disciplinary experts cannot. As a result of these considerations, polymaths think very creatively; this may, in fact, be their greatest strength of all.

5. **Conclusion 5: Polymathy develops due to a combination of nature and nurture and polymathy is maintained in adulthood by a willingness to continue to work to improve oneself through self-directed learning.** In answering the question, "How did polymaths come to be that way?" the answer is that it is due to a variety of factors. All participants felt that their polymathy emerged due to both nature and nurture – both genetics and environment. Several participants said they believe that polymathic approaches could be encouraged in anyone, though, and that the school system is an integral part of the equation to support the development of more polymaths. Some participants felt their polymathy was due to luck or chance. Others acknowledged the role that opportunity or privilege played in their development as a polymath, though this certainly still required a level of openness to have those experiences and say yes to pursue them.

Openness to experience is the "disposition to be imaginative, nonconforming, and unconventional" (Judge, Bono, Ilies, and Berhard, 2002, p. 765). It includes exploring multiple options, challenging assumptions, seeking different perspectives, combining different viewpoints, and actively evaluating different options (Shalley and Perry Smith, 2008). People high in the openness to experience personality trait are often more flexible and able to understand various perspectives more readily (Zhao and Seibert, 2006), and those people tend "to be imaginative, intellectually curious, and open to trying new things" (Burke and Witt, 2002, p. 712). A number of different studies over a period of many years link openness to experience with creativity at the individual level of analysis (McCrae, 1987; Feist, 1998; George & Zhou, 2001; McCrae & Costa, 1997).

For most polymaths, it is easy to learn, but it took discipline, time, and attention to develop a level of expertise in their fields; but it also took a level of openness as well. In sum, polymaths came to be polymaths because of both genetic and environmental considerations, but also from a willingness to be open to exploring new things and then pursuing them consistently over a long period of time to achieve excellence.

Polymathy also emerges through continued self-directed learning. For the purposes of this study, the definition of self-directed learning that fits best is Brockett's (1983), which defines self-directed learning as "a disposition to engage in learning activities where the individual takes personal responsibility for developing and carrying out learning endeavors autonomously without being prompted or guided by other people" (p. 16). Self-directed learning may be an interactive process, however, as self-directed learning may not even be well planned, and the environment, opportunities, or characteristics of the learner all interact together and impact one's self-directed learning (Merriam, Caffarella, & Baumgartner, 2007). Self-directed learning also allows for a large degree of personalization and diversity since students can design their own learning (Smith & Morrison, 2006). It is a complex and multi-faceted concept that emphasizes human capacity, the ability to change one's own behavior, and self-evaluation as opposed to these facets coming from external sources (Danis, 1992).

One facet of polymathy that became clear through this study is that it develops very much through self-directed learning. Nobody tells a polymath exactly what combination to pursue in architecting their learning journeys. Further, there is very little societal scaffolding to support the polymath's journey as a polymath. There are no professional purveyors of polymathy to whom an aspiring polymath can go to for assistance. It is truly a self-initiated effort. Given that there is no research regarding self-directed learning and polymaths, this study adds some new insights in this area.

6. **Conclusion 6: Polymath identity is discovered from not fitting in; polymath identity can be difficult to fully own and to explain to others.** In answering the question, "How did polymaths discover their identity?" the quick answer is that it was through being different. It was through noticing all the many out-groups of which they were not a part, and forging their own identity in relation to not fitting in those groups. This is in line with the basic tenets of Social Identity Theory, but it also adds a new perspective as well, because it provides an example of identity formation in the absence of an in-group. Social identity is "a person's knowledge that he or she belongs to a social category or group" (Stets & Burke, 2000, p. 225), although polymaths do not have a polymath group of which to be a part.

Polymaths feel like they cannot explain who they are very easily. Because of their multidisciplinarity, they cannot be easily contained or fit into "a box." They took a path that few pursue and that may be singularly unique to their personhood, and that may be hard to explain to others. Many polymaths realized their identity in comparison to not being narrow, like their counterparts are. Some polymaths feel comfortable with using that particular word while others do not. To some, calling oneself a polymath or a Renaissance man/woman sounds like boasting. In fact, many polymaths are self-conscious about putting off other people or coming across as threatening to others. Is it arrogant to consider oneself a polymath? Showing off too much about what one can do or what one knows can impact how one fits in socially, and so many polymaths think carefully about how they explain the story of who they are or what they know to others. It is frequently easier to not share too much about one's talents so as not to be threatening to others, or to simply share parts of one's personhood in small doses over time; and in this way, polymathy may remain in the shadows, not part of the larger societal discourse and not recognized as such, because for a polymath to share all of themselves may seem overwhelming to those on the receiving end and could further isolate polymaths as a result. Polymaths tread carefully in explaining who they are and what they are capable of to others.

Further, the narrative of one's own polymathy is a consistent challenge among polymaths, because outsiders may not understand if and how their varied interests relate or why someone would choose to pursue so many things as opposed to focusing more narrowly, professionally. Thus, owning and sharing one's polymath identity is challenging; it seems, based on this limited research, that the way to overcoming that challenge is through having a sense of self-confidence to own one's polymath identity and figuring out ways to tell the narrative in a way people can both understand and support. This involves a process of thoughtful sensemaking and sensegiving (Weick, 1995).

7. **Conclusion 7: Family and financial resources impact the emergence of polymathy.**

In answering the question, "What in a polymaths' environment impacted them becoming a polymath?" the biggest factors seem to be their upbringing and their financial resources. One of the example polymaths cited earlier in this dissertation was about Michael Polanyi (1891 – 1976), a British-Hungarian researcher whose skillsets spanned fields including science, philosophy, history, politics, art, economics, literature, ethics, values, and religion (Terjesen and Politis, 2015). He said that much of the reason he was a polymath was because of his upbringing and the way he was raised, which supported his polymathy (Terjesen and Politis, 2015, p 154).

However, in some ways, having difficult childhood experiences could also prompt young persons to pursue excellence through polymathy; in this way, polymathy could be rooted in childhood disfunction and polymathy is a route to overcoming and moving beyond those childhood difficulties. For others, having supportive, involved parents spurred on polymathy as they were encouraged to explore and learn as they wish. There is no single consistent tale regarding how family impacts polymathy. What is clear, however, from all the interview, is that the impact of family life plays a part in one way or another.

And related, financial resources also play a part, though for some polymathy is rooted in needing to be resourceful because of a lack of money; for others, polymathy is further enabled from having money to pay for various experiences, classes, etc. For some, being polymathic seems to increase their ability to generate revenue through multiple income streams. Highly curious people, such as polymaths, may have higher employability (Chamorro-Premuzic, 2014). For others, not being a narrow specialist expert may limit the kind of income they will earn; according to Wiens (2012). the more deeply one specializes, the more money they are likely to earn. There is no consistent story around whether polymathy ensures financial success or makes it harder—different people have different experiences depending on their situation and how they have been able to navigate their specific career journeys.

In both of these examples—family and finances—what is clear is that people who become polymaths are able to take what was in their environment and use it to their advantage. They are not victims of their circumstances. Whether what was in their environment was challenging or supportive, polymaths used these factors to bolster themselves forward into a better future.

Recommendations

This next section will present recommendations for theory, practice, and research because of the work done in this study. Recommendations are further broken down into two categories: those based out of this researcher's knowledge on the topic of polymathy, and recommendations that are directly from participants themselves. The recommendations are summarized in succinct tables, followed by more thorough explanation for each recommendation.

Recommendations From This Researcher

Table 5-1: Summary of Recommendations From This Researcher

	Recommendations
For Theory	Recommendation 1: Expand considerations of how not having a group to be a part of shapes identity formation.
	Recommendation 2: Recognize that academia, and therefore the scholarly literature, is mostly dominated by single-disciplinary experts, and this may have negative implications for the types of research being conducted.
	Recommendation 3: Broaden conceptions around what types of human diversity exist.
	Recommendation 4: Broaden conceptions around what intrapersonal diversity means.
For Practice	**Recommendations for Academia**
	Recommendation 1: In academia, encourage the development of more interdisciplinary expert scholars
	Recommendations for Organizations
	Recommendation 1: Organizations should put more effort into identifying, recruiting, and retaining polymaths into their companies, given the distinctive capabilities that polymaths possess to creatively solve difficult problems and add unique value.
	Recommendation 2: Organizations should think strategically about leveraging the unique capabilities of polymaths
	Recommendation 3: Create a central organization to certify polymaths and to create a sense of place for polymaths to meet others who are similarly intrapersonally diverse.
For Research	Recommendation 1: Study the relationship between polymaths and leadership.
	Recommendation 2: Study the role of genetic factors involved in polymathy.
	Recommendation 3: Study polymaths in other cultures or educational systems.
	Recommendation 4: Research ways that organizational leaders can leverage the talents of polymaths.
	Recommendation 5: Identify other factors correlated with polymathy such as personality types and educational backgrounds.
	Recommendation 6: Study polymaths who are also entrepreneurs.
	Recommendation 7. Further Study the Relationship between Openness to Experience and Polymathy.
	Recommendation 8: Study different subcategories of polymaths that may exist (i.e., which types of polymaths are most appropriate in leadership positions or not)
	Recommendation 9: Study polymaths who may not be as educated, accomplished, or as elite as those who were part of this study but who

	are skilled and capable in other still important ways.

For Theory

Recommendation 1: Expand considerations of how not having a group to be a part of shapes identity formation. This recommendation relates to Identity Theory and Social Identity Theory.

Briefly, Identity Theory says that it is through self-categorization or identification that a human being forms his or her identity (Hogg, Terry, & White, 1995). In other words, we learn who we are (our self-concept) and about normative behavior acceptable in society in relation to others (Hogg, Terry, & White, 1995). However, since people interact and are part of various different groups, they may have many distinct selves based on the distinct groups to which they belong and whose opinions matter to them (Hogg, Terry, & White, 1995). So an individual's identity is not just one thing, but a composite of various identities merged together, impacted by both internal and external forces, all of which may shift over time. These role identities provide meaning for the self, both because they refer to specific roles the person inhabits, but also because these roles allow them to distinguish from counterroles that they do not inhabit (Lindesmith and Strauss, 1956).

Social Identity Theory, a subset of Identity Theory, is slightly different. While Identity Theory is more focused on the role of the individual, in Social Identity Theory, the emphasis is on groups of people (Stets & Burke, 2000). According to Social Identity Theory, social identity is "a person's knowledge that he or she belongs to a social category or group" (Stets & Burke, 2000, p. 225). It is knowing what their in-group is, of which they are a part, and their out-group, of which they are not a part (Stets & Burke, 2000).

There are two important sub-aspects of Social Identity Theory: (1) self-categorization and (2) social comparison (Hogg & Abrams, 1988). Self-categorization involves a person perceiving who they have similarities with while also accentuating perceived differences between the self and members of the out-group (Stets & Burke, 2000). Individuals develop their identity or their sense of self, in large part, due to the social categories to which they belong (Stets & Burke, 2000). And because each person has a unique life experience, each person has a unique combination of social categories with which they identify (Stets & Burke, 2000). Social Identity Theory is largely about how different groups relate and compare—in other words, how people see themselves as part of their in-group in contrast to the out-group (Stets & Burke, 2000).

However, these theories falsely assume that an in-group exists for all identities, but this is not the case for polymaths. (This may also be the case for other types of identities.) In fact, one important consideration this research on polymaths brings to light is that for some individuals, there actually is no in-group of which to be a part. For polymaths, this may make identification as a polymath more difficult. In the specific case of polymaths, there is no formally structured group of polymaths with which to belong, but there are many out-groups. Through this research, it became clear that many polymaths' identity formation emerged from feeling different—from dis-identifying with the many outgroups. Polymaths may notice out-groups and be able to form identity in relation to what they are *not*. And there may be in-groups with which they may identify in part, but not fully. The fact that there was no bigger, overarching group of polymaths with which they could co-create a sense of identity made the polymath journey harder on many of them. Said differently, part of how polymath identity formation emerges is from recognizing the many out-groups of which a polymath does not belong to, and a willingness to forge one's polymathic identity in the absence of any polymathic in-group.

Of course, polymathic individuals may be a part of certain groups, such as a racial group, or feel a part of a group based in gender identity, and they must also navigate that intersectionality. However, in terms of broader conceptions around identity, having to do with career and capability—things that a person has some degree of choice over, Social Identity Theory should acknowledge that not all identities have an in-group. Said differently, the theory should take into account when there is no group with which a person may join and how that affects identity formation in those individuals.

This point is important so that Identity Theory and Social Identity Theory may be expanded. Essentially, this research on polymaths is an example that illustrates the importance of broader consideration being given regarding how identity formation develops when there is no formal group of which to be a part or with which to identify. Since Identity Theory and Social Identity Theory are based on in-group and out-group membership, these theories should also consider how identity is formed in the absence of an in-group because for some people—like polymaths—an in-group may not exist. Accordingly, these theories should be expanded to account for identity formation when there is no in-group with which to identify. Further, how does identity form when labels such as being "a polymath" is rarely even mentioned (as polymathy is rarely discussed and there is almost no societal discourse around it)? How does identity form when that identity is not part of the social discourse or when people do not have a word in their vocabulary to describe themselves? These are areas for future study.

This recommendation represents a contribution to the scholarly literature since it expands conceptions around identity formation, provides a justification for modifying an existing and prevalent theory, and provides a novel insight to help build new models in the future surrounding identity formation in the absence of an in-group. In other words, this research on polymaths can serve as a basis for further study on identity formation when there is no in-group. Understanding this process is an important area for future research, especially considering that the need to feel a sense of belonging is a fundamental human need (Baumeister & Leary, 1995), and something that many polymaths feel is somewhat lacking from their human experiences.

Recommendation 2: Recognize that academia, and therefore the scholarly literature, is mostly dominated by single-disciplinary experts, and this may have negative implications for the types of research being conducted. There is an important place for single-disciplinary experts in academia, who can dive deeply into a subject and master it, and find unique, well-informed solutions to the problems humanity faces. There is also an important role for broader experts who can forge connections between disciplines to reach different insights and find novel solutions, as well. However, very few multi-disciplinary experts exist in academia. Of those who do exist in academia, few are able to succeed on the same level as single-disciplinary experts can, particularly in an academic, research setting. An example of this trend in academia is in the tenure and promotion process which rewards deep specialization (Terjesen and Politis, 2015). Multidisciplinary scholars are viewed as being less expert and are therefore not promoted and respected at the same level that more narrow scholars are (Terjesen and Politis, 2015). Accordingly, there is very little incentive for an academic scholar to develop mastery in more than one field. Similarly, most academic journals also lack multi-disciplinarity, and if they do, it tends to be in fields that are different but closely related, like accounting and finance (Terjesen and Politis, 2015). As a general rule—whether inside academia or not—disciplinary specialization is common in our time (Ross, 2011). This reality may have severely negative implications for the type of research that is being conducted (or not being conducted, as the case may be). This begs the question: what research gaps exist in the literature that polymaths may be in unique positions to contribute towards? Further, what insights and innovations may be more possible through broad and interdisciplinary sensemaking as opposed to more narrow expertise? What problems can polymaths help to solve? I believe polymaths can add great value in many different settings, across myriad fields and disciplines including in academic research. We need more of them. (Obviously, this is a reflexive point, given this author is writing this dissertation as part of a university's doctoral program.)

Recommendation 3: Broaden conceptions around what types of human diversity exist. Most discourse and research around diversity considers what that means in groups of people, and focuses on racial, sex, and socio-economic disparities among different people from different groups. While those forms of diversity are important and deserve attention, there is more to what makes up someone's personhood besides these characteristics, over which individuals had no choice. While someone cannot pick which race, sex, or socioeconomic class they are born into, they can have a sense of autonomy and control, to some degree, regarding the types of activities and subjects they choose to explore and the subsequent intrapersonal diversity they develop in themselves as a result. This other kind of diversity—diversity within a person—should be more largely acknowledged. Diversity is studied at the meso and macro levels, but diversity at the micro level of analysis should also be given more credence in academic and professional circles. Intrapersonal diversity should be explored more, acknowledging that there is a type of diversity that can exist within a person, in addition to diversity among groups of different people. All kinds of diversity matter and are worthy of understanding.

Recommendation 4: Broaden conceptions around what intrapersonal diversity means. The scholarly literature around intrapersonal diversity focuses on *functional* intrapersonal diversity which has to do with the extent to which someone is a generalist or a specialist in their career, but it does not consider other types of diversity that might exist within a single individual but outside the confines of one's job requirements; for instance, what about intrapersonal diversity that one might have among hobbies, extracurricular activities, social networks, emotions, etc.? The idea of intrapersonal diversity needs to become more diversified itself. This is a major gap in the literature regarding these other types of intrapersonal diversity that exist and an area for further exploration. Might an instrument be created to measure intrapersonal diversity? This would be very useful because if one's level of intrapersonal diversity could be objectively measured, this would open the doors for it to be studied more rigorously as it pertains to myriad other related subjects and might allow for new theories around diversity and identity formation to be constructed.

For Practice

In this section, recommendations are broken down into three categories: first, recommendations for academia, and then for organizations.

Recommendations for Academia

Recommendation 1: In academia, encourage the development of more interdisciplinary expert scholars. Universities are an organization just like any other; they are in the business of education. Universities should also think strategically about how they might support polymathy amongst their staff, particularly researchers. Universities and other kinds of research institutions should support multi-disciplinary scholars. This may be done by, for instance, giving awards and recognition to researchers who become experts in two disparate fields and by doing more to help them publish, speak, and teach, even if the way they do this might be in somewhat non-traditional ways.

Recommendations for Organizations

Recommendation 1: Organizations should put more effort into identifying, recruiting, and retaining polymaths into their companies, given the distinctive capabilities that polymaths possess to creatively solve difficult problems and add unique value. Polymaths are very gifted individuals; some of them are geniuses. However, many polymaths feel underutilized in their jobs, and a lot of polymaths become self-employed entrepreneurs in order to leverage their full skill set and reach their fullest professional potential. They are frequently underutilized and underchallenged at work (which they experience negatively), or completely absent from traditional organizations as they pursue entrepreneurial ventures. Smith (2014) said, "Universities, companies, professional organizations, and individuals themselves need to promote and pursue the development and integration of all the diverse talents that are latent in each person." (p. 59). Companies should take steps to ensure that they are leveraging these diverse talents in their employees (whether those employees are polymaths or not). One sample way of allowing for this is to suggest an employee spend a certain amount of their time doing the critical, primary aspects of his or her job, and then the rest of the time, encourage employees to initiate new projects they are passionate about and where they feel they can add value using their unique strengths. This is a way to leverage the talents of an employee, as well as a way to help them feel fulfilled, challenged, and appreciated in their workplace.

Recommendation 2: Organizations should think strategically about leveraging the unique capabilities of polymaths. One way an organization can reach its fullest potential is, in fact, by leveraging the full potential of its employees. Polymaths are unique individuals who bring great prowess, insights, and creativity to their work. Polymaths will prefer to work for an organization that appreciates their talents and allows them some degree of flexibility to use their various strengths at work. They will prefer variety over monotony. They might like job rotations to learn about different areas within a company or even take short assignments outside the organization. Polymaths are voracious learners who want training and development opportunities. They prefer to be treated as equals rather than part of a hierarchy. Organizations should ask their polymathic employees what they can do to support them. There are certainly some approaches that organizations could implement that would appeal to polymaths and urge them to come and stay at an organization. Companies who take these sorts of thoughtful approaches will reap the benefits that polymaths bring, rather than miss out on them.

Recommendation 3: Create a central organization to certify polymaths and to create a sense of place for polymaths to meet others who are similarly intrapersonally diverse. Like Mensa is the High IQ Society, there should be an organization for Polymaths to join as well. Social identity theory explains how people form their individual identities in relation to larger groups of people who are like they are. This is very difficult for a polymath to do since there is no organization to which they may belong as a unified group. If polymathy was discussed more—if there was more discourse about what it is like to be a polymath, the strengths they bring to bear on problems, the challenges they face—and if there was an association to which they could belong, I believe that more people would begin identifying and owning their identities as polymaths. And they might, as a result, try to contribute more to the world in polymathic ways (i.e., forging interdisciplinary connections and solutions).

For Research

Recommendation 1: Study the relationship between polymaths and leadership. Do polymaths make more effective leaders? I believe, after studying polymaths, that they very well might because they are able to take a broader view and make connections in ways that deep specialists cannot. Consider Complexity Leadership Theory, which says that in a Complex Adaptive System, problems are solved in neural-like networks of distributed decision making (Uhl-Bien, Marion, & McKelvey, 2007). Are polymaths more effective in a hub (leadership) role as opposed to narrower, specialist leaders? The below graphic attempts to describe this idea.

Figure 5-1: Polymath Leader as a Hub of a Network

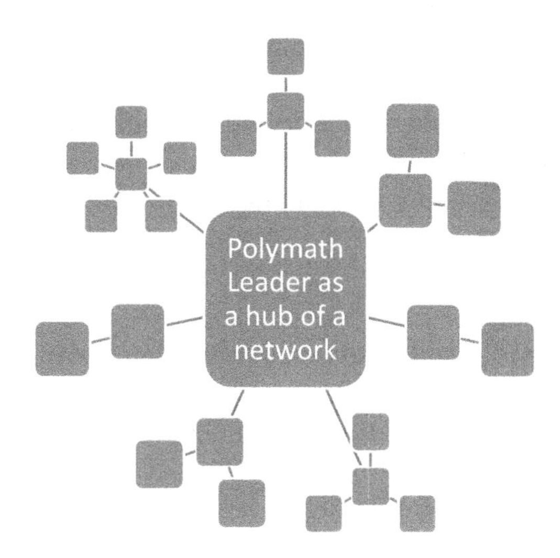

Research should be conducted to study polymaths as leaders. Does their polymathy enable them to be better leaders? How does their polymathy shape their leadership approaches? Under what circumstances does a polymath make an effective leader, and under what circumstances would a narrow specialist be more effective in a leadership role? This is an area for future exploration since very little research has been done in this area, and it would be quite useful information particularly for organizations when recruiting and selecting individuals for leadership positions.

Recommendation 2: Study the role of genetic factors involved in polymathy. The question of whether polymathy was due to nature or nurture was asked of all participants in this research. Although some participants felt that either genetic or environmental factors were stronger in their particular case, the vast majority felt that it was due to both factors to some degree. It is easy to understand the environmental factors that help support the development of polymathy in individuals. What is less understood is the role that genetics play. So for example, a study about identical twins raised separately (where one or both are polymaths) would help shed light on this issue further by isolating the genetic component and seeing what becomes evident as a result.

Recommendation 3: Study polymaths in other cultures or educational systems. This phenomenological study involved mostly American participants. One interviewee was raised in England and living in the USA at the time of the interview; another was born, raised, and living in Germany. Both of these countries are European. The rest of the interviewees were born and raised in the USA. This study also required that participants have native English fluency, which is a limitation of this work and an area for future research—to study polymaths from cultures that speak languages other than English. Do cultures that speak other languages value polymathy differently than cultures that speak English? Is the experience of polymathy similar or different than the experiences of American polymaths? There may be interesting findings that would emerge from doing a study like this one in a different cultural setting, such as in Asia, Africa, South America, etc. Are there aspects of polymathy that are universal human experiences, or are polymath experiences mediated by the cultural context in which the polymath exists? This is an area for exploration and would be a useful addendum to help inform this study further.

Recommendation 4: Research ways that organizational leaders can leverage the talents of polymaths. In this study, some participants gave some specific recommendations which were included in chapter 4. Those participants provided ideas for how organizations could support them to add the best value to the organization. However, this is an area that should be explored more comprehensively given how important of an issue it is. Purposeful exploration of this idea might illicit a whole host of behaviors that organizations could engage in to fully leverage their polymathy employees, so more should be done in this area particularly.

Recommendation 5: Identify other factors correlated with polymathy such as personality types and educational backgrounds. This particular study tried to understand the life histories, details of the experience of being a polymath, and the sensemaking polymaths did regarding their experiences as polymaths. The findings included educational, familial, social, financial, and other factors that interplay with polymathy in one way or another. But there may be other interesting variables associated with polymaths. For instance, is there a certain Myers-Briggs personality type that is more common among polymaths when compared to the general population? What might explain that sort of finding? Are there certain universities that attract and/or produce more polymaths than others? These are just two examples. There are myriad ways that mediators, moderators, or correlates of polymathy could be studied further, and endless variables (whether personality types, universities, etc.) that could be studied in this way to add a deeper, richer layer of understanding to the phenomenon of polymathy.

Recommendation 6: Study polymaths who are also entrepreneurs. A number of polymaths interviewed as part of this research have been or currently are self-employed entrepreneurs. Many of them chose that path out of the frustrations with employers who did not know how to properly leverage their unique skillsets and/or who did not appreciate them. Are most entrepreneurs polymathic in nature? Both polymaths and entrepreneurs must have a level of confidence and bravery in order to forge their own paths in the way they do—is this common link all that entrepreneurs and polymaths have in common, or is there more? This is an area worth exploring further, since it seems there may be some sort of link between those with polymathic tendencies and those with entrepreneurial tendencies

Recommendation 7: Further Study the Relationship between Openness to Experience and Polymathy. Although participants of this research were not measured for their levels of openness to experience, for example, by using a validated instrument, it seems obvious that they must have relatively high levels of openness, otherwise they would not be polymaths.

With that in mind, much of the literature on openness to experience was validated and very much in line with polymathic traits discovered in this research so it appears there very likely is some sort of relationship between the two constructs. For instance, openness to experience is correlated with high levels of innovation (Shane, 1995; Olikitan, 2011). Openness to experience is also correlated with creativity (Sung and Choi, 2009; Wolfradt & Pretz, 2001). McElroy and Dowd (2007) said that individuals high in openness to experience will be more likely to pay attention to multiple influences when making decisions. De Jong, et al., (2001) found that individuals high in openness to experiences tend to be dissatisfied in jobs low in skill variety; they become dissatisfied and frustrated if jobs are mechanical or unchallenging. All of these descriptions of openness to experience based in the scholarly literature are in line with the reports of polymaths in this phenomenological study. In other words, polymaths reported that they believe they are innovative, creative, more holistic in their views, and that they need variety in order to be happy. Clearly, there is a strong correlation between polymathy and openness to experience and this is an area for future study.

Given the scholarly literature as well as the experiences polymaths shared as part of this research, I believe that openness to experience may be a precursor to polymathic exposure; in order to have broad, varied learning experiences, it is of course necessary to be open to having them to begin with. What exactly is the connection between openness and experience and polymathy? Perhaps one way of thinking about this relationship is that openness to experience is a personality trait or an attitude, while polymathy is expressing that openness through actual behaviors. Essentially, this is their relationship: an attitude or personality trait versus behavior dyad. They are similar ideas but different; for instance, someone may be open to experiences but never actually engage in them, and as a result, never become polymathic.

This recommendation may represent a contribution to the literature, as well, as it attempts to explain the relationship between openness to experience and polymathy. To date, there has been no other research that attempts to explain the relationship between openness to experience and polymathy. (As a general rule, there has been very little research done on polymathy at all.)

While openness to experience is personality trait or an attitude, polymathy is expressing that openness through actual behaviors; they are interrelated. One way of further studying this relationship would be to measure Openness to Experience in polymaths and compare how they are rated, on average, compared to the general population. This would provide further support, besides the qualitative evidence found through this research, that polymaths are high in openness to experience. If this evidence was not found, this would also be a useful finding to further explore if and how openness to experience is related, or not, with polymathy. Polymathy, in general, is an area for future study, and this would just be another possible avenue to pursue to understand polymathy more.

Recommendation 8: Study different subcategories of polymaths that may exist (i.e., which types of polymaths are most appropriate for leadership positions or

not?). It may be the case that under the umbrella term, "polymath," there are different types of polymaths that exist. It is unclear at this time what those types may be exactly, but it is worth studying further to confirm if subtypes do exist, and if so, what they are. Names should be assigned as well as explanations describing each type, with evidence to support the different categories.

Recommendation 9: Study polymaths who may not be as educated, accomplished, or as elite as those who were part of this study but who are skilled and capable in other still important ways. This study focused on finding highly accomplished polymaths; the idea was to find the most extreme examples of polymathy in an attempt to identify the clearest themes among them—to really understand the experience of very strong polymaths. However, that is not to say that polymathy cannot and does not exist in more everyday forms. There may be individuals with little formal education, but who are still very learned and capable of doing many different types of things. There may be people whose polymathic tendencies shows up on a construction site or a beauty salon. Polymathy does not only exist among the elite, and more work should be done to elucidate their stories and experiences. Polymathy is not just the elite. There are many polymaths in our society who we need to recognize and support.

Recommendations from Study Participants

Throughout the course of the 13 interviews, there were a number of recommendations that participants themselves gave related to the educational system and family life. In an effort to recognize their ideas and contributions, those specific recommendations are summarized in the below table.

Table 5-2: Summary of Recommendations From Study Participants

	Recommendations
For Practice	**Recommendations for Schools**
	Recommendation 1: Create connections more explicitly between the disciplines to foster a more holistic education.
	Recommendation 2: In the school system, support the development of more polymaths.
	Recommendation for Parents
	Recommendation 1: Encourage children to become lifelong learners to learn broadly throughout the lifespan about a variety of topics that interest the child.
For Research	Recommendation 1. Study the role of childhood security in polymaths.
	Recommendation 2: Explore parental influence in the development of polymathy in offspring.

For Practice

In this section, recommendations are broken down into three categories: first, recommendations for schools, and secondly, recommendations for parents.

Recommendations for Schools

Recommendation 1: Create connections more explicitly between the disciplines to foster a more holistic education. Many of the interview participants said that the development of their polymathy would have been easier and felt more supported if connections were made more explicitly between different classes they took in school. A liberal arts education is an attempt to allow a learner to sample a variety of classes in different areas. The same is true for elementary, middle, and high schools in the United States (and likely elsewhere). Subject areas exist in relative silos, without linkages made between them.

More connectivity would advance systems thinking and perhaps polymathy itself: "Advancing the practice of integrative thinking entails realizing the principle of connectivity: that all things (data, information, knowledge, wisdom, ideas, experience, events, etc.) can be integrated to increase their meaning, purpose, and usefulness" (Siler, 2011, p. 419). A successful example of this is the *ArtScience Program for Realizing Human Potential* which was created in 1994 and integrates the arts and sciences by applying various methods of inquiry, critical thinking, problem solving approaches, and collaboration skills to meet modern day challenges (Siler, 2011).

There are a variety of ways to create these sorts of interdisciplinary connections. For example, one way of making linkages more between subjects is for educators to use information students already understand, and somehow relate it to something different they are trying to help the student to learn. In fact, prior experiences are the basis on which learners construct new information (Merriam, Caffarella, & Baumgartner, 2007; Mezirow, 1995; Pillay, 1998). As such, learning and development professionals at all levels should also encourage a wide variety of experiences for learners to engage in, even those outside the classroom. This will enrich the learner's internal database of experiences to draw lessons, information, and enrichment from, and may subsequently help in the learning process in other areas as well, as linkages between prior experiences and new information can be made to assist in the learning process. As Shavinina (2013) said, "Parents and teachers should also encourage the gifted to develop their talents to the fullest extent in all possible areas of human endeavor" (p. 62).

Recommendation 2: In the school system, support the development of more polymaths. Several different interviewees recommended that the school system support the development of more polymaths. Educators should make polymathy a topic of discussion more explicitly throughout the educational process beginning with elementary school; educational institutions should facilitate discussions around polymathy more with students. Sadly, most people have never heard of the term polymath and may have never really thought about it. What if children were taught what a polymath is and what it means? What if we lived in a culture where instead of asking children what they want to be when they grow up (which implies picking one profession), we asked them instead, "What different things do you want to be when you grow up?" Or "What combination of things do you want to have for jobs when you are older?" "Do you think you would enjoy being a polymath?" This sort of change in paradigm might help inform a youngster's thinking around what is possible for them in their life as they mature.

In fact, authors Beghetto and Kaufman (2009) argue that everyone has multicreative potential. "Although we acknowledge that eminent…forms of polymathy are rare, we maintain that everyone has multicreative potential—particularly when considered in more everyday activities and vocations" (Beghetto and Kaufman, 2009, p. 42). They believe that the most important question for educators is to ask: "How likely is multicreative expression and how might it be nurtured in schools and classrooms?" (Beghetto and Kaufman, 2009, p. 40).

Imagine what the world would be like if polymathy was identified as something young people could strive for, if it was discussed, and students were given the tools to explore their own potential polymathy. The University of

Southern California's *Academy for Polymathic Study* is a great example of this sort of effort, but more universities and learning institutions should follow suit. Imagine if polymathy was more consciously nurtured among the masses. Imagine if more teachers themselves were polymaths. Imagine the impact that a polymath like Da Vinci made. What if there were thousands of Da Vincis? The educational system should do more to support the development of polymaths for the benefits this brings the students as well as society more largely.

For Parents

Recommendation 1: Encourage children to become lifelong learners to learn broadly throughout the lifespan about a variety of topics that interest the child. During interviews, several participants spoke about the significant role that their parents played in the development of their polymathy. Parents should encourage their children to learn about things they are interested in, and to self-direct their own unique learning journeys. Based on what participants shared, it appears the best thing a parent could do to support the development of polymathy is to simply support the child learning about what interests them without trying to direct the child's learning too much towards any one thing or in any specific direction. If the child seems interested in something, be open to learning about it with him/her or at a minimum, supporting their own independent exploration.

For Research

Recommendation 1: Study the role of childhood security in polymaths. A number of participants felt that it was due to both nature and nurture that they became polymaths, though they were not completely sure how to explain this belief. They did describe, on the whole, having supportive parents, however. Secure attachment has been shown to help create a sense of confidence in individuals to go and explore the world (Bowlby, 1988). Since being a polymath requires a certain amount of bravery and confidence to explore multiple arenas (which is harder to do than exploring or having a career in just one), it may be worth better understanding how polymaths got to be secure and confident enough to traverse life in this fashion. Is polymathy rooted in early childhood development? Are children who have secure attachments more likely to develop into adult polymaths, or is this not the case? Understanding if secure attachment is a precursor to polymathy would enrich our understanding of the importance of secure attachment in early life and shed light on some of the necessary ingredients that help to support the development of polymaths later in life. The relationship between polymath confidence as an adult and secure attachment as a child is an area for further exploration.

Recommendation 2: Explore parental influence in the development of polymathy in offspring. All participants talked about how their parents and/or primary caregivers impacted their polymathy. Does a person usually become a mix of two parents to some degree? If so, then having parents who are opposite might be a way that polymathy becomes more likely to show up in offspring. Could it be that two parents with opposite skill sets widens the gene pool and allows for more intrapersonally diverse children? Could it be that having parents who are totally different exposes a child to more ideas, more possibilities, showing up in their environment? Could the old saying "opposites attract" be mother nature's way of encouraging the creation of people with polymathic potential, from both genetic and environmental standpoints? Intrapersonal diversity exists in bodies (i.e., in the gut microbiome) that adds to the health of the body; does intrapersonal diversity in terms of capabilities also add to the health of a personality in some ways? Is polymathy nature's way of ensuring survival ("survival of the fittest")? Further investigation into the relationship between polymathy in offspring and traits in their parents would be useful for future research on this subject. As it relates, it may be just happenstance, but most (though not all) participants in this study seem to have come from families with parents who did not divorce. Quite a few participants said that their dad would show them, engage with them, teach them about some technical area of expertise. So along these same lines of studying parental influence in polymaths more deeply, another area for further study would be to look at the role that fathers play, specifically, in the development of children with broad minds and diverse skillsets. Are children who grow up in a household with their father involved more likely to develop polymathic traits than those who do not have a father engaging with them? This would be an interesting avenue to pursue to see what might be found there.

Concluding Remarks

Human Potential

In many ways, the story of polymaths is a story about human potential in its broadest form. It is about people who choose the breadth in their personhood rather than restriction. Indeed, a polymath is not constrained by narrow fields of study but rather has a deep curiosity, finding almost everything interesting and worthy of understanding. Polymaths strive for mastery in themselves. They are daring curators of their own unique, full lives.

Inspiration for This Research

The inspiration for conducting this research came out of my own fascination with people who pursue the fullness of their potential, who have a zest for life, have a growth mindset, and try to make the most of their human experience; I aspire to be this sort of person myself. In retrospect, my early life felt quite limited—I was educated early on in what felt like a small bubble—but once I was in college, I was more broadly exposed to various types of thinking, different types of people, to other international cultures, to different cuisines, and just to generally different ways of being, thinking, and experiencing the world. This is probably a common occurrence for many young people who experience college as a time of expansion. It was at that time, in my late teenage years, that I came to develop a deep appreciation for soaking in the fullness of life in all its variety. I credit professor Eric Trules at the University of Southern California for planting the seed and encouraging me to try new things, just for the sake of having new experiences. However, for many years, I did not have any word to place upon what it was I was striving towards; now I know what I was wishing to someday become was a polymath.

Polymathy Should Become Part of Societal Discourse

Regrettably, polymathy is not currently part of discourse in American society much, and polymathy is not adequately appreciated nor understood. Polymaths are rarely even acknowledged. In my experience, most people do not even know the word "polymath." Many polymaths struggle with their identity as such, and I believe this is due in large part to the lack of conversation around the phenomenon. This is unfortunate, and hopefully this will change at some point in the future.

Polymaths Are Well Suited to Face Modern Problems & Enrich Society

Polymaths on the whole are remarkable people; some of them are also wonderfully suited to meet the demands of our time. We live in a world that is becoming increasingly connected, complex, and chaotic. Polymaths who are positioned at the intersection of different fields can help bridge the gap between them, acting as a sort of translator and forging new insights and innovations in the process due to their varied aptitudes. Polymaths can add great value to the world. As shown throughout this dissertation, polymaths can bring disparate fields together, in concert, and develop unique insights as a result. Their broadness can help inform problems they face personally as well as professionally. Polymathy is a valuable trait, and polymaths possess a large toolkit of skills as they navigate life.

Both Monomaths and Polymaths Have Value

Being a polymath is not better than not being one; everyone has the right to select and work towards the type of person they want to become. Both narrow, deep specialist experts and polymaths have a place in our society. Polymaths are not superior to non-polymaths. Narrow specialists may also get deep joy and satisfaction and may also add tremendous value to society through that path. Truth be told, being a polymath does not guarantee success nor happiness; in fact, several participants of this study talked about struggling with depression. But certainly, both approaches—being a narrow specialist expert or being a broad polymath—have value, although in our society, polymaths are not adequately appreciated for the insights and skills they can offer while narrow specialists are valued and lauded. It is precisely this imbalance that is problematic.

Intrapersonal Diversity as a Tool to Support Intergroup Diversity

The kind of intrapersonal diversity this dissertation has focused on is very different from traditional notions of diversity, which are typically focused on the oppression of certain ethnic groups or unfair gender biases. Although these kinds of diversity are qualitatively different – one about individuals becoming broader-minded with a wide variety of work and life experiences, the other about trying to provide equal access and opportunity to entire groups of people regardless of their sex or race—there is a possible relationship between the two.

For example, could racial separations and tensions be alleviated if individuals from different racial groups were able to bond over experiences they have in common? Imagine a scenario where a black man and a white man meet for the first time and are learning about one another. If they are able to find a common interest, similar hobby, or another way of connecting over something they have in common, how might this affect their ability to relate to one another and to connect over their commonalties, instead of focusing on the differences between them? Imagine an alternative scenario where these two men meet, and they cannot find anything they have in common. It is likely that the difference between them will be validated, reinforced, and perpetuated, which does not help race relations at all, in my view.

I am not suggesting that simply sharing a common hobby is a way to solve hegemonic forces impacting race relations in our society. What I do wonder, however, is if on an individual, personal basis, intrapersonal diversity—as a tool for commonality and connection with others who are also intrapersonally broad—might help make positive strides somehow in the larger context. It is simply a tool that allows us to focus on what we have in common as people, instead of emphasizing what makes us different which can sometimes serve to create a further divide.

Indeed, striving to be an intrapersonally diverse person is a way to expand parts of one's personhood, which makes it easier to connect with other people based on common experiences, knowledge, or interests. It provides a way to bridge the gap between social constructions of difference. In fact, one of the polymath's greatest strength is their ability to find something in common and connect with nearly anybody.

What if more people were polymaths, and were able to forge these sorts of connections with more people—spanning all the races? It is possible if society had more quantities of highly intrapersonally diverse people that this would help people from all the races come together more as they find commonalities between themselves rather than focusing on differences?

In other words, more intrapersonally diverse people provides a foundation for more connection amongst more people. It creates a different kind of "in-group" not based on race, but rather based on their passions—from the heart. However, if people have narrower experiences and mindsets, then the likelihood of connecting with other people who are from a different racial group may be challenging and less likely to occur. In other words, if there was more intrapersonal diversity in the population, this could possibly serve to enhance race relations in this country and elsewhere.

Polymathy and Brain Health

Another possible benefit of polymathy and in general, lifelong learning, is that it is actually good for brain health. Studies have shown (Baroncelli, et al., 2010) that continual learning and having enriching experiences actually enhances brain plasticity and helps to ward off Alzheimer's Disease and dementia, as well as a whole host of other neurological disorders. It seems then that expanding one's intrapersonal diversity is a way to enhance not only one's capabilities and perhaps confidence, but also possibly brain health. "Strong correlative and epidemiological evidence shows that lifestyle, including occupation, leisure activities and physical exercise, has a direct effect on the risk of cognitive decline. Results indicate that a higher level and ***variety*** (emphasis added) of mental and physical activity is associated with a lower cognitive decline and a reduced risk for dementia. These results encourage stronger efforts in the application of EE [environmental enrichment] paradigms, alone or in combination with pharmacological treatments, for the therapy of neurological disorders" (Baroncelli et al., 2010, p. 1099).

Regarding The Future of Work

As we consider the future of work in the modern world, I believe that we should think about how we can develop and support more polymaths. This is a way to better deal with unforeseen factors of a certainly complex future. We should think about how we can develop polymaths more largely in both the school system and in industry as well. Although, despite this fact, in the internet age, where information is readily available and virtually free, anyone with a desire to learn and the discipline to do it can develop their own polymathy.

What is true for anybody is that the more tools we have in our toolkit, the better prepared we will be to face the challenges that lie ahead. This is particularly relevant in the 21st century, as industries themselves continue to overlap and impact one another, creating new career fields in the process that can benefit from multidisciplinary expertise. Whereas in the past, jobs were situated within siloed industries, jobs of the future may very well be more and more at the intersections, where innovation can occur. In that world, polymaths are in a unique position to add value, where their cross-disciplinary expertise is needed. Said differently, there is reason to believe that the job market of the future will be a job market that may demand polymaths. We should prepare for this eventuality by fostering the fullest possible development of more polymaths wherever possible, whether through education or professional practice.

Polymaths Are an Untapped Resource

However, understanding polymathy is mostly a nascent field of study and polymaths themselves are an untapped resource to push humanity forward. What will the world look like when this is no longer the case? I believe a world with better understanding of polymaths and more of them will be a better world. Much remains to be seen, but one thing is certain: polymathy is a route to understanding the world we live in more broadly and helping support innovations across myriad fields; it is a worthy pursuit to understand and support the development of more polymaths so we, as a society, and reap the rewards that polymaths offer.

Anybody Can Express Polymathic Values

For anyone reading this who may think becoming a polymath is too much, too arduous, too daunting but who are intrigued by the idea, consider efforts to simply move in that direction, to become more polymathic, to express polymathic values. Anybody can decide to expose themselves to broader experiences and ideas on purpose to enhance their life and capacities; this can be considered a life-design process (Setlhare-Meltor & Wood, 2015). People are "constantly in the process of change and development" (Ornstein, 1993, p. 8), so it is worth considering how individuals can proactively, consciously choose what they are exposed to which may cause them to change and develop further.

In other words, people can choose to design who they become, on purpose. Of course, "Life experiences have a profound effect on the cultivation of the self," and it is therefore worth considering "how can one guide one's life to enhance one's development" (Ornstein, 1993, p. 9) and how we can "remake ourselves through conscious choice, even in adulthood" (Ornstein, 1993, p. 12). Polymaths remind us that through curating our lives with an open mind and conscious choice, by choosing to learn, experience, and expand, we can give rise to our fullest, most authentic selves.

References

Abd-El-Fattah, S. (2010). Garrison's model of self-directed learning: Preliminary validation and relationship to academic achievement. *The Spanish Journal of Psychology*, 13, p. 586-596.

Albert, M., Laberge, S., Hodges, B.D., Regehr, G., and Lingard, L. (2008). Biomedical scientists' perception of the social sciences in health research. *Social Science and Medicine*, 66(12), p. 2520-2531.

Amabile, T. (1983). The social psychology of creativity: A componential conceptualization. *Journal of Personality and Social Psychology*, 45, p. 357-377.

Amabile, T. (1996). *Creativity in context.* Boulder, CO: Westview.

Angriawan A. and Adebe M. (2001). Chief executive background characteristics and environmental scanning emphasis: an empirical investigation. *Journal of Business Strategies,* 28, pp. 75-96.

Arbesman, S. (2013). Let's bring the polymath—and the dabblers—back. *Wired.* Retried on July 23, 2017 from https://www.wired.com/2013/12/165191/.

Bantel, K. and Jackson, S. (1989). Top management and innovations in banking: Does the composition of the top team make a difference? *Strategic Management Journal*, 10 (Supplemental 1), p. 107-124.

Barczak, G., Lassk, F., and Mulki, J. (2010). Antecedents of team creativity: An examination of team emotional intelligence, team trust and collaborative culture. *Creativity and Innovation Management,* 19, p. 332-345.

Baroncelli, L, Braschi, C., Spolidoro, M., Begenisic, T., Sale, A., and Maffei, L. (2010).

Nurturing brain plasticity: Impact of environmental enrichment. *Cell Death and Differentiation*, 17, p. 1092–1103

Baumeister, R. & Leary, M. (1995). The need to belong: desire for interpersonal attachments as a fundamental human motivation. *Psychological Bulletin*, 117(3), p. 497-529.

Baveye, P., Palfreyman, J., & Otten, W. (2014). Research efforts involving several disciplines: Adherence to a clear nomenclature is needed. *Water Air Soil Pollution,* 225, p. 1-5.

Beghetto, R. & Kaufman, J. (2009). Do we all have multicreative potential? *Mathematics and Education*, 41, p. 39-44.

Bhat, P. P., Rajashekar, B. B., & Kamath, U. (2007). Perspectives on self-directed learning—the importance of attitudes and skills. *Bioscience Education e-Joumal.* doi: 10.3108/beej.l0.c3

Bing M. and Lounsbury J. (2000). Openness and job performance in U.S.-based Japanese manufacturing companies. *Journal of Business and Psychology*, 14, pp. 515-522.

Bloom, B. (1985). Developing talent in young people. New York: Ballantine Books.

Boden M. (2004). *Creative Mind: Myths and Mechanisms*, 2nd Edn. London: Routledge.

Boisot, M. (1998). *Knowledge assets: Securing competitive advantage in the information economy.* New York, NY: Oxford University Press.

Bowlby, J. (1988). A secure base: Clinical applications of attachment theory. New York: Routeldge.

Brockett, R. (1983). Self-directed learning and the hard-to-reach adult. *Lifelong learning: The adult years,* 6(8), p. 16-18.

Brockman, B. and Morgan, R. (2003). The role of existing knowledge in new product innovativeness and performance. *Decision Sciences*, 34(2), p. 385-419.

Bryant, S. (2005). The impact of peer mentoring on organizational knowledge creation and sharing: an empirical study in a software firm. *Group and Organization Management*, 30(3), p. 319-338.

Bunderson, J. and Sutcliffe, K. (2002). Comparing alternative conceptualizations of functional diversity in management teams: Process and performance effects. *Academy of Management Journal*, 45(5), pp. 875-893.

Burke, L.A. and Steensma, H.K. (1998). Toward a model for relating executive career experiences and firm performance. *Journal of Managerial Issues,* 10, pp. 86-102.

Burke, L., and Witt, L. (2002). Moderators of the openness to experience-performance relationship. *Journal of Managerial Psychology*, 17(8), p. 712-721.

Caffarella, R. (1993). 'Self-directed learning,' in S. Merriam (ed.) *An Update on Adult Learning Theory: New Directions in Adult and Continuing Education,* San Francisco: Jossey-Bass.

Cahoon, B. (1995). Computer skill learning in the workplace: a comparative case study. *Dissertation Abstracts International*, 56/05A, 1622 (UMI No. AAI9531174).

Campion, M.A., Cheraskin, L., and Stevens, M.J. (1994). Career-related antecedents and outcomes of job rotation. *Academy of Management Journal*, 37, pp. 1518-1542.

Candy, P.C. (1991). *Self-direction for lifelong learning: A comprehensive guide to theory and practice.* San Francisco: Jossey-Bass.

Cannella, A., Park, J., and Lee, H. (2008). Top management team functional background diversity and firm performance: Examining the roles of team member colocation and environmental uncertainty. *Academy of Management Journal,* 51(4), pp. 768-784.

Chamorro-Premuzic, T. (2014). Curiosity as important as intelligence. *Harvard Business Review*, retrieved from https://hbr.org/2014/08/curiosity-is-as-important-as-intelligence on February 24, 2017.

Chemg-Jyh, Y., & Simon, L. (2009). Learner autonomy as a predictor of course success and final grades in community college online courses. *Journal of Educational Computing Research*, 41, p. 347-367.

Chiocchio, F., Kelloway, E.K., and Hobbs, B., (2015). *The Psychology and Management of Project Teams.* Oxford, England: Oxford University Press.

Choi, B. and Pak, A. (2006). Multidisciplinarity, interdisciplinarity and transdisciplinarity in health research, services, education, and policy: Definitions, objectives, and evidence of effectiveness. *Clinical and investigative medicine*, 29(6), p. 351-364.

Colquitt, J. and George, G. (2011). Publishing in AMJ: Topic choice. *Academy of Management Journal*, 54(3), p. 432-435.

Cooley, C. (1902). *Human nature and social order.* New York: Scribners.

Cranefield, P. (1966). The philosophical and cultural interests of the biophysics movement of 1847. *Journal of the History of Medicine,* 21, p. 1 – 7.

Creswell, J. (2007). *Qualitative inquiry and research design: Choosing among five traditions*. Thousand Oaks, CA: Sage Publications, Inc.

Creswell, J. W. (2013). *Qualitative inquiry & research design: Choosing among five approaches* (3rd edition). Thousand Oaks, CA: Sage.

Creswell, J. (2014). *Research Design: Qualitative, quantitative, and mixed methods approaches* (4th edition). Thousand Oaks, CA: Sage.

Crotty, M. (1998). The foundations of social research: Meaning and perspective in the research process. Allen & Unwin, St Leonards, NSW.

Csikszentmihalyi, M. (1996). *Creativity, flow, and the psychology of discovery and invention.* New York: Harper Perennial.

Da Vinci, L. (2013). *Leonardo's Notebooks: Writing and Art of the Great Master.* New York: Hachette Books

Danis, C. (1992). Advances in research and practice in self-directed learning. In G.J. Confessore & S.U. Confessore (Eds.), *Guideposts to self-directed learning: Expert commentary on essential concepts* (p. 160-174). King of Prussia, PA: Organization Design and Development.

Day, D. and Dragoni, L. (2015). Leadership development: An outcome-oriented review based on time and level of analysis. *Annual Review of Organizational Psychology and Organizational Behavior*, 2, pp. 133-156.

De Jong, R., Velde, M., Jansen, P. (2001). Openness to experience and growth need strength as moderators between job characteristics and satisfaction. *International Journal of Selection and Assessment,* 9 (4).

Dewey, J. (1916). *Democracy and Education.* New York: The Macmillan Company.

Erikson, E. (1950). *Childhood and society*. New York: W. W. Norton.

Erikson, E. (1963). *Childhood and society.* (2nd ed.). New York, NY: Norton.

Feist, G. (1998). A meta-analysis of personality in scientific and artistic creativity. *Personality and Social Psychology Review,* 2, p. 290-309.

Feist, G. and Barron, F. (2003). Predicting creativity from early to late adulthood: Intellect, potential, and personality. Journal of Research in Personality, 37, p. 62-88.

Freire, P. (1968). *Pedagogy of the oppressed.* New York: Herder and Herder.

Fromm, E. (1955). *The Sane Society.* London: Routledge Classics.

Garrison, D.R. (1997). Self-directed learning: Toward a comprehensive model. *Adult Education Quarterly*, 48(1), p. 18-33.

George, J. and Zhou, J. (2001). When openness to experience and conscientiousness are related to creative behavior: An interactional approach. *Journal of Applied Psychology*, 86, p. 513-524.

Gheorghe, S., Dinu, V., & Laurentiu, T. (2014). An inter-, trans-, cross- and multidisciplinary approach to higher education in the field of business studies. *Amfiteatru Economic,* 16 (37), p. 707-725.

Gibson, C., Folley, B. and Park, S. (2009). Enhanced divergent thinking and creativity in musicians: A behavioral and near-infrared spectroscopy study. *Brain and Cognition*, 69, p. 162-169.

Goldstein, K. (1939). *The Organism: A holistic approach to biology derived from pathological data in men.* Salt Lake City, UT: American Book Publishing.

Grant, R. (1997). The knowledge based view of the firm: Implications for management practice. Long Range Planning, 30(3), p. 450-454.

Guglielmino (1977). "Reliability and validity of the self-directed learning readiness scale and the learning preference assessment (LPA)." In H.B. Long and associates (eds), *Expanding Horizons in Self-Directed Learning.* Norman: Public Managers Center, University of Oklahoma.

Guglielmino, L. (2008). Why self-directed learning? *International Journal of Self-Directed Learning*, 5(1), p. 1-14.

Harding, T. (2010). Fostering creativity for leadership and leading change. *Arts Education Policy Review*, 111(2), p. 51 – 53.

Harrison, D. and Klein, K. (2007). What's the difference? Diversity constructs as separation, variety, or disparity in organizations. *Academy of Management Review*, Vol. 32(4), pp. 1199-1228.

Helson, R., Roberts, B., and Agronick, G. (1995). Enduringness and change in creative personality and the prediction of occupational creativity. *Journal of Personality and Social Psychology*, Vol. 69(9), pp. 1173-1183.

Hitt, M.A. and Tyler, B.B. (1991). Strategic decision models: Integrating different perspectives. *Strategic Management Journal*, 12, pp. 327-351.

Hogg, M. & Abrams, D. (1988). *Social identifications: A social psychology of intergroup relations and group processes.* London: Routledge.

Hogg, M., Terry, D., & White, K. (1995). A tale of two theories: A critical comparison of identity theory with social identity theory. *Social Psychology Quarterly*, 58(4), p. 255-269.

Houle, C. (1961). *The Inquiring Mind.* Madison: University of Wisconsin Press.

Huckman, R. and Staats, B. (2011). Fluid tasks and fluid teams: The impact of diversity in experience and team familiarity on team performance. *Manufacturing and Service Operations Management*, 13(3), pp. 310-328.

Huxley, Aldous. Lecture entitled Integrated Education, 1959, Santa Barbara, CA. Retrieved from http://brobjerg.net/docs/wp-content/uploads/2015/07/19590209Integrateeducation.pdf

Ibarra, H. (2005). Identity transitions: Possible selves, liminality, and the dynamics of career change. INSEAD Working Paper. Fountainebleau, France: INSEAD.

Ivcevic, Z. and Brackett, M. (2015). Predicting creativity: Interactive effects of openness to experience and emotion regulation ability. *Psychology of Aesthetics, Creativity, and the Arts*, 9(4), p. 480-487.

Ivcevic, Z. & Mayer, J. (2006). Creative types and personality. *Imagination, Cognition and Personality,* 26(1-2), p. 65-86.

Jarvis, P. (1987). *Adult learning in the social context.* London: Croom Helm.

Jones, B. (2009). The burden of knowledge and the 'death of the renaissance man': Is innovation getting harder? *The Review of Economic Studies*, 76(1), p. 283-317.

Judge, T., Bono, J., Ilies, R., and Gerhardt, M. (2002). Personality and leadership: A qualitative and quantitative review. *Journal of Applied Psychology*, 87, p. 765-780.

Kaufman, J., Beghetto, R., Bae, J., and Ivcevic, Z. (2010). Creativity polymathy: What Benjamin Franklin can teach your kindergartener. *Learning from Individual Differences,* 20, p. 380-387.

Kickul, J. and Neuman, G. (2000). Emergent leadership behaviors: The function of personality and cognitive ability in determining teamwork performance and KSAs. Journal of Business and Psychology, 15(1), pp. 27-51.

Kolb, D. (2015). Experiential learning: Experience as the source of learning and development. New Jersey: Pearson FT Press.

Knight, D., Pearce, C.L., Smith, K.G., Olian, J.D., Sims, H.P. Smith, K.A., Flood, P. (1999). Top management team diversity, group process, and strategic consensus. Strategic Management Journal, vol. 20, pp. 445-465.

Knowles, M. (1975). *Self-directed learning: A guide for learners and teachers.* Chicago: Follett.

Lang, R. (2014). The protean scholar and multi-disciplinary polymath: Lessons from Michael Polanyi. Available at: https://villasophiasalon.wordpress.com/2014/01/19/the -protean-scholar-multidisciplinary-polymath. Accessed February 1, 2017.

Leahey, E. (2007). Not by productivity alone: How visibility and specialization contribute to academic earnings. *American Sociological Review*, 72(4), p. 533-561.

Leahey, E., Keith, B., and Crockett, J. (2010). Specialization and promotion in an academic discipline. *Research in Social Stratification and Mobility*, 28(2), p. 135-155.

Levi, D. (2001). *Group dynamics for teams. Thousand Oaks: Sage Publications.*

Lindesmith, A. & Strauss, A. (1956). *Social Psychology.* New York: Holt, Rinehart and Winston.

Locke, L., Spirduso, W., & Silverman, S. (2013). *Proposals that work: A guide for planning dissertations and grant proposals* (6th ed.). Thousand Oaks, CA: Sage.

Lounsbury, J. W., Levy, L. J., Park, S., Gibson, L. W., & Smith, R. (2009). An investigation of the construct validity of the personality trait of self-directed learning. *Learning and Individual Differences*, 19, p. 411-418.

MacLachlan, M. (2009). Rethinking global health research: Towards integrative expertise. *Globalization and Health,* 5(6).

Manson, S. (2001). Simplifying complexity: a review of complexity theory. *Geoforum*, 32, p. 405-414.

Martindale, C. (1989). Personality, situation, and creativity. In: Handbook of Creativity. New York: Springer, pp. 211 – 232.

Maslow, A. (1970). *Motivation and Personality.* New York: Harper and Row.

Maxwell, J. (2005). *Qualitative research design: An interactive approach.* (2nd ed.). Thousand Oaks, CA: Sage.

McCrae, R. (1987). Creativity, divergent thinking, and openness to experience. *Journal of Personality and Social Psychology*, 52(6), p. 1258-1265.

McCrae, R. (1994). Openness to experience: Expanding the boundaries of factor V. *European Journal of Personality*. Vol. 8(4), pp. 251-272.

McCrae, R. and Costa, P. (1997). Conceptions and correlates of openness to experience. In R. Hogan, J. Johnson, and S. Briggs (Eds.), Handbook of personality psychology. San Diego, CA: Academic Press.

McCreary, E. (1990). Three behavioral models for computer-mediated communication. *Online Education: Perspectives on a New Environment* (Ed.), p. 117-130. New York: Praeger.

McElroy, T. and Dowd, E. (2007). Susceptibility to anchoring effects: How openness-to-experience influences responses to anchoring cues. *Judgment and Decision Making*, 2(1), p. 48-53.

McWilliam, E. (2008). *The creative workforce: How to launch young people into high-flying futures.* Sydney: University of New South Wales Press.

Mead, G. (1934). *Mind, self, and society: From the standpoint of a social behaviorist*, edited and with an introduction by C.W. Morris. Chicago: University of Chicago Press.

Merriam, S. B. (2009). Qualitative research: A guide to design and implementation. San Francisco: Jossey-Bass.

Merriam, S.B., Caffarella, R.S., & Baumgartner, L.M. (2007). *Learning in adulthood: A comprehensive guide* (3rd ed.). San Francisco: Jossey-Bass.

Mieg, H., Bedenk, S., Braun, A., and Neyer, F. (2012). How emotional stability and openness to experience support invention: A study with German independent inventors. *Creativity Research Journal*, 24(2-3), p. 200-207.

Merriam, S. & Tisdell, E. (2016). *Qualitative Research: A guide to design and implementation* (4th Edition). San Francisco, CA: Jossey-Bass.

Mezirow, J. (1985). A critical theory of self-directed learning, *New Directions for Continuing Education,* 25, p. 17-30.

Mezirow, J. (1995). Transformation theory of adult learning. In M. R. Welton (Ed.) In defense of the lifeworld: Critical perspectives on adult learning (p. 39-70). New York: State University of New York Press.

Moustakas, C. (1994). *Phenomenological research methods.* Thousand Oaks, CA: Sage Publications.

Myers, M. (2008). *Qualitative research in business & management.* Los Angeles: CA Sage Publications.

Naisbitt, N. (1984). *Megatrends: Ten new directions transforming our lives.* London: Macdonald.

Nobel, 2002. The Sveriges Riksbank Prize in Economic Sciences in Memory of Alfred Nobel 2002: Daniel Kahneman, Vernon L. Smith. Available at http://www.nobelprize.org/ nobel_prizes/economic-sciences/laureates/2002/Accessed February 23, 2017.

O'Neill, J. and McGinley, S. (2014). Operations research from 1913 to 2013: The Ford assembly line to hospitality industry innovation, *International Journal of Contemporary Hospitality Management,* 26(5), p. 663-678.

Oakes, D.W., Ferris, G.R., Martocchio, J.J., Buckley, M.R., and Broach D. (2001). Cognitive ability and personality predictors of training program skill acquisition and job performance. *Journal of Business and Psychology*, 15(4), pp. 523-548.

Oldham, G. (2002). Stimulating and supporting creativity in organizations. In S.E. Jackson, M.A. Hitt and A.S. DeNisi (Eds.), *Managing knowledge for sustained competitive advantage* (p. 243-273). San Francisco: Jossey-Bass.

Olakitan, O. (2011). An examination of the impact of selected personality traits on the innovative behavior of entrepreneurs in Nigeria. *International Business Management*, 3(2), p. 112-121.

Orlikowski, W. & Baroudi, J. (1991). Studying Information technology in organizations: Research approaches and assumptions. *Information Systems Research, 2, p. 1 – 28.*

Ornstein, R. (1993). *The roots of the self.* New York: Harper Collins.

Owen, T. (2002). *Self-directed learning in adulthood: A literature review.* (Report number CE 082822). Morehead, KY: Morehead State University. (ERIC Document Reproduction Services No. ED 441000).

Park, M.H., Lim, J.W. and Birnbaum-More, P. (2009). The effect of multi-knowledge individuals on performance in cross-functional new product development teams. *The Journal of Product Innovation Management,* 26, pp. 86-96.

Pillay, H. (1998). Adult learning in a workplace context. In P. Sutherland (Ed.), *Adult learning: A reader* (p. 122-134). Sterling, VA: Kogan Page.

Polymath. In the British Dictionary. Retrieved February 24, 2017 from http://www.dictionary.com/browse/polymath

Richardson, J. (2005). Leonardo: why the inventor failed to innovate. *Foresight: The Journal of Futures Studies, Strategic Thinking, and Policy*, 7(5), p. 56-62.

Roberson, Q. (2013). *Oxford handbook of diversity and work.* New York: Oxford University Press.

Robinson, A. (2005). A polymath's dilemma. *Nature*, 438, p. 291.

Robinson, A. (2006). Everyone hates a know-all. *Nature,* 441, p. 409.

Rogers, J. (1989). *Adults learning* (4th ed.). Philadelphia: Open University Press.

Root-Bernstein, R. (2015). Arts and crafts as adjuncts to STEM education to foster creativity in gifted and talented students. *Asia Pacific Education*, 16, p. 203-212.

Root-Bernstein, R. (2009). Polymathy. In B. Kerr (Ed.)., *Encyclopedia of giftedness, creativity and talent* (p. 685-687). New York: Sage.

Root-Bernstein, R., Allen, L, and Beach, L., et al. (2008). Arts foster scientific success: Avocations of Nobel, National Academy, Royal Society and Sigma Xi Members. *Journal of Psychology and Science and Technology*, 1(2), p. 51-63.

Root-Bernstein, R., Bernstein, M., & Garnier, H. (1995). Correlations between avocations, scientific style, and professional impact of thirty-eight scientists of the Eiduson Study. *Creativity Research Journal*, 8, p. 115-137.

Rosenberg, J. (2015). How Google Manages Talent [Interview]. Retrieved from https://hbr.org/2014/09/how-google-manages-talent on February 24, 2017.

Ross, C. (2011). "Trying all things": Romantic polymaths, social factors, and the legacies of a rhetorical education. *Texas Studies in Literature and Language*, 53(4), p. 401-430.

Rossing, B.E. & Long, H.B. (1981). Contributions of curiosity and relevance to adult learning motivation. *Adult Education,* 32(1), p. 25-36.

Rulke, D.L. (1996). Member selection strategy and team performance: Cognitive integration vs. social integration in cross-functional teams. *Academy of Management Best Paper Proceedings*, pp. 424-428.

Saldana, J. (2009). *The coding manual for qualitative research*. Thousand Oaks, CA: Sage.

SavinBaden, M. & Major, C.H. (2004). *Foundations of problem-based learning.* Berkshire: SRHE & Open University Press.

Schachtel, E. (1959). *Metamorphosis: On the development of affect, perception, attention, and memory.* New York: Basic Books.

Schilpzand, M., Herold, D., and Shalley, C. (2011). Members' openness to experience and teams' creative performance. *Small Group Research*, 42(1), p. 55-76.

Schmidt, H., Cohen-Schotanus, J., & Arends, L. (2009). Impact of problem-based, active learning on graduation rates for 10 generations of Dutch medical students. *Medical Education*, 43, p. 211-218.

Scott, S. and Bruce, R. (1994). Determinants of innovative behavior: A path model of individual innovation in the workplace. *Academy of Management Journal*, 37, p. 580-607.

Seidman, I. (2013). *Interviewing as qualitative research: A guide for researchers in education and the social sciences*. New York and London: Teachers College Press.

Setlhare-Meltor, R. & Wood, L. (2015). Using life design with vulnerable youth. *The Career Development Quarterly*, 64, pp. 64 – 74.

Shane, S. (1995). Uncertainty avoidance and the preference for innovation championing roles. *Journal of International Business Studies,* 26(1), pp. 47-68.

Shalley, C. and Perry-Smith, J. (2008). The emergency of team creative cognition: The role of diverse outside ties, sociocognitive network centrality, and team evolution. *Strategic Entrepreneurship Journal,* 2, p. 23-41.

Shalley, C, Zhou, J., and Oldham, J. (2004). The effects of personal and contextual characteristics on creativity: Where should we go from here? *Journal of Management,* 30, p. 933-958.

Schutz, A. (1967). *The phenomenology of the social world* (G. Walsh & F. Lenhert, Trans.). Chicago: Northwestern University Press.

Shavinina, L. (2013). How to develop innovators? Innovation education for the gifted. *Gifted Education International,* 29(1), p. 54-68.

Shibayama, S. (2008). Effect of knowledge diversity on technological innovations in scientific research. From a conference called Entrepreneurship and Innovation – Organizations, Institutions, Systems and Regions, Copenhagen, Denmark, June 17 – 20, 2008.

Siler, T. (2011). The ArtScience Program for Realizing Human Potential. Leonardo, 44(5), p. 417-424.

Smith, R. (2014). Leonardo: Bridging the gap. *Research-Technology Management*, 57(1), p. 58-59.

Smith, V. (2008). *Discovery: A memoir.* Bloomington, Indiana: Authorhouse.

Smith, K., Collins, C., and Clark, K. (2005). Existing knowledge, knowledge creation capability and the rate of new product introduction in high-technology firms. *Academy of Management Journal*, 48(2), p. 346-357.

Smith, P., & Morrison, J. (2006). Clinical clerkships: students can structure their own learning. *Medical Education*, 40, p. 884-892.

Spear, G.E. & Mocker, E.W. (1984). The organizing circumstance: Environmental determinants in self-directed learning. *Adult Education Quarterly*, 35(1), p. 1- 10.

Spender, J. (1996). Making knowledge the basis of a dynamic theory of the firm. *Strategic Management Journal*, Vol. 17, special issue (winter), p. 45-63.

Sriraman, B. (2009). A historic overview of the interplay of theology and philosophy in the arts, mathematics and sciences, *Mathematics and Education,* 41, p. 75-86.

Stets, J. & Burke, P. (2000). Identity theory and social identity theory. *Social*

Psychology Quarterly, 63(3), pp. 224-236).

Stryker, S. & Serpe, R. (1982). Commitment, identity salience, and role behavior (p. 199-218) in *Personality, Roles, and Social Behavior,* edited by W. Ickes and E.S. Knowles. New York: Springer-Verlag.

Sung, S. and Choi, J. (2009). Do big five personality factors affect individual creativity? The moderating role of extrinsic motivation. *Social Behavior and Personality,* 37(7), p. 941-956.

Swan, J., Scarbrough, H., and Robertson, M. (2002). The construction of 'communities of practice' in the management of innovation. *Management Learning*, 33(4), p. 477-496.

Taylor, A. and Greve, H. (2006). Superman or the fantastic four? Knowledge combination and experience in innovative teams. *Academy of Management Journal,* 49(4), p. 723-740.

Terjesen, S. and Politis, D. (2015). In Praise of Multidisciplinary Scholarship and the Polymath. *Academy of Management Learning and Education*, 14(2), p. 151-157.

Tetlock, P. and Gardner, D. (2015). *Superforecasting: The art and science of prediction.* New York: Crown Publishers.

Tough, A. (1971). *The adult learning projects: A fresh approach to theory and practice in adult learning.* Toronto, Canada: Ontario Institute for Studies in Education.

Tsoukas, H. and Mylonopoulos, N. (2004). Introduction: Knowledge construction and creation in organizations. British Journal of Management, 15(1), p. 1-8.

Turner, J., Hogg, M. Oakes, P., Reicher, S. & Wetherell, M. (1987). *Rediscovering the social group: A self-categorization theory.* Oxford: Blackwell.

Turner, M., Pratkanis, A., Probasco, P., & Leve, C. (1992). Threat, cohesion, and group effectiveness: Testing a social identity maintenance perspective on groupthink. *Journal of Personality and Social Psychology,* 63(5), p. 781-796.

Uhl-Bien, M., Marion, R., & McKelvey, B. (2007). Complexity leadership theory: Shifting leadership from the industrial age to the knowledge era. *The Leadership Quarterly*, 18, p. 298-318.

Vagle, M. (2014). *Crafting phenomenological research.* Walnut Creek, CA: Left Coast Press.

Van Manen, M. (1990). *Researching lived experience: Human science for an action sensitive pedagogy.* London, Canada: The University of Western Ontario.

Van Manen, M. (2014). *Phenomenology of Practice.* Walnut Creek, CA: Left Coast Press, Inc.

Vissers, G. and Dankbaar, B. (2002). Creativity in multidisciplinary new product development teams. *Creativity and Innovation Management*, 11(1), p. 31-42.

Von Stumm, S., Hellk, B., and Chamorro-Premuzic, T. (2011). The hungry mind: Intellectual curiosity is the third pillar of academic performance. *Perspectives on Psychological Science*, 6(6), p. 574-588.

Vygotsky, L. (1978). *Mind in society.* Cambridge, Massachusetts & London, England: Harvard University Press.

Ward, T. (1995). What's old about new ideas? In S.M. Smith, T. Ward, and R. Finke, (Eds.), *The creative cognition approach*: p. 157-178. Cambridge, MA: MIT Press.

Weick, K. E. (1995). *Sensemaking in organizations* (2nd ed.). Thousand Oaks, CA: Sage.

Wenfu, L., Xueting, L., Huang, L., Kong, X., Yang, W., Wei, D., Li, J., Cheng, H., Zhang, Q., Qiu, J., and Liu, J. (2014). Brain structure links trait creativity to openness to experience. *Social Cognitive and Affective Neuroscience*, 10(2), p. 191-198.

White, H. (2009). Cultivating students' curiosity quotient with problem-based learning. Biochemistry and Molecular Biology Education, 37(4), p. 249.

Whitman, W. (2005). *Walt Whitman's Leaves of grass: The first* (1855) edition. New York: Penguin Books.

Wiens, K. (2012). In defense of polymaths. *Harvard Business Review.*

Wolfradt, U. and Pretz, J. (2001). Individual differences in creativity: Personality, story, writing, and hobbies. *European Journal of Personality*, Vol. 15(4), pp. 297-310.

Yap, C., Chai, K., and Lemaire, P. (2005). An empirical study on functional diversity and innovation in SMEs. *Creativity and Innovation Management*, Vol. 14(2), pp. 176-190.

Yardley, S., Teunissen, P., and Dornan, T. (2012). Experiential learning: Transforming theory into practice. *Medical Teacher,* 34, p. 161-164.

Young, J. &Marzano, M. (2010). Embodied interdisciplinarity: What is the role of polymaths in environmental research? *Environmental Conservation,* 37(4), p. 373-375.

Zhao, H. and Seibert, S. (2006). The Big Five personality dimensions and entrepreneurial status: A meta-analytical review. *Journal of Applied Psychology*, 91, p. 259-271.

Zollo, M. and Winter, S. (2002). Deliberate learning and the evolution of dynamic capabilities. *Organization Science*, 13(3), p. 339-351.

APPENDIX A: SOLICITATION TO PARTICIPATE IN THE STUDY

Angela Cotellessa
(213) 804-5151
ACotellessa@gwmail.gwu.edu

Greetings,

Do you have varied interests and skill sets across disparate domains? Have you had at least two unrelated, totally different career paths? Are you more of a broad generalist as opposed to a narrow specialist in your career? Do your personal hobbies span many subjects requiring different skill sets and/or ways of thinking? When you have been a student, did you study a number of different fields deeply? Do you like to continue learning and growing across various domains of knowledge? Have you achieved a level of success and/or notoriety in two or more domains? If you answered "yes" to all of these questions, you may be a great polymath, more commonly known as a Renaissance person. You're somebody I would love to speak with more!

About me: I am a doctoral student with the George Washington University currently working on my dissertation to get my doctoral degree in Human and Organizational Learning; the dissertation research is the last big, final step in order to get my doctorate.

My research is on the experiences of modern day polymaths. I will be gathering information by conducting one on one interviews with people who fit the above description; if you do, I would like to request that you consider being a part of the study.

A few things you should know, should you choose to participate: although the interview will be audio recorded so the conversation can be transcribed later so I may study more closely what was said, you will be able to stop the recording at any point. You will also have an opportunity to review the typed transcript afterwards to correct, delete, and/or add any information you wish. Your identity will be kept strictly confidential. And I will provide you with a copy of the final dissertation.

If you agree to let me interview you, I anticipate it will take approximately 90 minutes of your time. We can find a date and time that works for both of us and I believe the experience could be quite enjoyable for you to share your story of what makes you the person you are today!

I look forward to hearing your response and hopefully meeting with you. Thank you for your consideration!

Best wishes,
Angela Cotellessa

Attachment: Research Study Overview

APPENDIX B: RESEARCH STUDY OVERVIEW

In Pursuit of Polymaths: Understanding Renaissance Persons of the 21st Century

Problem addressed:
Problems facing humanity in the modern era are frequently very complex and often involve multiple dimensions, not all of which can be solved within a single discipline or narrow, limited silo (Terjeson and Politis, 2015). Indeed, "the world's problems require a multi-disciplinary skillset—that is, the combination and involvement of several academic disciplines or professional specializations to a topic or problem." Despite the need for this way of thinking in order to solve major societal and worldwide problems, few incentives exist for individuals to become multi-disciplinary experts (Terjeson and Politis, 2015, p. 151).

Purpose of the study:
The primary purpose of this phenomenological study is to help fill in the gap in the scholarly literature by better understanding how Renaissance men and women in the 21st century (polymaths) got to be adept in multiple, disparate areas—what motivated or led them to do so—and more generally what their experiences are of being this way. Of particular interest, this researcher also aims to understand how their varied skillsets impacts their ability to solve real-world problems creatively (or not) as well as how their identity is emerged in relation to and how it has been impacted by their polymathy. This study explores the shared experiences—common themes—among a variety of different polymaths.

Significance of the study:
This research adds a new perspective to a somewhat limited body of knowledge on the subject and takes a new perspective in doing so. There is ample literature exploring the individual experiences of one polymath at a time, but almost no literature that aims to find common themes among different polymaths. Of the literature that does exist, much of it looks at Renaissance men from history; very little looks at Renaissance persons living in the 21st century. Regarding polymaths who do currently exist in current day, there is scant scholarly literature exploring how and why they got to be that way and what their experiences are as a result. In fact, "very few (if any) attempts have been made to isolate the qualitative aspects of thinking that adequately describe" the term polymath (Sriraman, 2009, p. 75).

Participants sought for the study and participant expectations:
This research will look at 12 – 15 different polymaths. Interviews will be conducted once with each person for approximately 90 minutes each. Interviews will be recorded but will remain confidential. Participants must be at least 30 years old and have native English fluency. Participants should have distinguished capabilities in at least two disparate areas (i.e., in the arts and also the sciences).

About the researcher:

Angela Cotellessa is a doctoral candidate at the George Washington University within the Graduate School of Education and Human Development. Her doctoral degree (Ed.D.) will be in Human and Organizational Learning. Angela has worked in the federal government for over 10 years, including 6 years as a non-political employee at the Executive Office of the President, and over 4 years at the Office of Personnel Management, working in the field of adult education with a focus on leadership development.

APPENDIX C: INTERVIEW PROTOCOL

Primary Research Questions:

- RQ1: What is the lived experience of polymaths?
    - Sub-question: What is it like being a polymath? How does it feel?
    - Sub-question: How does polymathy impact creativity and creative problem solving?
- RQ2: How did polymaths come to be that way?
    - Sub-question: How did polymaths discover their identity?
    - Sub-question: What in a polymath's environment impacted them becoming a polymath?

Instructions:

Good morning (or afternoon). My name is Angela Cotellessa. Thank you for agreeing to let me interview you as part of my doctoral dissertation research with George Washington University. The purpose of this interview is for me to understand your experience as a polymath. There are no right or wrong, desirable or undesirable answers. I want you to feel comfortable telling me whatever comes to mind and how you really think and feel about the questions I ask. I anticipate this interview will take 60 -90 minutes, approximately.

Recording:

If it is okay with you, I will be recording our conversation. The purpose of this is so that I can capture all of the details of what you're saying but at the same time be able to pay close attention to our conversation together today (recording, of course, allows me to go back to gather details more carefully at a later date). I assure you that all of your comments will be confidential. I may quote you in my dissertation or may summarize themes among various interviews, but no one will have any way of knowing it was you who said anything in particular or even that it was you who participated in my research. Do I have your permission to record this session?

(If yes – begin recording now.)

Okay, I am recording our discussion now. Thank you.

Do you have any questions for me before we get started?

Interview questions:

PART I: BACKGROUND/GATHERING DATA ON THE INTERVIEWEE:

- What term do you prefer (i.e., polymath, Renaissance man/woman, etc.)? What does that label/term mean to you?
- In what ways do you consider yourself a polymath (use whatever term they prefer)?
- In what areas do you feel you excel? What do you define as success with in science (or whatever scientific topic they are skilled in) arena? In the arts (or whatever scientific topic they are skilled in) arena?
- Tell me about your interests. What types of things are you curious about and/or interested in both now and over the course of your lifetime?
- Tell me about the jobs you've had over your career (and also how they're similar and/or different from one another).
- What kinds of hobbies do you have or have you had?
- Do you consider yourself to be more of an introvert or an extrovert? Tell me why you think this is the case.

PART II: BECOMING A POLYMATH:

- Walk me through the first time you realized you were a polymath.
- Do you think you were born a polymath (or at least with polymathic tendencies early in your youth), or was this more something that your environment spurred in you?
- Do you think you naturally became this way or did you have to work at it?
- Are you a self-directed learner? Please explain.
- How did you become a success in science area? In the arts area?
- What in your environment impacted your becoming a polymath? Why did you become this way?
- Was there any particular person who impacted you to become a polymath? Or who discouraged you?
- Do you identify as a polymath? How did you discover your identity as someone with these tendencies?

- Do you associate (professionally or personally) with other polymaths? If so, why?

- What thinking led you to become this way?

- Were there any impediments to pursuing being a polymath? Were you able to overcome those impediments? If so, how?

PART III: THE EXPERIENCE OF AND IMPLICATIONS OF BEING A POLYMATH:

- How does being a polymath affect your day to day life?

- What does it mean to you to be this way?

- What is it like being a polymath? How does it feel?

- What benefits have you experienced from being a polymath?

- Are there any benefits that perhaps you have not experienced personally but which you think might be the case for other polymaths?

- What drawbacks have you experienced being a polymath?

- Do you think being a polymath has made your professional life easier or harder? Do you think employers have known how to leverage your varied skill sets adequately? What characteristics in a workplace/organization/environment do you feel bolster your set of skills?

- Are there any drawbacks that perhaps you have not experienced personally but which you think might be the case for other polymaths?

- Do you think your polymathy is in any way related to self-actualization (becoming your best self)?

- Do you think being a polymath impacts your creativity and creative problem solving? Please explain how.

- Is there anything else you think I should know about the experience of being a polymath?

PART IV: DEMOGRAPHIC DATA:

- Lastly, I'd like to gather some quick demographic data. Can you confirm your age, race, and gender?

PART V: CLOSING:

Thank you so much for talking with me. I really appreciate your support of my doctoral dissertation research and I enjoyed talking with you!

APPENDIX D: RESEARCH CONSENT FORM

Principal Researcher: Angela Cotellessa

Principal Investigator: Dr. Michael Marquardt

Research Title: In Pursuit of Polymaths: Understanding Renaissance Persons of the 21st Century

Under the guidance of Principal Investigator, Dr. Michael Marquardt of The George Washington University, you are invited to participate in a research study that seeks to gain greater understanding of the experience of modern day Renaissance men and women—also known as polymaths. Your participation in this study requires one interview during which you will be asked questions about your perception of how you became this way, your identity, and the ramifications/impact of being this way. The duration of the interview will be approximately 90 minutes. With your permission, the interview will be digitally recorded and transcribed in order to capture and maintain an accurate record of our discussion. Your formal name will not be used or referred to on any documentation. On all transcripts and data analysis you will be referred to by a pseudonym.

This study will be conducted by the researcher, Angela Cotellessa, a doctoral candidate at George Washington University. The interview will be conducted at a time and location that is mutually suitable. Approximately 12 – 15 participants will be interviewed for this study.

Risks and Benefits:
This research will contribute to the understanding of the influence of the experience of polymaths in modern day. Participation in this study carries the same amount of risk that individuals will encounter during a usual meeting of colleagues.

Data Storage to Protect Confidentiality:
Under no circumstances, whatsoever will you be identified by name in the course of this research study, or any publication thereof. Every effort will be made that all information provided by you will be treated as strictly confidential. All data will be coded and securely stored, and will be used for professional purposes only.

How the Results Will Be Used:
This research study is to be submitted in partial fulfillment of requirements for the degree of Doctor of Education at George Washington University, Washington, DC. The results of this study will be published as a dissertation. In addition, information may be used for educational purposes in professional presentations and/or publications in the future as well.

Participant's Rights

- You have read and discussed the research description with the researcher. You have had the opportunity to ask questions about the purposes and procedures regarding this study.
- My participation in the research is voluntary. You may refuse to participate or withdraw from participation at any time.
- The researcher may withdraw me from the research at her professional discretion.
- Any information derived from the research that personally identifies me will not be voluntarily released or disclosed without my separate consent, except as specifically required by law.
- If at any time you have questions regarding the research or my participation, you can contact the researcher, Angela Cotellessa, who will answer your questions. The researcher's phone number is (213) 804-5151. You may also contact the researcher's faculty advisor, Dr. Michael Marquardt at (703) 726-3764.
- If at any time you have comments or concerns regarding the conduct of the research, or questions about my rights as a research subject, you should contact the George Washington University Office of Human Research at (202) 994-2715 or ohrirb@gwu.edu.
- You should receive a copy of this document.
- Digital recording is part of this research. Only the principal researcher and the transcriptionist will have access to written and taped materials. You will be given an opportunity to review the transcription at a later date and make edits/deletions if you wish.
- Once transcriptions have been validated, original audio recordings will be deleted.
- Approximately 12 – 15 polymaths will be interviewed as part of this study. Data will be aggregated across participants and summarized as "themes" found, but some individual information may also be highlighted and described in the dissertation, in order to provide rich descriptions of the experiences of polymaths. By signing this consent form, you acknowledge that you understand that individual results may be highlighted, though those results will be anonymous and not tied to your identity in any way.

Please check one:

( ) You consent to be audio taped.
( ) You DO NOT consent to be audio taped.

My signature indicates that I freely agree to participate in this study, based on the terms and conditions described above.

Participant's signature: ______________________________ Date: / / ____

Name (Please print): ______________________________

Made in the USA
Coppell, TX
08 December 2023

25600698R00164